Theologizing *in the* Radical Middle

Theologizing *in the* Radical Middle

Rethinking How We Do Theology for Spiritual Growth in Word and Spirit

RYUN H. CHANG

Foreword by Keith Park

WIPF *&* STOCK · Eugene, Oregon

THEOLOGIZING IN THE RADICAL MIDDLE
Rethinking How We Do Theology for Spiritual Growth in Word and Spirit

Wipf & Stock
An Imprint of Wipf and Stock Publishers
199 W. 8th Ave., Suite 3
Eugene, OR 97401

www.wipfandstock.com

PAPERBACK ISBN: 978-1-5326-5149-6
HARDCOVER ISBN: 978-1-5326-5150-2
EBOOK ISBN: 978-1-5326-5151-9

Manufactured in the U.S.A.   09/13/18

This book is dedicated to

My wife, Insil Chang, who has been putting up with me for the past thirty-one years.
I have seen no better example of Christlikeness than her, hands down!

And to my three children: Christy, Joshua, and Justin,
who remind me of God's constant favor bestowed upon my life
because it has been through their gracious forbearance of their father's many faults
that I've often understood what God's forgiveness in his Son Christ is truly like.

Contents

Foreword

FOR AS LONG AS I've known him, Ryun has devoted himself to the idea of the "Radical Middle," although he did not call it by that name at the time. Having graduated from Talbot Seminary, which was considered one of the bastions of cessationism at the time, he had to somehow make peace with the fact that his personal mentor was also considered by many to be the embodiment of Pentecostalism. Thus, I was not at all surprised but in fact more than happy to hear the news that he was writing a book on this topic. My excitement for this book goes beyond Ryun's early interest and struggle for the Radical Middle, but I deeply believe that he can shed a light on this subject from a uniquely advantageous vantage point, not only because he had struggled as a seminarian, but also faced hardships as a church planter in southern California, trying to formulate a biblically balanced philosophy of ministry as a young pastor. I believe Ryun is uniquely qualified to bring different angles on this subject because his theology is not just academic but is something that he is living and practicing in life. After his doctorate studies, he then served as a missionary in Mexico, teaching and discipling local pastors from all denominations, reconciling them to one another by pointing to the Bible through expository studies. Currently, several theological courses he produced are used in various seminaries and churches in several cities in Mexico, along with one text book that is used nationally (also in Peru). His decade of service as a teacher and missionary who crossed over various denominational boundaries has given him much wisdom, knowledge, and familiarity on the topics of common misunderstandings between different schools of thoughts. Even now, Ryun serves as a mission and resource pastor for our interdenominational community of churches, which now endeavors to apply the Radical Middle to our own doctrine. His work for us currently takes him to many overseas teaching posts in Central and South America, Southeast Asia, Central Asia, and the Middle East. Ryun's book collects many views commenting on the topic of Radical Middle theology, and is a diligent study coming from an honest desire to not only teach but to live according to the overall teaching of the Bible, through a multicultural and multidenominational approach. May we all learn to live in the tension and the exhilarating joy of the Radical Middle as we learn to worship God in Spirit and truth!

Keith Park
Sydney, Australia

Preface

THERE IS NO DENYING that the way we theologize has led to divisiveness in the face of Christ's call for his followers to "become perfectly one" (John 17:23b). Regardless, attempts to systematize Scripture under the rubric of one overarching idea (e.g., "God is sovereign"; "once saved, always saved"; "miracles only happened in the past") will continue because, if truth be told, we do not value unity much. Neither is God's word, in effect, very valued, since our theologizing requires that the many antithetic and antinomic propositions in the Bible are distorted or ignored in support of the overarching idea. This book challenges our toleration of disunity engendered by the improper hermeneutics responsible for the way we theologize.

My awareness of this issue dates to my Pentecostal and cessationist seminary days in the 1980s when, amid confusion and doubts, a deeper understanding began to take root in my mind. One clarifying moment came after I almost lost my faith while attending a liberal seminary. After being graciously restored by the Lord, I realized that the real danger to our faith is theological liberalism that impugns Scripture itself, not theological differences among those who nevertheless agree on the essentials of the Christian faith. But, the recent escalation of cessationist and continuationist conflicts prompted by the Strange Fire Conference and the 2013 book bearing the same title, which rocked the unity of church, indicates that we are as divisive as ever and Scripture is still read very partially.

In view of this, this book presents the hermeneutics of the Radical Middle as a viable alternative to interpret Scripture in accordance with how it is actually structured, so that we may grow in word and Spirit to embody humility and love to desire unity in Christ. I believe that thirty-five years in public ministry as a pastor and teacher—including ten years spent abroad to train pastors of all denominational backgrounds and studying in several seminaries with varying theological backgrounds— has uniquely prepared me to prepare this material.

Ryun Chang
Philadelphia

Introduction: An Overview

WHO INCITED DAVID TO take a census of Israel that later led to God's judgment against the king? Second Samuel 24:1 says it was the LORD, but 1 Chronicles 21:1 says just the opposite of that: "Then Satan stood against Israel and incited David to number Israel." How could that be? And what does that have to with this book? You may be saying to yourself, "I thought this book is about word and Spirit, and the tension existing between those who favor one over against the other." Yes, you are right; these matters may appear disjoined. But it is my aim to show that the remedy for one problem might just be the cure for another. Before proceeding, note that most of what is discussed in the introduction, including the terms used, is amplified in chapter 1. This is an overview of the main thesis and its supporting arguments to be developed in the book.

THE CONVERGENCE

Perhaps a bit of the elitist in me could not help but compare the East Coast to Oklahoma City, but I was genuinely surprised to see a crowd of nearly fifteen hundred in town for the biblical conference I was attending. To be sure, Oklahoma City is not a large city, so I wondered to myself where all these folks had come from. Most undoubtedly came from nearby states, but some participants had traveled from as far as Oceania. In any case, we had all come together in "The Passionate Pursuit of Word and Spirit," the theme of the Convergence Conference (October 2017), which was plastered on the cover of every program guide handed out.

Sam Storms, the senior pastor at Bridgeway Church in Oklahoma City and the brains behind the conference, has long placed the Holy

Spirit, along with the faithful exposition of God's word, as the focus of his ministry, becoming the figurehead for what is called "the Third Wave" wing of the larger Charismatic Movement. In 2017, after forty-four years of ministry, Storms put together the Convergence Conference, the first national conference of its kind. Perhaps he felt that now is the right time to do so. His perception was timely if anything, as indicated by the crowd's reaction following an address by Matt Chandler. At face value, Chandler, the lead pastor of a Dallas megachurch and author of *The Explicit Gospel*, seemed out of place at a charismatic conference; neither he nor Francis Chan, another speaker at the conference, are visible leaders of the movement.

As we soon discovered, both had been invited to share, among other things, their own struggles to incorporate the Spirit into their respective ministries. Chandler, even though he has "identified himself as Reformed charismatic"[1] admitted to being a "coward" for hesitating to do so in his church. Later that evening, Storms, perhaps sensing that Chandler hit a nerve with the audience, asked people if they identified with his struggles; a large portion of the auditorium stood in response. The response was telling and indicative of symptoms across the evangelical world as a whole. Most Christians know the roles of the Father and the Son in doctrine, but they are unsure of how to integrate the Holy Spirit into their lives and ministries.

A PENTECOSTAL AND REFORMED IN THE SAME ROOM

In the 1990s, I spent my entire thirties pastoring a church in Southern California, an English-speaking congregation attended mostly by young Korean-Americans. One day, while praying about whom to invite as the speaker for our annual summer retreat (1998), an idea arose in my mind that led me to do something I had never done before: invite two speakers—instead of the customary one—whose theological orientations were as different as night and day; so I invited both a Pentecostal and a Reformed speaker.

The first speaker I invited was a Pentecostal missionary named Kim. Ironically enough, while he would be in a room full of Korean-Americans with the same name, Kim was actually a Caucasian missionary serving in Mexico, whom I had known from the very day I became a Christian at

---

1. McCraken, "Rise of Reformed Charismatics," para. 9.

a Los Angeles Pentecostal church in 1981. I also invited John, a student attending Westminster Theological Seminary in Escondido, California, who would many years later become a Reformed seminary professor. If Kim was an unapologetic Pentecostalist, then John, who was on my youth ministry staff while I attended Talbot School of Theology, could be his mortal enemy, an unswerving five-point Calvinist. Both accepted my invitation. As countless Pentecostalists have done before him, Kim proceeded to poke a little fun at John's religious training (to paraphrase: "Seminary? More like cemetery, am I right?!"). He then went on to share compelling anecdotes of all the divine miracles he had witnessed in Mexico, including one case of resurrection from the dead. John, on the other hand, gave collegiate lectures on divine covenants, and his handouts included excerpts from the Westminster Confession of Faith from 1646, as well as the London Baptist Confession of Faith of 1689.

I do not recall anyone accusing me of purposely trying to confuse the retreat attendees; although some folks were probably scratching their heads as to why such opposites were invited. Once Kim and John had their say, I gave a final talk to clear the air; hopefully, my congregation had a better grasp of what their pastor had in mind. So what did I say? I do not remember too much of what I told them twenty years ago, but I did stress our obligations to pursue a serious study of God's word, as well as to allow the Spirit to do his works in our lives. In some ways, Kim and John captured this tension when they shook hands at the end (with slightly wary smiles). I just did not know what to call this tension until, several years later, a pastor friend of mine for the past thirty years, Keith Park, gave me a book entitled *The Quest for the Radical Middle* (1999).

THE RADICAL MIDDLE

What does the "Radical Middle" mean? One pastor, being unfamiliar with the term, commented that this phrase was a contradiction. He was not wrong to assume this since the word "middle" or "middling" implies moderating two or more contending positions to forge a compromise, that is, a middle position acceptable to everyone involved. No one would likely call that middle position "radical." But neither is the paradigm of the Radical Middle "radical," if what is meant by radical is to be extreme on account of advocating one position at the exclusion of another.

So why did Billy Jackson, a proponent of the charismatic Vineyard Movement founded by John Wimber in 1982, write *The Quest for the Radical Middle*? The description on the book jacket explains his reason:

> *The Quest for the Radical Middle* provides an in-depth look at the history of one of the fastest growing church movements in the last twenty years. The Vineyard story is a fascinating case study of those that would attempt to hold in tension the great historical doctrines of the Christian faith with an ardent pursuit of the Spirit of God.[2]

What drew my interest was the phrase, "the Radical Middle," and the stated purpose of the Vineyard movement: equally upholding God's word, which would appeal to cessationists, and pursuing the Spirit, which would appeal to continuationists. However, while the Vineyard Church may have done its part, the situation between cessationists and continuationists has not improved; in fact, it has gotten worse since 2013, when cessationist pastor John MacArthur held a conference and published a book bearing the same name, *Strange Fire*, to disown the brotherhood with continuationists.

But, upon hearing me say, "This book will figure out who is at fault and how to reconcile this mess," someone may say, "Has not that already been done by others who have dealt with this same subject?" Yes, of course. *Authentic Fire* by Michael Brown (2013), *Holy Fire* by R. T. Kendall (2014), and *Strangers to Fire* (2014), whose contributors include scholars Craig S. Keener and Jack Deere, immediately come to mind.[3]

---

2. Jackson, *Quest for the Radical Middle*, back blurb.

3. The full title of Kendall's book is, *Holy Fire: A Balanced, Biblical Look at the Holy Spirit's Work in Our Lives*. Keener, in his review of *Holy Fire*, writes: "Whereas Pastor MacArthur's *Strange Fire* offers a polemical Reformed cessationist approach, Pastor Kendall's work offers instead an irenic Reformed charismatic approach. Lest one misunderstand me, I strongly appreciate MacArthur's calling the church back to the Scriptures; as a biblical scholar, I have devoted my life to the same calling. I believe, however, that MacArthur's theological presuppositions regarding the Spirit's activity have obscured for him some key portions of the Bible. Here Kendall offers a better way. Kendall's humble and gracious style invites dialogue, and his central objective is one that all readers should appreciate." (Keener, "Holy Fire," paras. 3–4.) The full title of Brown's book is, *Authentic Fire: A Response to John MacArthur's Strange Fire*. One reviewer writes: "Dr. Michael Brown in his work *Authentic Fire* confronts the misinformation of Pastor John MacArthur's outspoken zeal against all things charismatic in his book, *Strange Fire*. While Dr. Brown admits that on some points Dr. MacArthur is right on, his language is radically abusive in tone . . . Brown carefully separates the message from the messenger in addressing charismatic abuse before proceeding to the

Thus, if the intent of this book is to respond *directly* to MacArthur's *Strange Fire*, then I am about four years late in joining others who have already done that. I do have much to say about MacArthur's response to continuationism in later chapters, but as a microcosm of the larger problem of how we theologize.

WHY I WROTE THIS BOOK

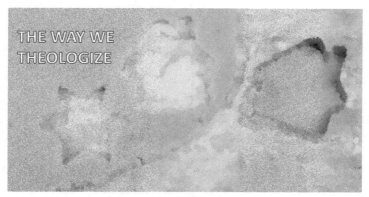

I wrote this book as a small step toward rethinking how we theologize. My concern stems from our efforts to systematize Scripture under the rubric of one overarching idea, whether it be Calvinism ("God's sovereignty"), Free Grace ("once saved, always saved"), or cessationism ("miracles only happened in the past"). The typical way this is handled results in the disunity of the church, and no believer should be given to think that this is a small, inconsequential matter.

The Problem

So what is behind the problem? Systematic theology, by its nature, imparts more of a particular theological knowledge, mostly based on selective Scriptures, rather than "the whole counsel of God" (Acts 20:27b). This then has the effect of justifying the very overarching idea responsible for the passages preferred. But, when Scripture is neatly systematized in accordance to one dominant thought, the many antithetic and antinomic propositions in the Bible must be ignored or distorted as a theological expediency; Scripture, as a result, is not allowed to speak for itself.

_____

good stuff: how to burn with authentic fire." (King, "Authentic Fire," para. 1.)

Certainly, there are theologians who, after presenting opposing views in a fair manner, articulate their disagreements in a cogent manner, perhaps even tweaking their views in the process. Perhaps no one better exemplifies this than Robert L. Saucy, professor of systematic theology at Talbot School of Theology (La Mirada, California) for a half decade, who taught me and (likely MacArthur also).[4] While no book should be judged by its cover, in the case of two of Saucy's works, much is suggested by their titles. As a systematic theologian who studied at the dispensational and cessationist Dallas Theological Seminary in the late 1950s, he penned a book entitled, *The Case for Progressive Dispensationalism: The Interface Between Dispensational and Non-Dispensational Theology* in 1993. A cautious cessationist when he taught me in 1987, Saucy later contributed a chapter called, "An Open but Cautious Response" in *Are Miraculous Gifts for Today? Four Views* (1996). What this shows is a theologian who remained open to dialogue with those whom he disagreed with, theologically, even recalibrating his position as his understanding of Scripture deepened.[5]

But some theology is so rigid by design that it can hardly avoid a partial reading of Scripture. For instance, consider Ultradispensationalism that takes a theological idea of "dichotomy between Israel and the church"[6] "throughout eternity"[7] to such an extreme degree that "whatever church is mentioned before Paul [Acts 9] is said . . . to be the Jewish Church and not the body of Christ."[8] This theology certainly would fall into this rigid category, but not necessarily Progressive Dispensationalism that posits "God . . . [as having] a single purpose—the establishment of the kingdom of God—in which Israel and the church will both share."[9]

"Hyper-Calvinism" that denies "all human responsibility in both believing and preaching"[10] would also fall into this intractable category,

---

4. Saucy began teaching at Talbot Theological Seminary in 1961. MacArthur graduated in 1963; I graduated in 1988.

5. His son Mark, who now teaches at Talbot, told me that "it would be incorrect to label [his father] a cessationist," given that whereas he was open and cautious regarding the sign gifts, "cessationists are not 'open' to the possibility of those gifts continuing." Mark Saucy, email sent to author, May 1, 2018.

6. Bass, *Backgrounds to Dispensationalism*, 23.

7. Fuller, *Hermeneutics*, 25, cited in Ryrie, *Dispensationalism Today*, 45.

8. Ryrie, *Dispensationalism Today*, 200.

9. Grudem, *Systematic Theology*, 860.

10. Hodges, *Reformed Theology Today*, 24.

but not necessarily "what may be called the moderate Calvinist view"[11] that upholds election without diminishing man's responsibility to believe and preach. And as for cessationism, what Keener calls the "hard cessationism" of MacArthur is a departure from the cessationist views articulated by Richard B. Gaffin in *Are Miraculous Gifts for Today? Four Views* (1996). In this work, Gaffin, being mindful of "our common bond in Christ," cautions against "overlook[ing] . . . the genuine work of God's Spirit in and among believers who identify themselves as charismatic or Pentecostal."[12] Such charitable spirit is almost completely absent in hard cessationism.

The Outcome

What then is its outcome? Note that Ultradispensationalism and hyper-Calvinism are intragroup differences, but often that is all it takes to pit one subgroup against another even within the same systematic theology. Obviously, the level of acrimony escalates rapidly when one systematic theology tries to justify and defend its core beliefs against another system at the macro level, be it the Reformed against Dispensationalism, or Calvinism against Arminianism, or New Perspective (N. T. Wright) against "Old" Perspective (John Piper). Despite agreeing on the essentials of the Christian faith (for the most part), they become suspicious of each other, sometimes even denying their brotherhood in Christ. Ironically, long before MacArthur disowned continuationists, some in the Free Grace did the same to him for preaching what is, to them, a false gospel of Lordship Salvation (chapter 4).

Still none of them behave all that differently than the apostle John, who expected Jesus to applaud him for stopping a man from doing God's work for not being like him (i.e., one of the twelve). Instead, Jesus told John, "Do not stop him, for the one who is not against you is for you" (Luke 9:50). John called for disunity; the Lord, the unity of the body. The larger issue, then, is not simply rectifying the conflict between cessationists and continuationists, but to rethink how we theologize so that we can remain united in Christ.

---

11. Hammond, *In Understanding Be Men*, 88.
12. Gaffin, "Cessationist View," 63.

FOCUS AND PLAN OF STUDY

What is at the root of such theological rigidity? There may be several factors responsible for this, such as worldview, personality, and background (e.g., family, church, etc.), to name a few; but this study is largely focused on the matter of hermeneutics (i.e., the interpretation of Scripture.) That is to say, I do not question the heart, for that is what God does (Jer 11:20), but I do question the improper hermeneutics of what is called "logocentrism" (chapter 3) of those who, in effect, "tamper with God's word" (2 Cor 4:2b). In the same vein, while several factors are responsible for cessationist and continuationist conflicts (e.g., the misuse of spiritual gifts for the latter and naturalism for the former), the book's focus is largely delimited to hermeneutics. Why? It is because of inadequate exegesis, the result of unsound hermeneutical principles rooted in logocentrism, that hard cessationism and flawed versions of continuationism have been produced. In fact, without relying on the hermeneutics of logocentrism, the advocates of these opposing views would not be able to insist on the rightness of their respective pneumatology (i.e., the study of the Holy Spirit) to the exclusion of all others.

The Strategy

This book attempts to point out the inherent weakness of systematic theology in general. To do that, both hard cessationism and flawed aspects of continuationism, as a microcosm of the larger problem stemming from rigid theology, are presented to demonstrate this weakness in the form of the hermeneutics of logocentrism—an essential component to all theological systems.

The first step in this process is the recognition that Scripture, for the most part, is framed antithetically and antinomically (chapter 2), as evidenced by the example given at the outset (Who ordered the census? God or Satan?). Antithesis also affects other doctrinal matters such as Christology, ecclesiology, and soteriology (chapter 3). In reaction, the rigid adherence to systematic theology ends up privileging the interpretation they favor, while ignoring all those that do not fit their system (chapter 4). Instead of logocentrism, I present the hermeneutics of the Radical Middle as a viable alternative to properly theologize the Bible. This is to say, the study seeks to extract principles of the Radical Middle from the very way Scripture is framed, and then apply those principles to our hermeneutics in order that our exegesis reflects what Scripture actually purports, instead of privileging our preferred systematic theology.

As noted earlier, this study has a great deal of interest in the ongoing conflicts between cessationists and continuationists, between word and Spirit. This interest is not merely theological or doctrinal; rather, it stems from the desire to embody a humble and loving disposition, that values unity with fellow believers. By the end of this book, I hope that the readers will see that when both specific arguments for hard cessationism and flawed aspects of continuationism are examined according to the Radical Middle, the result will be the privileging of both word and Spirit in a healthy tension. This, then, will be presented as the optimal way to reach the kind of spiritual growth that leads to humility, love, and unity (chapter 11).

The Three Goals

The three goals of this book are: first, to present the hermeneutics of the Radical Middle as best suited to theologize Scripture in accordance with how it is structured, so that it is the Bible that is taught, and not the entirety of a particular systematic theology; second, to put forward a pneumatology with respect to the sign gifts that reflects the entire Scripture with hopes of narrowing the gap between cessationists and continuationists; and third, to present the upholding of both word and Spirit in healthy tension as the condition for optimal spiritual growth.

The Four Objectives

To ascertain the three goals, the study seeks to meet the following four objectives: The first is to recognize the antithetic and antinomic nature of Scripture, and then the typical ways it is handled under the rubric of the hermeneutics of logocentrism. The second objective is to understand the paradigm of the Radical Middle and how the hermeneutics of the Radical Middle differs fundamentally from logocentrism. The third objective is to appraise the hermeneutics of hard cessationism and certain flawed aspects of continuationism in accordance with the hermeneutics of the Radical Middle, as a prelude to presenting what I deem a pneumatology that is closer to Scripture. The final objective is to compare inadequate and optimal approaches to word and Spirit tension, after which the latter is presented as the approach that is best suited to nurture the kind of spiritual growth that leads to humility, love, and unity.

Structure of the Book

Before discussing the Radical Middle and logocentrism as they relate to theologizing in chapters 2–5, the first chapter presents the long version of the ongoing feud between cessationists and continuationists, with an eye towards pointing out both the inherent weakness and potential danger in systematic theology. In chapters 6–10, the specific arguments of hard cessationism and flawed versions of continuationism are examined through the hermeneutics of the Radical Middle. The final chapter deals with the proper attitude necessary for desiring and upholding the paradigm of the Radical Middle. Interspersed throughout the book are discussions on spiritual growth in word and Spirit.

1

Urgency for the Paradigm of the Radical Middle

IT WAS SAID THAT the reason Bill Jackson wrote *The Quest for the Radical Middle* is because cessationists who advocate word and continuationists who pursue Spirit have not been getting along. This chapter then is a longer version of that, which for the most part should be familiar to those who read the earlier responses to *Strange Fire*. Therefore, please allow me to present this discussion under the rubric of how two old theological rivals became fast friends after finding out that they had a common foe. In light of the first goal of the study—rethinking how we theologize—the amplification of cessationist and continuationist conflicts highlights the inherent weakness and potential danger in systematic theology, especially when it becomes very rigid and partial.

ONGOING CONFLICT BETWEEN CESSATIONISTS AND CONTINUATIONISTS

Since the inception of Pentecostalism in 1906, Reformists and dispensationalists took little time to begin criticizing Pentecostalism and the related charismatic movement (i.e., traditionally those in non-Pentecostal churches who believe in and practice the sign gifts). According to the Center for the Study of Global Christianity (2011) at Gordon-Conwell Theological Seminary, there are 584 million Pentecostal and charismatic believers in the world. Naturally, this impressive worldwide growth has only deepened the concern of cessationists over a movement they feel is unbiblical in many regards.

So what are they fighting about? For most, the main issue at stake is the gifts of the Holy Spirit. Regarding these gifts (namely, the gift of tongues, prophecy, healing, and apostolicism), the discourse may be neatly separated into two camps: continuationists—who uphold that all spiritual gifts as delineated in the Bible continue to exist today—and cessationists—who believe that these signs or miraculous gifts have long ceased to operate in the church, as far back as the first century.

The Main Cessationist Argument

Evidently, the conviction held by cessationists against continuationism is so strong that it has had the effect of turning two long-time theological nemeses into allies.

Strange Bedfellows

Now it is no secret that the Reformed and dispensationalist theologians do not see eye to eye on many theological matters.

Regarding ecclesiology (i.e., the study of churches), while Reformists see the church as the true Israel, dispensationalists see them as separate entities. And many theologians would agree that this difference alone affects how the Bible is understood more than any other biblical issue (see chapter 4). In fact, they disagree on the very premise upon which God's redemptive plan is established: five or six covenants for the Reformed[1] and seven dispensations for the dispensationalist. A renowned dispensationalist, Charles Ryrie, irked by "opposition to Dispensationalism"[2] on the part of Louis Berkhof, a Reformed theologian of equal prominence, writes:

> After rejecting the usual dispensational scheme of Bible distinc-
> tions, [Berkhof] enumerates his own scheme of dispensations
> or administrations, reducing the number to two—the Old

1. Showing the subjective nature of systematic theology even within the same branch is the difference in the number of covenants identified by Reformed theologians Louis I. Hodges and Louis Berkhof. Hodges identifies six: the Edenic, Noachian, Abahamic, Sinaitic, Davidic, and new covenant (Hodges, *Reformed Theology Today*, 41–43). Berkhof omits the Davidic covenant in his list (Berkhof, *Systematic Theology*, 293–301).

2. Ryrie, *Dispensationalism Today*, 15.

Testament dispensation and the New Testament dispensation. However, within the Old Testament dispensation Berkhof lists four subdivisions which, although he terms them "stages in the revelation of the covenant of grace," are distinguishable enough to be listed. In reality, then, he finds these four plus the one New Testament dispensation, or five periods of differing administrations of God.[3]

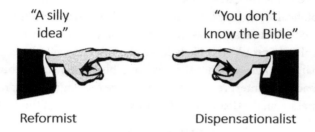

"A silly
idea"

Reformist

"You don't
know the Bible"

Dispensationalist

Ryrie's response to Berkhof is quite tame when compared to how Thomas Ice, a dispensationist theologian and rapture expert, responded to the renowned Reformed theologian R. C. Sproul, who called rapture a "silly idea."[4] The doctrine of rapture posits that any day now Jesus will descend from heaven and meet the church in the air, and then they will return to heaven (1 Thess 4:15–17), at which point the seven-year tribulation will commence on earth.[5] Ice said of Sproul, "Someone who thinks that rapture is a silly concept doesn't know the Bible."[6]

It is interesting how a biblical scholar says this about another of a different theological persuasion; in fact, even British theologian N. T. Wright felt like he was subject to it. His "New Perspective" view has garnered criticism for saying that "Paul was not countering legalistic Jewish individuals who were attempting to earn their salvation through works-righteousness,"[7] but targeting instead their ethnocentrism and exclusivism which threatened to divide the church and keep the gentiles away. Now regardless how you feel about that view, I believe Wright knows

3. Ibid., 15–16.

4. Ice, "When Will the Rapture Come?" conference presentation, Calvary Chapel Prophecy Conference "Israel and Final Days," August 2006, Chino Hills, California, CD. Note: The contacted individual serving at this ministry was not completely certain about the exact date and place of the conference.

5. Grudem, *Systematic Theology*, 1113.

6. Ice, "When Will the Rapture Come?" 2006.

7. Saucy and Gomez, "Justification and the New Perspective," 14.

the Bible rather well. Nevertheless, he felt that "some critics of [his view] write as if they are the ones who know 'what the Bible says' while others of us play fast and lose with it."[8]

What happened? As is often the case when adherents of two differing theological systems discuss theology, the discussion becomes personal. Inasmuch as Ice felt chagrined by Sproul's comment that denigrated a doctrine he values, had Sproul heard Ice's comment about his lack of biblical knowledge, the Reformed theologian would have been just as irked—Wright sure was. In fact, this may be the only time anyone said *that* about Sproul, who likely knew the Bible as well as Ice. In truth, what separated them was not the level of biblical knowledge, but different approaches to interpreting Scripture. Once theological disagreements become personal, the disunity of the body of Christ is not too far behind.

Continuationists

Pentecostals

Charismatics

Reformed
Cessationists

Dispensational
Cessationists

Evidently, there is no love lost between Reformists and dispensationalists when it comes to theology. Howbeit, despite all these theological differences, they become immediate allies under the rubric of cessationism when encountering claims of the supernatural today.

Reformed Cessationists

Speaking on behalf of the Reformed view, Louis I. Hodges, in his *Reformed Theology Today* (1995), first states that "the extraordinary gifts (often called *charismata*), involving miraculous elements, . . . were given to confirm the gospel and to authenticate the apostles as God's messengers (Hebrews 2:3–4)."[9] As to whether these gifts still operate today, he adds, "the majority of Reformed theologians . . . have insisted that the extraordinary gifts ceased with the original certification of the gospel

8. Wright, *Justification*, x.

9. Hoekema, *Tongues and Spirit-Baptism*, 104, 109, cited in Hodges, *Reformed Theology Today*, 112.

during the time of the apostles."[10] Accordingly then, the sign gifts ceased to exist around the late first century, when the book of Revelation was penned. How does this Reformed theologian then account for millions of continuationists who purportedly speak in tongues, one of the most prominently mentioned sign gifts in the Bible? To that question, he summarily says, "For the most part the phenomenon is merely a human reaction, prompted by neither the Holy Spirit nor demons, but psychologically induced."[11]

Dispensational Cessationists

As for the renowned dispensationalist Pastor John MacArthur,[12] in agreement with this Reformed position, states in reference to the apostle Paul's Letter to the Corinthians: "First Corinthians 13:8[13] states plainly that 'tongues will cease'. . . I am convinced beyond any reasonable doubt that tongues ceased in the apostolic age and that when they stopped, they stopped for good."[14] Before proceeding, it is worth noting that while Paul certainly denotes the eventual end of these gifts, he does not say when this will happen. While MacArthur himself notes this, saying, "The passage does not say *when* tongues were to cease" (italics his),[15] he attempts to back his conclusion with an argument from Greek grammar, which will be examined in chapter 6.

In this manner, cessationists from the Reformed and dispensationalist camps have been brought together by their continued questioning of the validity of the self-described ministry of the Holy Spirit among continuationists. (For instance, Reformed theologian Sproul also spoke at the *Strange Fire* conference through video feed.)

---

10. Hodges, *Reformed Theology Today*, 112. Hodges lists multiple sources to make this point, including Hoekema.

11. Hoekema, *Tongues and Spirit-Baptism*, 128–29, cited in Hodges, *Reformed Theology Today*, 114.

12. Although many now consider MacArthur as a Reformed pastor, he graduated from Talbot Theological Seminary, a dispensationalist school, and continues to hold to premillennialism, which is not part of the Reformed eschatology.

13. "Love never ends. As for prophecies, they will pass away; as for tongues, they will cease; as for knowledge, it will pass away."

14. MacArthur, *Charismatics*, 166.

15. MacArthur, *Charismatic Chaos*, 389.

The Main Continuationist Argument

Meanwhile, Pentecostals and charismatics have insisted that their movement is the fulfillment of the prophecy from Joel 2:28–32. Verse 28 states, "And it shall come to pass afterward, that I will pour out my Spirit on all flesh; your sons and your daughters shall prophesy, your old men shall dream dreams, and your young men shall see visions." The fact that this promise was fulfilled on the day of Pentecost in Jerusalem 2,000 years ago, (the apostle Peter cited it specifically to validate what occurred on that day), not in 1906, fails to deter continuationists. They believe they are part of the movement from God that has restored the biblical sign gifts (the gift of tongues, prophecy, healing, and apostolicism), long dormant in the church, once again in the light of modern day. To that effect, Kenneth E. Hagin, one of most influential charismatic leaders in history, states: "If I received the same Holy Ghost they [i.e., one hundred twenty in the upper room] received I would have the same initial sign they had—the Bible evidence—speaking with tongues."[16]

Evidently, a considerable theological gap exists between these two pneumatological systems—enough to warrant heated debates between cessationists and continuationists. But arguments between the proponents of two diametrically opposing systems seldom remain objective and civil. In the Middle Ages, matters would become political as the outcome for some believers, who stood on the opposite side of the reigning theological structure of the time, was a death sentence, decreed by the church and carried out by the state—just ask the Anabaptists.[17] While any outcome is better than that, our theological exchanges typically become very personal.

Escalation of the Conflict: Getting Personal

We saw a glimpse of objective arguments becoming personal from the bantering between the Reformist Sproul and dispensationist Ice. An

---

16. Hagin, *Why Tongues?*, loc. 29 of 48.

17. Among several teachings of the Anabaptists that irked both the Catholics and Reformers, one was their conviction that believer's baptism, not infant baptism, is biblical, and therefore the believers baptized as infants should be rebaptized. As a result, "thousands of Anabaptists were put to death (by fire in the Catholic territories, by drowning and the sword under Protestant regimes)." Yoder and Kreider, "Anabaptists," 402.

undeniable truth is that the more you believe in the rightness of your *entire* system, it becomes harder to tolerate those who theologize out of a different system. And that is one inherent weakness of systematic theology when one embraces it lock, stock, and barrel. Evidently cessationist and continuationist conflicts have not been an exception to the rule. One major reason for the heightened animosity between them is that their arguments have become quite disparaging; that is to say, they impugn one's faith or intellect, or both. I know about this all too well.

Continuationists as Aggressors

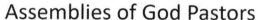

Assemblies of God Pastors

I served as a missionary teacher in the city of Chihuahua, Mexico for ten years from 2001 to 2011, and among other ministries, I most of all enjoyed training fellow pastors and church leaders in continuing education. From the three weekly classes of this type, two were strictly segregated between the Baptist and Assemblies of God pastors; I knew going in (and it was confirmed later by a friend) that they would not get along. Several years into teaching these pastors, many of whom had become personal friends by this time, I asked Pastor Javier, then the senior pastor of the largest Baptist church in the city, why he did not see eye to eye with Pentecostals.[18] As he was laboring for a response, I asked him whether any Pentecostal pastor had ever made him feel like a second-class Christian of sorts for not speaking in tongues. Breaking into a smile as if to say, "How did you know?" Javier admitted to feeling insulted some years back when told by an Assemblies of God pastor that he was not baptized with the

18. During my recent visit to Javier (April 2018), now retired, he confirmed several stories cited in this book that involve him. He also granted permission to use them.

Holy Spirit, since he did not speak in tongues. Javier then readily agreed that his default stance against Pentecostals and charismatics was more personal in nature than doctrinal, since he admittedly had not grasped all the theological nuances of the conflict.

So how then did I guess what the nature of his problem with Pentecostals was? Because I was one of them, having been converted to the faith at a Pentecostal Holiness church in Los Angeles. There, responding to the criticism leveled by cessationists (usually Baptists), we often called them out for not being Spirit-filled and mocked them by purposefully mispronouncing seminary as "cemetery." Even worse, a small Pentecostal denomination known as Unitarian Pentecostals have said that "one must speak with tongues to be saved."[19] Suffice it to say, apart from its obvious doctrinal incorrectness, such belief would be an affront and insult to any nontongue-speaking believers.

Cessationists as Aggressors

Not to be outdone, cessationists have called out Pentecostals and charismatics as "feelers," who put more emphasis on seeking the manifestations of the Spirit than teaching the Bible and upholding the important doctrines of the church. More to the point, cessationists do not hold continuationists in very high regard with respect to their knowledge of the Bible. Is this a fair and accurate appraisal? The answer is yes and no.

As for yes, "viewing the past with hindsight, we can see how it is often the unexpected, the unknown, the insignificant, the marginalized who lead the way into renewal."[20] Much like Peter and John, these people, such as Patrick, a former slave whom God used to initiate Celtic monasticism that, in time, evangelized Western Europe, were "uneducated, common men" (Acts 4:13b).[21] The same can be said about those whom God used to initiate Pentecostalism—a renewal movement that has become a movement of its own—such as William J. Seymour of the Azusa Revival fame (1906–1909), a black clergyman born to former slaves with modest theological training. But since that time continuationists have been catching up with the theological erudition of those who have been at it longer than they have (such as Reformists and dispensationalists).

19. Synan, Spirit Said "Grow," 8.
20. Pierson, "Historical Development of the Christian Movement," 32.
21. Neill, History of Christian Missions, 49–50, 59–64.

I can also testify to the same on behalf of the organization to which I belong: Acts Ministries International (AMI), a consortium of eighteen panasiatic churches in several states and East Asia. Every lead pastor in our fellowship is a continuationist and almost all of them have a Master of Divinity degree or higher from major US seminaries.[22] I mention educational pedigree only to suggest that we are just as committed to, and care about, God's word as are cessationists. So it would be insensitive, even insulting, to continue to see continuationists as theologically challenged.

Little Room Left for Further Dialogue

Amid this already heated environment came MacArthur's *Strange Fire* conference and book in 2013 that launched a no-holds-barred denunciation of the charismatic movement. In effect, he left little or no room for further dialogues between cessationists and continuationists.

Ironically, in contrast to his recent writing, MacArthur was not always so acrimonious toward Pentecostals and charismatics. In his first book against continuationism published in 1978, *The Charismatics: A Doctrinal Perspective*, MacArthur, after critiquing the movement at length, praised them in the final chapter entitled, "What Can We Learn from the charismatic movement?" He writes:

> [A charismatic] wants to believe that God is really at work in his life—right now and right here. Dead orthodoxy can never satisfy, and that is why many people look for satisfaction in the charismatic movement. We can thank God for charismatic and Pentecostal people who believe in the word of God.[23]

This gracious cessationism (from which Gaffin, mentioned in the introduction, apparently has not departed, since Keener, in his 2014 work, cites him as "a very charitable example of a cessationist")[24] certainly is not the MacArthur of today who is firmly committed to hard cessationism. Thirty-five years after penning that mildly promising book, MacArthur is no longer in any mood to continue any type of positive dialogue with Pentecostals and charismatics, whom he denounced as

---

22. Talbot School of Theology, Golden-Conwell Theological Seminary, Westminster Theological Seminary, Biblical Theological Seminary, Fuller Theological Seminary, Columbia Biblical Seminary, etc.

23. MacArthur, *Charismatics*, 180.

24. Keener, "Are Spiritual Gifts for Today?," 158.

not being part of the movement of the Holy Spirit (in effect, not true Christians). We already saw the writing on the wall when the chapter praising Pentecostals and charismatics in his first book was omitted in his second, *Charismatic Chaos* (1992). In *Strange Fire*, he states:

> In Jesus' day, the religious leaders of Israel blasphemously attrib-
> uted the work of the Spirit to Satan (Matt 12:24). The modern
> charismatic movement does the reverse, attributing the work
> of the devil to the Holy Spirit. Satan's armies of false teachers,
> marching to the beat of their own illicit desires, gladly propa-
> gate his errors . . . What we are seeing is *in reality* the explosive
> growth of a false church, as dangerous as any cult or heresy
> that has ever assaulted Christianity. The charismatic movement
> was a farce and a scam from the outset; it has not changed into
> something good.[25] (italics his)

So what is really bothering MacArthur? Is it the continuationist movement itself? Or perhaps something else which he thinks is *neces-sarily* part of it?

A KEY FACTOR BEHIND THE ESCALATION

To properly analyze what truly alarms MacArthur about continuation-ism, it would be helpful to do so against the backdrop of what typically develops within a particular systematic theology: subgroups that become either more flexible or inflexible than the original theological vision.

And if an outsider to that system is seeking to correct it because he disagrees with the system itself, then the wise thing to do is first identify with whom he can work from within. For instance, if one disagrees with Calvinism, it would be wise to begin the conversation with the moderate Calvinists whose "flexibility gives them more tolerance toward non-Re-formed churches" than those who adhere to "hyper-Calvinism."[26] If one disagrees with Dispensationalism, it would be wise to start the discussion with the progressive dispensationalists rather than the ultradispensation-alists who believe that, as hinted earlier, "the Body Church [i.e., the body of Christ] did not begin until after Paul came on the scene."[27] In light of this, it ought to be said that there are also subgroups within continu-

25. MacArthur, *Strange Fire*, xiii, xvii.

26. Hodges, *Reformed Theology Today*, 24–25.

27. Ryrie, *Dispensationalism Today*, 198.

ationism and, considering what truly bothers MacArthur, he should have recognized one subgroup that he could have worked with to clean up the mess that they both see. Let me now explain what this is about.

The Truth about the Prosperity Gospel

What truly raises the ire of MacArthur is prosperity theology, as evidenced by the fact that one-fifth of *Strange Fire* is dedicated to exposing the excess of this health-and-wealth gospel,[28] which he sees as being part and parcel of Pentecostalism and the charismatic movement. And it is not an overstatement to say the strong association between the two in MacArthur's mind is a major factor that negatively affects his cessationism, making it harsher than it needs to be. Before proceeding, allow me to explain what the prosperity gospel is really like.

The Prosperity Gospel I Witnessed

While reading sections in *Strange Fire* that expose the extremes of prosperity theology, I experienced the same sensation I eventually felt while trying to follow the teachings of charismatic stalwarts such as Fred Price and Kenneth Copeland in the early 1980s. That feeling, however, pales in comparison to what I often felt while serving in Mexico and visiting several other Latin American countries. There, I experienced firsthand how the prosperity gospel can undermine true faith.

> Undoubtedly, no Latin American church represents this theology better than the Universal Church of God's Kingdom of Brazil that has grown from a small group in 1977 to 3.5 million members and affiliates in close to 6,000 churches by 2010[29]; it is found in major cities in ninety different countries.[30]

Their theology, known also as *Pare de Sufrir* ("Stop the Suffering"), teaches that "prosperity is a promise of God and must be part of the life of all who are faithful and act in agreement with Holy Scriptures."[31] "The first

28. In *Strange Fire*, pages 8–18, 55–66, and 155–76 are focused on the antics of the prosperity gospel preachers.

29. Chang, "Hola, the Koreans are Here!," 183 (the figures obtained from Mandryk, Operation World, 163).

30. González and González, *Christianity in Latin America*, 292.

31. Ibid., 291.

step toward receiving this blessing, [coincidentally enough], requires one to give all to the church. This message of health-and-wealth, often televised through their well-established media outlet, has reached the point"[32] where

> some look on the poor as a curse . . . In a land where poverty is rampant, high unemployment and bankruptcy are everywhere, and the health system is inadequate, it is no surprise that people flock to churches and crusades that promise all kinds of cures and blessings from God.[33]

Profound disappointment typically settles on many who adhere to the prosperity gospel when it dawns on them that their promised material blessing may not come. "In the end, many give up on their faith in bitterness while mired in even deeper poverty, which then tears families apart even further."[34]

Turning the Prosperity Gospel into a Wedge Issue

So what does MacArthur think about the health-and-wealth gospel? After noting that "the vast majority of Pentecostals and charismatics—measuring in the hundreds and millions—embrace some form of the prosperity gospel,"[35] he declares, "the health-and-wealth prosperity gospel may be popular, but it is *not* the true gospel"[36] (italics his). MacArthur is, of course, absolutely correct and has reasons to be concerned about this disturbing development.

But, he fails to notice two additional developments surrounding continuationism that are changing what it means to be a continuationist

32. Chang, "Hola, the Koreans are Here!," 184.

33. Barro, "Wrestling with Success," 71.

34. Chang, "Hola, the Koreans are Here!," 184.

35. MacArthur, *Strange Fire*, 15. MacArthur's statement is based on a 2005 survey from the Pew Forum on Religion and Public Life that found that 95 percent of Pentecostals in Nigeria and 99 percent in the Philippines, agree with statements, "God will grant material prosperity to all believers who have enough faith" and "God will grant good health and relief from sickness to believers who have enough faith," respectively. (Olsen, "What Really Unites Pentecostals?," 19). In response, Craig Keener says that "it is questionable whether the 'vast' majority of charismatics support prosperity teaching" because "many Africans do not read the survey question about the connection between faith and prosperity the way the Western evangelicals expect, that is, against the backdrop of materialistic teaching." (Keener, "Review of MacArthur's Strange Fire," 40).

36. MacArthur, *Strange Fire*, 15.

today. And because MacArthur does not see them, the prosperity gospel, to him, looms as a key component to continuationism. This is a pivotal question that needs to be accurately addressed, because as long as cessationists believe the health-wealth gospel is accepted by *all* continuationists, any meaningful dialogue between the two groups is not likely to happen.

Subgroups Within Continuationism

As hinted earlier, continuationism, as a systematic pneumatology, consists of subgroups; and one way to identify them is their stance on prosperity teaching.

Subgroup 1:
Not as Open to the Spirit but Open to the Prosperity Gospel

Now of the two additional developments that affect continuationism, one of them challenges MacArthur's insinuation that there is a strong correlation, if not full equation, between an openness to the Spirit and embracing the prosperity gospel. While there is no denying that Pentecostals and charismatics have embraced the prosperity gospel, it is also true that many of them no longer speak in tongues, which, according to classical Pentecostalism is "the initial evidence of the Baptism of the Holy Spirit"[37] and one clear, but certainly not the only, indicator of openness to the Spirit. According to a survey done in the mid-2000s, "at least 40 percent of Pentecostals in six of the ten countries surveyed said they had never prayed or spoken in tongues. Only half of U. S. Pentecostals had spoken in tongues."[38]

What does this imply? It suggests that there are numerous advocates of prosperity theology who are not all that interested in pursuing the Spirit even if cessationists implicate them as full-fledged continuationists. In view of MacArthur's allusion that anyone open to the Spirit—which to him certainly includes speaking in tongues, supports the prosperity gospel—how does he account for many Pentecostals who are not as open to the Spirit (perhaps continuationists in name only) but uphold prosperity teaching? Admittedly, many of them still believe in prophecy, which may be construed as openness to the Spirit, but only the type that promises health and wealth. Suffice it to say, the correlation between an openness

37. Sherrill, *They Speak with Other Tongues*, 80.
38. Olsen, "What Really Unites Pentecostals?," 18.

to the Spirit and embracing the prosperity gospel is not as strong as suggested by MacArthur.

Subgroup 2:
Open to the Spirit, but Not Open to the Prosperity Gospel

Before considering the second of the two additional developments surrounding continuationism, I wonder whether MacArthur has ever considered the possibility of continuationists who are open to the Spirit without advocating the prosperity theology. It appears that he has because MacArthur acknowledges so-called "theologically respectable conservative continuationists [who] represent a very small minority within the charismatic movement."[39] And he laments that "they provide the entire movement with an aura of theological credibility and respect."[40] Meaning what? The presence of a very few theologically respectable leaders among continuationists—like John Piper and Wayne Grudem, who obviously do not back the prosperity theology—is drawing attention away from, among other things, the overwhelming majority of continuationists who adhere to the "name-and-claim it" theology.

But MacArthur should have looked closer at continuationists because, as Craig Keener has observed, "there are far more charismatics like MacArthur's continuationist friends than he recognizes."[41] Consider what Randy Clark writes in *Strangers to Fire* (2014), an anthology of twenty-six continuationists responding to *Strange Fire*, on behalf of Revival Alliance, a large of coalition of continuationists to which his group belongs:

> There is among us an understanding of blessings and curses related to covenant lifestyles. However, there is a majority opinion that this message is not to be perverted by focusing on the overtly material aspect of this truth to the point that our focus is our kingdom instead of His kingdom. Our focus is on being blessed to give, not what kind of car we drive, how large our homes are, or what kind of jewelry or watch we wear."[42]

This is one group of continuationists with whom MacArthur could have initiated a dialogue to clean up the mess created by the

---

39. MacArthur, *Strange Fire*, 234.

40. Ibid., 234.

41. Keener, "Review of MacArthur's *Strange Fire*," 48.

42. Clark, "Strange Fire," 61–62.

health-and-wealth wing of the charismatic movement. There is yet another subgroup within continuationism that offers the same opportunity.

Subgroup 3:
Continuationists but Not Part of the Larger Charismatic Movement

As said before, while most Pentecostals and charismatics—many of whom are not as open to the Spirit—adhere to some form of the prosperity gospel, MacArthur and other cessationists ought to consider the subtle nuances, particularly with respect to terms used in the discussion. One reason MacArthur fails to recognize a larger segment among continuationists who renounces the prosperity gospel is due to his indiscriminate usage of the term "continuationist" to refer to all Pentecostals and charismatics. Consequently, he does not see those continuationists/charismatics who, while upholding the perpetuity of all spiritual gifts, neither attend Pentecostal churches nor self-consciously identify with the charismatic movement as a whole (as represented by the likes of Trinity Broadcasting Network, televangelists, etc.). This is the Third Wave represented by the likes of continuationist Sam Storms mentioned at the outset of the book.

And this development is as significant to the changing face of continuationism as the other two (the adherence to the prosperity gospel by most Pentecostals and those who self-identify with the charismatic movement; two-fifths of Pentecostals no longer speaking in tongues). For instance, consider Southern Baptist and Reformed pastors, most of whom are theologically conservative: denominationally they are not Pentecostals and most of them do not send money to televangelists in the hope of getting rich. I think it is safe to say that MacArthur would not put these Baptists and Reformists in the category of "a false church, as dangerous as any cult or heresy,"[43] as he has done to Pentecostals and charismatics under the rubric of unbiblicality of continuationism. But the truth is that numerous Baptist and Reformed pastors are not only sympathetic to continuationism, but are seeking to pursue it.

A 2007 study by LifeWay Research of Southern Baptist Church pastors—typically noncharismatic and against prosperity theology—found that "half believe the Holy Spirit gives today the private use of tongues."[44] More recently, *Christianity Today*, following the conclusion of the Convergence Conference, put out an article full of oxymoronic phrases (to

43. MacArthur, *Strange Fire*, xvii.

44. Lovelace, "LifeWay Releases Prayer Language Study," lines 50–51.

cessationists, that is): "the Reformed charismatics," "Calvinist continu-ationists," "Reformed & Revived," and "100 percent committed to both word and Spirit."[45] Apparently, this group is growing: the header of the article says, "The Rise of Reformed Charismatics."[46]

On this list I would also include all ministers belonging to Acts Ministries International who adhere to continuationism. As the teaching pastor of the fellowship who works extensively with all pastors and their staff, I know of no one in this group who adheres to prosperity teaching (1 Tim 6:5–10; 2 Cor 2:17; 1 Thess 2:5) and identifies him- or herself as a part of the greater charismatic movement.

The Unfortunate Outcome

This section began by raising the question of what key factor has been behind the escalation of cessationist and continuationist conflicts punc-tuated by *Strange Fire*. It is none other than the lumping together of all continuationists as being one and the same, people who adhere to the health-and-wealth theology within the charismatic movement.

Now it is not as if MacArthur is completely unaware of more than one type of charismatic within continuationism. He admits that "there are sincere people within the charismatic movement who . . . recognize that salvation is not about health and wealth, and . . . genuinely desire to be rescued from sin, spiritual death, and everlasting hell."[47] As noted earlier, he also "ha[s] good friends . . . who label themselves as 'reformed charismatics.'"[48] MacArthur's key mistake, then, is failing to consider the implication of his own admission. Since these continuationists are true believers who shun prosperity teaching as much as he does, he should not have made blanket statements that, in effect, put all continuationists in the same category of a false church. But this very influential leader did, and to many who look to him for answers, continuationism is part and parcel of the health-and-wealth gospel and vice versa.

---

45. McCraken, "Rise of Reformed Charismatics," paras. 7, 8, and 11.

46. McCraken, "Rise of Reformed Charismatics."

47. MacArthur, *Strange Fire*, 81.

48. Ibid., 231.

Suspicion

So then, what has been the unfortunate outcome of grouping all continuationists into this unpleasant, one-size-fits-all category? One outcome is unwarranted suspicion that can hurt the local church.

As mentioned earlier, one ministry objective I had while serving in Mexico was to help forge some unity between the Baptist and Assemblies of God pastors. Thus, I was dismayed to find that upon returning to Chihuahua some years after leaving, two prominent Baptist leaders were already reading through MacArthur's *Strange Fire*. Evidently, they had received a copy as a gift when they attended MacArthur's annual international conference which followed the *Strange Fire* event. If I wondered then how the book may affect the faith of Mexican believers, I got my answer the following year when I returned to conduct a seminar for the Assemblies of God pastors. During this trip, Pastor Hugo, an Assemblies of God pastor and a faithful colleague, expressed his displeasure with John MacArthur. When I asked why exactly, Hugo told me about a wealthy man who came to his congregation after being fleeced by a prosperity gospel church in the city. Feeling very upset and discouraged, he sought help from Pastor Hugo. But after reading *Strange Fire,* he abruptly left his church after becoming suspicious that Hugo was part of the prosperity gospel movement, even though Hugo does not promote prosperity teaching.

Disheartenment

As Hugo experienced, this sort of thing has the effect of disheartening those continuationists who greatly disapprove of what MacArthur sees happening in the charismatic movement, such as the misuse of spiritual gifts and questionable doctrines like the health-and-wealth gospel. Sadly, continuationists in this group have been alienated by hard cessationism since it categorizes them as part of a false church. This also means an opportunity is being lost. Meaning what?

A Lost Opportunity

Let me share my personal story here. I left my Pentecostal church after three years of hardcore discipleship and attended Talbot School of Theology, a cessationist seminary (then anyway) in the mid-1980s. While I learned valuable lessons from my pastor then, which are helpful to this day, I also witnessed the messy side of the charismatic movement pointed out in *Strange Fire*. So, while studying at Talbot, I slowly found myself agreeing with most of what I heard. The turning point came when I began reading MacArthur's *The Charismatics: A Doctrinal Perspective*. I was so convinced of the cessationist argument that I stopped praying in tongues for several months during my seminary days, a daily practice I had kept since the day I became a believer in May 1981. Now while I did not stay that way—that is, after studying the Bible more judiciously—I still remember what can go wrong with continuationism. Therefore, without agreeing with the hermeneutics and theology of hard cessationism of MacArthur, there is still much in his criticism of continuationism that I would agree with. Thus, I would like to believe that continuationists like me are that subgroup within continuationism with whom cessationists can work together. But, I am afraid that *Strange Fire* has put a big dent in that possibility. And that is a great opportunity lost.

A Key to De-escalation

It was said earlier that as long as cessationists believe continuationism and the health-and-wealth gospel go hand in hand, having meaningful dialogues with continuationists is very unlikely and the fractured relationship will remain unamended. But, what has been presented thus far shows that that characterization is not entirely correct. First, there are a sizable number of continuationists (mainly in name only) who pursue the prosperity gospel, and second, there are more than "a very small minority"[49] among continuationists who disavow the "name-and-claim" it theology.

So what do these factors indicate? They suggest that prosperity theology is neither a necessary nor intrinsic component to the theology of continuationism since it is predicated upon the perpetuity of all spirit gifts and being open to them. The material blessing that is truly from God is indeed a gift "from above" (Jas 1:17b), but it is not a spiritual gift. In light of this, I would appeal to cessationists to cease from perceiving the health-and-wealth gospel as an essential aspect to continuationism; it is not.

---

49. MacArthur, *Strange Fire*, 234.

THE ULTIMATE FALLOUT
FROM THEOLOGICAL DISSENTIONS

What then is the ultimate fallout from dissentions among the adherents of competing systematic theologies in general and between cessationists and continuationists in particular? In short, the loss of the unity of the church.

Valuing Unity

Among conservative Christians, the word "ecumenism" conjures up the unsavory image of fellowshipping with mainstream liberal Christians at best, and the even more distasteful image of religious pluralism at worst. In any case, the unity that Christ often talked about should not necessarily be equated with modern-day ecumenicalism, which may not always see Christ as the center of its belief system. As long as Pentecostals and charismatics do believe that Jesus is the Lord and Savior (and most of them do), cessationists should not easily dismiss them, especially considering how Christ pleaded the night before his crucifixion: "That they may all be one, just as you, Father, are in me, and I in you, that they also may be in us, so that the world may believe that you have sent me" (John 17:21). In a time of fractious hostility in America, it does no service to the world when Christ's representatives act just as divisively and acrimoniously toward one another as anybody else. Doing so has the effect of weakening our witness and thereby dishonoring the Trinity, whose essence is unity. It is for this reason that the apostle Paul tells the believers to be "eager to maintain the unity of the Spirit in the bond of peace" (Eph 4:3). Seeing how important unity is to a credible witness to the world, believers should not so easily break bonds because of differences or even errors, which of course should be addressed, but "with gentleness" (2 Tim 2:25b).

Examples of Disunity

It goes without saying that disunity between cessationists and continuationists was around long before the arrival of *Strange Fire*. While the examples are too numerous to count, the two that immediately stand out in my mind are especially personal in nature. In 2005, when "the

Southern Baptist Convention's International Mission Board (IMB) dis-qualified candidates who spoke in tongues,"[50] I was four years into my time in Mexico, which included teaching Baptist pastors weekly while attending a church pastored by one of them. Thus, even though the ruling itself had no effect on my life, how the Baptist pastors would respond if they found out that I spoke in tongues certainly did. That question was eventually raised in a class I was teaching. How did it go? I will return to that story in the final chapter.

The second example felt even more personal. A year after arriving in Mexico, on the night before my wife and I were to be interviewed by the board of an American missionary school, we prayed that they would not ask us whether we spoke in tongues. Why? Because another mis-sionary family, sent by an Assemblies of God Church in America, told us that their children were denied admission after the board found out that they spoke in tongues.[51] While we were very happy that God answered our prayer, it did concern me that other Mexican churches would take this example of a sectarian attitude (in a school for children!) to heart. You might call this a catalyst that influenced the eventual direction of my ministry in Mexico: to forge unity between the feuding Baptist and Pentecostal pastors in Chihuahua.

Unfortunately, to what was already a discordant relationship be-tween cessationists and continuationists, the aftermath of *Strange Fire* has driven a deep wedge to further divide them. It is the time for remedy-ing the situation and I hope this book can play a small part.

THE REMEDY

So what shall we do to fulfill Christ's exhortation for unity? As mentioned earlier, while teaching and serving with cessationists and continuation-ists in Mexico for many years, I had a deep desire to reconcile the two. I will share what happened as a result of those efforts at the very end of the book. While practical and face-to-face reconciliation and unity between cessationists and continuationists should continue to be the highest goal, what I present as a remedy to rectify the division over word and Spirit may seem more intellectual than practical. But that is not true—it is

50. Smietna, "International Mission Board Drops Ban," para. 1. This ban was lifted in 2015.

51. In time I became friends with everyone on this board who diligently taught our children for many years.

practical with several concrete examples to show how (chapters 6–10). Ultimately, I want to show that this can only come about as we grow spiritually in word and Spirit.

To do that, the next three chapters will lay down the theoretical framework for the hermeneutics of the Radical Middle, beginning with recognizing the antithetic nature of Scripture and why that matters to the word and Spirit conflict. This is the part that may seem somewhat abstractive and academic. Please bear with it. After that, MacArthur's specific arguments against the viability of the sign gifts for today will be examined through the hermeneutics of the Radical Middle.

QUESTIONS FOR REFLECTION & DISCUSSION

1. Why do you think that two individuals who love the Lord and his word can be so diametrically opposed to one another in their thinking? If you were given a chance, what would you say to the likes of MacArthur and Hagin?

2. What are negative outcomes of the hostile contention between cessationists and continuationists?

3. Why is unity in Christ among the believers so important to the triune God? Has this matter concerned you in the past? How can we improve our unity in the Lord?

4. What is meant by pursuing the great historical doctrines of the Christian faith? What is meant by ardently pursuing the Spirit of God? Why is there struggle or tension between these two pursuits?

5. Pastor John MacArthur has been a faithful servant of the Lord for nearly fifty years. But no one bats a thousand, and he certainly has not done so with respect to his treatment of continuationists. Nevertheless, we must be careful not to dishonor God's servants with whom we may disagree (1 Tim 5:17).

   a. Would you pray that the Lord will guard your heart as you read this book? Whether you lean toward cessationism or continuationism, I encourage you to pray for our hearts to be open, and against being easily offended.

   b. Would you pray for Pastor MacArthur to finish well and reconsider his approach to continuationism?

2

The Antithetic/Antinomic Nature of Scripture and the Need for the Hermeneutics of the Radical Middle

Duck or Rabbit?

Young or old woman?

WHAT DO YOU SEE in these familiar pictures? Do you see a young maiden or an old woman? Do you see a duck or rabbit? Of course, what you see depends on where you are looking. To argue over whose vision is more correct would be foolish since each picture presents two different yet related realities; therefore, the proper response here is to recognize them both.

In the context of a book like this, the language of recognizing multiple views may raise the alarm of some conservative Christians who see an illustration like the one above as letting relativism into the church through the back door. Worse still, my credentials as an evangelical might be called into question were I to say that there is much in Scripture, though certainly not everything, that talks out of both sides of the mouth (i.e. seems to present conflicting truths). Whether we classify those conflicting truths as antithetic or antinomic, that is, contradictory (a point which I will elaborate on later), we must accept this unmistakable reality of Scripture and then adjust our hermeneutics accordingly.

The truth is, no one will see the need for the Radical Middle paradigm of both/and unless we first recognize how God's revelation in Scripture is structured and framed. One consequence of our failure to recognize this textual reality has been the dogmatic and ideological interpretation of the Bible that pits one systematic theology against another. The Radical Middle paradigm avoids this by allowing the entirety of Scripture to speak for itself. The outcome, however, will not neatly conform to any theological system, whether it be dispensational, Reformed, Pentecostal, or Arminian. Putting it differently, if we are already committed to a particular systematic theology whose formation is influenced by the privileging of preferred passages and the ignoring or distorting inconvenient ones, then we cannot do the hermeneutics of the Radical Middle.

HERMENEUTICS

The term "hermeneutics" derives from *hermes* of Greek mythology who was known as a messenger of the gods. As a verb, *hermaneuō* means "to interpret, to explain."[1]

Its Goal and Objectives

The main goal of hermeneutics is "to ascertain what God has said in Sacred Scripture; to determine the meaning of the word of God."[2] While that is the expressed desire of every student of the Bible, desire alone is far from sufficient to uncover the intended meaning of Scripture: we need a method.

Now hermeneutics is sometimes referred to as "a *science* in that it can determine certain principles for discovering the meaning of a document, and in that these principles are not a mere list of rules but bear *organic* connections to each other"[3] (italics his). The first objective of hermeneutics, therefore, is to become familiar with these principles

---

1. Ramm, *Protestant Biblical Interpretation*, 10.

2. Ibid., 2.

3. Ibid., 11.

which are further divided into specific[4] and general hermeneutics. The second objective is to skillfully apply hermeneutical principles to extract out the meaning of the text.

Specific and General Hermeneutics

What is the main difference between specific and general hermeneutical rules? Having taught hermeneutics courses on numerous occasions, I liken specific hermeneutics to actual tools, such as a drill and a hammer, that are needed in order to build. Whether dealing with prose, poems, or narratives, the specific rules of hermeneutics are instruments that are regularly utilized to extract the meaning. Among the most common ones are context, cross-reference, and word-study.

On the other hand, I equate general hermeneutics to the building philosophy of an architect (e.g., Gregorian style or colonial). Advisedly, it would be beneficial to speak to the architect before grabbing tools and to begin building in order to understand his or her philosophy, even quirks and nuances, and ensure that the final product conforms to what the architect has in mind. No construction crew ever wants to present a completed building that appears right to them but ends up displeasing the architect. The ultimate architect of Scripture is God and it is in the interpreter's best interest to discover, and this before commencing the actual work of exegesis, *how* and *why* God put together the Bible the way he did.

So what is God's building philosophy? To know that is to understand general hermeneutics. In a typical hermeneutics course, students learn general hermeneutics such as accommodated revelation, progressive revelation,[5] and Scripture interprets Scripture,[6] to name a few. Now,

---

4. Ramm refers to it as "special," but I prefer to call it "specific" because it is a definite and concrete maneuver. See the text for an explanation.

5. This principle posits that God's revelations to humans were not disclosed all at once because of their inability to understand and properly handle them; instead, they were imparted gradually, from the shadows of the Old Testament to the reality of the New Testament (Heb 10:1). This rule can keep us from improperly using the Old Testament.

6. This principle posits that the Bible is its own commentary unto itself. It is knowing which books of the Bible should be studied together because of, among other things, their thematic similarities. For instance, Ezra 1–6 should be studied together with Haggai and Zechariah because they deal with the matter concerning building of Zerubbabel's temple.

consider the example of accommodated revelation (a.k.a., anthropomorphism), which is attributing bodily characteristics to God. For instance, while several biblical writers say that God cares for us (1 Pet 5:7; Nah 1:7), the psalmist puts it differently: "O God, . . . in the shadow of your wings I will take refuge" (Ps 57:1). Does God have wings? Certainly not, since "God is spirit" (John 4:24a). So how the Lord accommodates the psalmist is to allow him to portray God as if he had flesh (e.g., eyes, ears, face—Ps 34:15–16). In the next breath, we need to ask *why* would an infinite God permit himself to be portrayed as having flesh with all of its limitations? The answer, of course, is so that finite humans through a familiar visual can know and feel God's message, which in this case is that God truly cares for us. And, lest anyone misunderstand as the Mormons evidently have, I always remind the students, "Don't literally interpret anthropomorphism."[7]

HOW BIBLICAL REVELATION IS REALLY FRAMED IN SCRIPTURE

The first general rule of hermeneutics that I learned in seminary is called "the clarity of Scripture." It simply states that when a text is understood literally, except when figurative language is employed (e.g., "I am the bread of life"), its meaning can be clear to the common reader. This is certainly true since the meaning of most texts seems self-evident, such as what Jesus says in John 14:27a, "Peace I leave with you; my peace I give to you," and in John 12:47b, "I did not come to judge the world but to save the world."

The Unclarity of Scripture

However, evidently not all Scriptures are *that* clear. The apostle Peter, speaking of the apostle Paul's letters, wrote, "Some things in them are hard to understand" (2 Pet 3:16b). If I was asked to pick Paul's most difficult passage, I would choose 1 Corinthians 15:29: "Otherwise, what do

---

7. Once I told Mormon missionaries who came to my house, "If you are going to interpret anthropomorphic verses literally, then you should present your god as having wings since Psalm 57:1 says, "I will take refuge in the shadows of your wings." One of them retorted, "Since we are made in God's image, God must have a body since we do!"

people mean by being baptized on behalf of the dead? If the dead are not raised at all, why are people baptized on their behalf?"[8] While I am not sure whether Peter was thinking of what I am about to share, what makes the understanding of Scripture difficult is its antithetic nature. And the reason we rarely feel this difficulty or tension (aside from our failure to actually read the Bible) is because many of us are unaware of how most biblical revelations are framed.

Two Types of Revelations in the Bible

What is an antithesis? The *Merriam-Webster Dictionary* defines it as "being in direct and unequivocal opposition: directly opposite or opposed." What, then, is an antinomy? "*The Shorter Oxford Dictionary* defines it as 'a contradiction between conclusions which seem equally logical, reasonable or necessary.'"[9] While some thesauruses list antithesis and antimony as synonyms, there is a difference: antithesis highlights a contradiction between pairs of opposites (i.e., thesis and its antithesis), while antinomy confirms that they are in themselves reasonable despite the contradiction.[10]

In applying antithesis and antinomy to Scripture, are they synonymous? It depends because, evidently, there are two types of antithetic revelations in Scripture: one type is antinomic, the other is not.

---

8. It could be that the believing relatives of Christians, who died before getting baptized, underwent baptism on their behalf. At a time when baptism was taken utmost seriously, these well-meaning family members might have overextended themselves by making sure that their believing relatives who died without being baptized would spiritually benefit by their vicarious act—even if, in reality, it made no difference.

9. Packer, *Evangelism and the Sovereignty of God*, 18.

10. For instance, thesaurus.com lists "antithesis" as a synonym for "antinomy."

The First Type of Antithetic Revelation

First Type

Thesis: True

Antithesis: True

The first type is one in which pairs of opposite Scriptures that contradict each other are equally true. This constitutes an antinomy since both are reasonable and true in and of themselves. In this way the first type of antithesis and antinomy are synonymous. This is the reason J. I. Packer, an influential Reformed theologian, in addressing *The Shorter Oxford*'s definition of antinomy, says,

> For our purpose, however, this definition is not quite accurate; the opening words should read 'an *appearance* of contradiction'. For the whole point of antinomy—in theology, at any rate—is that it is not a real contradiction, though it looks like one."[11] (italics his)

Although Packer's words might reassure the inerrantists who may feel threatened by the charge of Bible contradictions, it does not make interpreting antithetic/antinomic revelation any easier. Yes, on the surface, it appears difficult if not impossible to handle them if our goal is to interpret. Yet one thing is clear: both must be accepted and included in our hermeneutics. This, then, is the premise of the hermeneutics of the Radical Middle of both/and.

The Second Type of Antithetic Revelation

What then is the second type of antithetic revelation? Unlike the first type in which both thesis and antithesis are equally true, with the second type, while the thesis is true, its antithesis is presented in Scripture as

11. Ibid., 18.

unequivocally false. And not all false antitheses are actually stated in the Bible as such but are the result of either misunderstanding certain Scriptures or simply ignoring them. The second type of antithetic revelation, therefore, is not antinomic (thereby, they are not synonymous) because the contradiction between pairs of opposites is real, necessary, and irreconcilable. The hermeneutics of the Radical Middle of both/and does not apply to the second type of antithetic revelation; instead it calls for the hermeneutics of either/or.

What will be helpful at this point in clarifying the two types of antithetic revelations is to see their differences by way of examining biblical examples. The objective of this discussion is to set a proper framework through which the conflict between word and Spirit is better analyzed and understood. A total of eleven examples, eight for the first type and three for the second, are introduced in the following section.

THE FIRST TYPE: EQUALLY TRUE THESIS AND ITS ANTITHESIS

As eight sets of the first type of antithetic Scriptures are presented here, consider whether it would be easy or difficult to interpret them. The degree of difficulty, however, varies because some antithetic Scriptures are easier than others to handle and vice versa, which is largely due to the context (as we will see in chapter 5). The first set of four examples is characterized by antithetic statements made by the same person; the second set of antithetic remarks is made by two different individuals.

Did God Keep the Promise Made to Abraham?

As for the first set, we begin with the question of whether God fulfilled his promise made to Abraham while he was alive. The Hebrews writer says,

> For when God made a promise to Abraham, since he had no one greater by whom to swear, he swore by himself, saying, "Surely I will bless you and multiply you." And thus Abraham, having patiently waited, obtained the promise. (Heb 6:13–15)

However, the same writer, in chapter 11 of Hebrews, where Abraham is prominently featured, states, "And all these," which includes Abraham, "though commended through their faith, did not receive what was promised, since God had provided something better for us, that apart from us they should not be made perfect" (Heb 11:39–40).

This is a case of the same author presenting two different accounts in the same book:

While one account says Abraham received what God promised him (thesis), another says he did not (antithesis). Which one is true? Which do you prefer? No doubt, I would prefer the proposition declaring that God kept the promise made to Abraham; but, if we are to accept both as true, how, then, do we make sense of it?

Did Jesus Come to Bring Peace or a Sword?

The next three examples pertain to the antithetic words of Christ recorded in the Gospels.

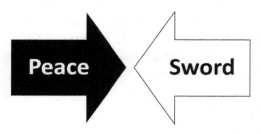

Let's begin with a question that most of us would feel confident to answer correctly. Did Jesus come to give us peace? Certainly yes, since Jesus says, "Peace I leave with you; my peace I give to you" (John 14:27a); "so that in me you may peace" (John 16:33a NIV). Referring to Christ, the apostle Paul says, "He himself is our peace" (Eph 2:14a). End of discussion, right? No, not really, because elsewhere Christ makes a diametrically opposing statement, saying: "Do not think that I have come to bring peace to the earth. I have not come to bring peace, but a sword" (Matt 10:34). On the one hand, Jesus came to give us peace (thesis), but on the other hand, "not peace, but a sword" (antithesis). Which proposition is true? Which one is preached more frequently from the pulpit? Which one do you prefer? Do we really get to choose, or do we accept both propositions as true even though they sure look contradictory?

Did Jesus Come to Judge?

Another set of statements made by Jesus that causes us to scratch our heads again has to do with what Christ said regarding why he came to earth. There is a collective sigh of relief upon reading John 12:47 where Christ says, "If anyone hears my words and does not keep them, I do not judge him; for I did not come to judge the world but to save the world." However, a little earlier, Jesus had declared, "For judgment I came into this world, that those who do not see may see, and those who see may become blind" (John 9:39). So which is it: Did Christ come to judge (thesis) or not (antithesis)?

Is Jesus Equal to the Father or the Father Greater than Jesus?

The third example, as far as the degree of doctrinal significance is concerned, ranks very high. It is the question of whether Jesus is equal to God the Father or lower than him, that is, God the Father is greater than Jesus. Yes, this has implications for the doctrine of Trinity in which the Father, the Son, and the Spirit are absolutely equal in divine essence and importance. There is no reason to question this doctrine upon seeing that, according to the apostle John, "[Jesus] was even calling God his own Father, making himself equal with God" (John 5:18b), saying, "I and the Father are one" (John 10:30). However, Christ, a day before his crucifixion, declared, "You heard me say to you, 'I am going away, and I will come to you.' If you loved me, you would have rejoiced, because I am going to the Father, for the Father is greater than I" (John 14:28). As readily seen, the statements, "Making himself equal with God" and "I and the Father are one," on the one hand, and "the Father is greater than I," on the other, are polar opposites. Again, this is a very significant doctrinal matter, and we are left with an apparent contradiction that, in all honesty, looks like a real one. So which is true: Is Jesus equal to God the Father (thesis) or lower than him (antithesis)?

Who Incited David to Take the Census: God or Satan?

While you are still mulling that one, consider the next set of four examples that involve multiple writers. Since they were inspired by the same Spirit (2 Tim 3:16; 2 Pet 1:20–21), shouldn't their stories match?

As mentioned at the outset of the book, another doctrinal quandary—certainly more consequential, if true, than the Trinity—is whether God and Satan refer to the same entity. King David, at the latter stage of his reign, ordered general Joab to take a census of the nation to identify those able to fight (2 Sam 24:2), thereby relying more on them than God. Later, God punished David for his sinful act by taking the lives of 70,000 Israelites (2 Sam 24:15–17).

So then, who incited David to take the census? The writer of 2 Samuel says, "Again, the anger of the LORD was kindled against Israel, and he incited David against them, saying, 'Go number Israel and Judah'" (2 Sam. 24:1). But, the writer of 1 Chronicles says that "Satan stood against Israel and incited David to number Israel" (1 Chr 21:1). Unless one believes that God and Satan are synonymous, this presents a big problem: God (thesis) is not Satan (antithesis), but these antithetic Scriptures attribute the inciting of the census to both. This is quite unsettling. So who incited the infamous census: God (thesis) or Satan (antithesis)?

Did Moses Fear Pharaoh?

Next is a question of what motivated Moses to leave behind the life of a prince in Egypt and go to the deserts of Midian where he would live and work as a shepherd for forty years. The following is what Moses himself said about what occurred on one fateful day in Egypt that led to his departure:

> One day, when Moses had grown up, he went out to his people and looked on their burdens, and he saw an Egyptian beating a Hebrew, one of his people. He looked this way and that, and seeing no one, he struck down the Egyptian and hid him in the sand. When he went out the next day, behold, two Hebrews were struggling together. And he said to the man in the wrong, "Why do you strike your companion?" He answered, "Who made you a prince and a judge over us? Do you mean to kill me as you killed the Egyptian?" Then Moses was afraid, and thought, "Surely the thing is known." When Pharaoh heard of it, he sought to kill Moses. But Moses fled from Pharaoh and stayed in the land of Midian. And he sat down by a well. (Exod 2:11–15).

According to Moses, he fled Egypt out of fear that Pharaoh was about to kill him for the murder of an Egyptian guard; however, what the writer of Hebrews says differs from Moses' account: "By faith he left

Egypt, not being afraid of the anger of the king, for he endured as seeing him who is invisible" (Heb 11:27).[12] Since fear is the polar opposite of faith, these narratives are antithetic to each other. So did Moses flee Egypt out of fear (thesis) or by faith (antithesis)?

Are Believers Aliens and Strangers?

Next is the question of whether believers are aliens and strangers while living in the world. According to the apostle Peter, believers are indeed so, for he writes, "Dear friends, I urge you, as aliens and strangers in the world, to abstain from sinful desires, which war against your soul" (1 Pet 2:11 NIV). The writer of Hebrews agrees with Peter, referring to those living by faith in God as "aliens and strangers on earth" (Heb 11:13b NIV). However, the apostle Paul says the exactly opposite: "So then you are no longer strangers and aliens, but you are fellow citizens with the saints and members of the household of God" (Eph 2:19).

So who is right? Peter, who insists that the believers are aliens and strangers (thesis), or Paul, who says that we are no longer aliens and strangers (antithesis)? While astute readers may quickly notice that Paul and Peter are talking about two different things (believers' relationship to the world and God, respectively), the antithetic use of the same terms can, at least initially, raise some concerns over Scripture being contradictory.[13]

Are Good Works Needed for Salvation?

The final example is as important doctrinally as whether Jesus is equal to or lower than God the Father. It is the question of whether good works are needed for salvation. The apostle Paul adamantly says no when he tells the Ephesian believers, "For by grace you have been saved through faith. And this is not your own doing; it is the gift of God, not a result of works, so that no one may boast" (Eph 2:8–9). However, the apostle

12. This verse does not seem to refer to the exodus (i.e., Moses' second departure from Egypt), since the subsequent passage (Heb 11:28) alludes to the Passover that occurred just prior to the exodus (further explained in chapter 5).

13. In the NIV, the two Greek words used in 1 Peter 2:11, *paroikos* and *parepidēmos*, are translated "aliens" and "strangers," respectively. In Hebrews 11:13, *xenos*, not *paroikos*, is used for "aliens" while the same *parepidēmos* is used to denote "strangers." As for Ephesians 2:19, a combination of *paroikos* and *xenos* is used, but in the ESV *xenos* is translated "strangers" instead of "aliens."

James seems to contradict Paul when he writes, "You see that a person is justified by works and not by faith alone . . . For as the body apart from the spirit is dead, so also faith apart from works is dead (Jas 2:24, 26). Again, who is telling the truth: Paul who declares, "Not by works" (thesis), or James who says, "Not by faith alone" (antithesis)?

Many Antithetic Statements in the Bible

These eight pairs of Scriptures are representative, though by no means exhaustive, of the way much of Scripture is framed antithetically. Noticing this, the renowned French thinker Jacques Ellul (whose work has been cited by luminary evangelical thinkers such as Charles Colson and J. P. Moreland) writes:

> We have to recognize that everything in revelation is formulated in antithetical fashion (in a dialectical way from certain standpoints) . . . We *never* find a single, logically connected truth followed by another truth deduced from it. There is no logic in the biblical revelation. There is no "either/or," only "both/and." We find this on every level.[14] (italics his)

While I agree with Ellul's view for the most part, he overstates his case by failing to recognize the second type of antithetic revelation in Scripture. It must firmly be stated that the hermeneutics of the Radical Middle is pertinent to the first type of antithetic revelation—what Packer describes as having "an *appearance* of contradiction," (italics his) but "not a real contradiction"[15] (i.e., being antinomic). Is this also true for Scriptures that pit word and Spirit against each other, or does Scripture really do that? We will return to this matter shortly.

14. Ellul, *Subversion of Christianity*, 43–44.
15. Packer, *Evangelism and the Sovereignty of God*, 18.

THE SECOND TYPE: TRUE THESIS, FALSE ANTITHESIS

Second Type

Thesis: True

Antithesis: False

With respect to the second type of antithetic revelation, it was said earlier that if the thesis is true, then its antithesis, whether stated in Scripture or incorrectly assumed, is unequivocally false. For this reason the second type of antithetic revelation is not antinomic because the contradiction is real and irreconcilable. This would mean that, contrary to Ellul's sweeping generalization of the entire Bible as a book that needs to be understood in terms of both/and, numerous antithetic revelations of the second type are to be interpreted in terms of either/or, not both/and. Consider the following three examples.

Does God Exist or Not Exist?

The writer of Hebrews declares that "for whoever would draw near to God must believe that he exists" (Heb 11:6b). While this thesis is accepted as true, its antithesis, the proposition that "there is no God" (Ps 14:1b) is dismissed as something a fool would say. Therefore, logically, the proposition that God exists, on the one hand, and the proposition that God does not exist, on the other, are not equally true: if one is true then the other is necessarily false.

Is Jesus the Only Name or is there Anyone Else?

The second example has to do with the exclusivity of Christ for salvation. Before the Sanhedrin, the apostle Peter declared, "This Jesus is the stone that was rejected by you, the builders, which has become the cornerstone. And there is salvation in no one else, for there is no other name under heaven given among men by which we must be saved" (Acts 4:11–12). While Scripture alludes to other names ("Indeed there are many 'gods' and many 'lords'"—1 Cor 8:5b), at no time are they deemed as equivalent or complementary to Christ in his role as Savior of humankind. The apostle Paul seconds Peter by saying, "Yet for us there is one God, the Father, from whom are all things and for whom we exist, and one Lord, Jesus Christ, through whom are all things and through whom we exist" (1 Cor 8:6). Therefore, religious pluralism, the belief that all religions lead to the same God, is an irreconcilable contradiction to the thesis that Jesus is "the way, and the truth, and the life. No one comes to the Father except through [Christ]" (John 14:6).

Are Humans Inherently Sinful or are They Not?

The third example, having to do with the fundamental nature of humans, is different from others in that while the thesis is presented in the Bible, its antithesis is not actually stated in the Bible as such but is the result of either misunderstanding certain Scriptures or simply ignoring them.

The apostle Paul states that "just as sin came into the world through one man, and death through sin, and so death spread to all men because all sinned" (Rom. 5:12). Thus, based on this and other related verses (Rom 7:17–18), Calvin drew the conclusion that "through Adam's Fall and rebellion, the whole human race has been cursed and has degenerated from its original state."[16]

But, no verse in the Bible counters the notion of inherently sinful nature of humans by saying something like humans are born either neutral or good. Yet Pelagius, a fifth-century British monk, denied original sin, saying, "Everything good and everything evil, in respect of which we are either worthy of praise or of blame, is *done by us*, not *born with us*"[17] (italics his). This is to say, Adam's "fall into sin injured no one but himself,

---

16. Lane and Osborne, *Institutes of Christian Religion*, 85.

17. Bettenson, *Documents of the Christian Church*, 53.

and left human nature unimpaired for good."[18] This antithetic view that opposes the biblical thesis was swiftly denounced by the early church led by Augustine.

Of course, the sinful nature does not prevent humans from doing moral as well as natural good—evil fathers, according to Jesus, will seek to meet their children's needs (Matt 7:11)—but it does keep them from doing so perfectly. And "whoever keeps the whole law but fails in one point has become guilty of all of it" (Jas 2:10), meaning no one who has ever lived except for Christ can escape charge that "all have sinned and fall short of the glory of God" (Rom 3:23).

PIVOTAL MISTAKES ESCALATING
THE CONFLICT BETWEEN WORD AND SPIRIT

The objective of discussion up to now has been to establish a proper framework to gauge the conflict between those who stress either word over Spirit, or Spirit over word. Recall that with respect to the first type of antithetic revelation, both thesis and its antithesis are equally true despite contradicting each other. The contradiction, however, is apparent, not real; it is antinomic in nature because both propositions are biblically valid in and of themselves. However, the second type of antithetic revelation is not antinomic, because the rightness of the thesis makes its antithesis necessarily false.

A False Dichotomy

But, what about word and Spirit? Does Scripture pit word and Spirit against each another in an antithetic manner? If so, does the conflict between the two belong to the first or second type of antithetic revelation?

Scriptural Justification for Both Sides

One thing is for certain: those who favor either Spirit over word, or word over Spirit do not have to look far before finding Scriptures that would justify their respective stances.

---

18. Berkhof, *History of Christian Doctrines*, 132.

The apostle Paul, in his final epistle written to his protégé Timothy, who was serving as the pastor of the church in Ephesus, reminded him to "do [his] best to present [him]self to God as one approved, a worker who has no need to be ashamed, rightly handling the word of truth" (2 Tim 2:15). In fact, Paul, in an earlier epistle, told Timothy, "Watch your life and doctrine closely. Persevere in them, because if you do, you will save both yourself and your hearers (1 Tim 4:16 NIV). The cessationist crowd would certainly favor these and other similar passages that stress the importance of correctly studying God's word and upholding the doctrines of the Christian faith.

However, continuationists are not without their own scriptural recourses. The same apostle Paul, a few years before penning his final letter to the Ephesian church, told the same church, "Be filled with the Spirit" (Eph 5:18b). Much earlier, the apostle reminded the Thessalonian congregation not to "quench the Spirit" (1 Thess 5:19).

What Scripture Actually Advocates

Inasmuch as I can remain objective, these Scriptures are not antithetic—meaning, nothing in the Bible says one must choose between word and Spirit. However, their relationship has become antithetic only because cessationists and continuations have made it so, since scripturally there is no warrant for it. Meaning what? It is a false dichotomy. As shown earlier, Matthew 10:34 and John 14:27 are a true antithesis of the first type since, while in the latter Jesus says, "My peace I give to you," in the former he says exactly the opposite: "I have not come to bring peace, but a sword." But there is no Scripture that says, "Do not think that I have come to bring 'word' to the earth. I have not come to bring 'word,' but 'Spirit.'" Neither is its opposite found in the Bible: "I have not come to bring 'Spirit,' but 'word.'" Instead, the same believers in Ephesus were told to "be filled with the Spirit" (Eph 5:18b), as well as to correctly handle God's word and uphold sound doctrines.

Its Relation to Spiritual Growth

And for our spiritual life to grow—fueled and marked by humility, love, and unity—while the embracing of word and Spirit may not be sufficient, they are absolutely necessary. Jesus makes this point clear in John 6:33: "It is the Spirit who gives life . . . The words that I have spoken to you are spirit and life." Since the Greek word used here for "life" derives from *zōē*, "referring to the principle life in the spirit and soul,"[19] it seems reasonable to say that the growth of our spiritual life is fueled by the combined work of the Spirit and Christ's words. However, the way cessationists and some continuationists argue their cases forces a choice between the two, which then becomes a prelude to an abnormal spiritual growth. Some have faith in reason itself, which, in time, makes them susceptible to doubts and rationalism. The faith of some can only be described as faith apart from reason that makes them vulnerable to "every wind of doctrine" (Eph 4:14b) and emotionalism.

A Confusion over Essentials and Nonessentials

What makes the conflict between word and Spirit and its concomitant consequence worse than it needs to be is the failure to consider one vital factor before attempting to correct a brother over an error, doctrinal or otherwise, and to what degree if it is carried out. What is it? The clarity of Scripture. As cited earlier, "some things" in Scripture "are hard to understand" (2 Pet 3:16b). Obviously, this implies that it would be harder to extract the exact meaning of those biblical texts that fall under the "hard to understand" category than those texts that do not. The first type of antithetic revelation, in which both thesis and its antithesis are equally true, certainly would qualify as harder to understand than the second type of antithetic revelation of either/or, which is considerably clearer in meaning. And one of the characteristics that distinguishes the first from

---

19. Zodhiates, *Complete Word Study*, 919.

the second type of antithetic revelation is the kind of doctrine generated from each.

First, let me briefly distinguish between essential and nonessential doctrines in relation to the clarity of Scripture. For the most part, the more essential the doctrines, which I define as those that affect salvation,[20] the clearer the Scriptures from which those doctrines are generated. By that definition, whereas the rapture[21] would be a nonessential doctrine, since whether one believes it or not does not affect salvation, "believ[ing] that Jesus is the Christ, the Son of God" (John 20:31b) is essential since it does affect salvation. In terms of scriptural support, while the doctrine regarding the identity of Jesus is backed by many clear verses in the New Testament, the doctrine regarding the rapture does not enjoy the same level of support. For instance, Hal Lindsey, the most renowned rapture expert in the late twentieth century, says in his book, *The Rapture*: "The truth of the matter is that neither a post-, mid-, or pre-tribulationist can point to any single verse that clearly says the Rapture will occur before, in the middle of, or after the Tribulation."[22] The timing of the rapture, he admits, largely depends on whether one believes Israel and the church to be the same or different.

The Second Type of Antithetic Revelation: Clear and Essential

Now, it is from the second type of antithetic revelation, which embodies more scriptural clarity than the first type, that most—if not all—of essential doctrines proceed. And, where there is a strong clarity of Scripture, doctrinal unity is found right along with it. That is why cessationists and most continuationists do not fight over the doctrine of the Trinity, justification by faith, divinity, and the humanity of Christ since, to theological conservatives, which both are, these are clear matters. But, given that it

20. For instance, a belief in the existence of heaven or hell would be an essential matter since if they do not exist, one would wonder why Jesus had to die. Whether scriptural descriptions of heaven and hell are to be understood literally or analogically is another matter that can be debated. The Trinity is essential since the Father, the Son, and the Spirit are all intimately involved with the planning and the implementation of the redemptive plan.

21. As noted in chapter 1, the rapture of the church postulates that Jesus will one day descend from heaven and meet the church, which just ascended from earth, in the air, and then they will return to heaven (1 Thess 4:13–17)

22. Lindsey, *Rapture*, 37.

took two to three centuries for the early church to nail them down, the more agreeable examples for the clarity of Scripture to Christians of all stripes (except for theological liberals) may be doctrines such as incarnation, death, and the resurrection of Christ.

The First Type of Antithetic Revelation: Not as Clear and Not as Essential

In contrast, most doctrines stemming from the first type of antithetic revelation tend to be nonessential ones, like issues of church governance, which can separate a Presbyterian church (ruled by the presbytery) from a Baptist congregation (locally governed), or eschatology.[23] The recognition that different things can be perceived from Scripture that may lead to drawing different conclusions in the nonessentials ought to foster an attitude and atmosphere of tolerance. If this is ignored, that is, everything taught in the Bible is seen as a matter of the second type of antithetic revelation of either/or, then this will lead to building a comprehensive airtight system that sees all other systems as unfaithful to God's word.

Implications for the Cessationist and Continuationist Conflicts

The two key takeaways from this discussion, which are related, are as follows.

Two Takeaways

First, just as there is a greater commandment among all commandments (Matt 22:38) and a greater sin among all sins (John 19:11), some doctrines are weightier than others. This is to say, while all doctrines taught in Scripture are valid, they are not all equally valuable. So it stands to reason that while Scriptures related to spiritual gifts are valuable, those biblical texts dealing with the doctrine of atonement are weightier since our response to it affects our eternal destiny.

Second, not only are teachings related to spiritual gifts not as consequential, they are not backed by the same level of scriptural clarity that

---

23. Amillennialists and premillennialists who disagree on several key issues, including the rapture and millennial kingdom, agree on the second coming of Christ, which, most would agree, is an essential doctrine of the church.

upholds essential doctrines. And this lack of clarity appears to be the reason Robert Saucy, professor of systematic theology at Talbot (mentioned in the introduction), went from writing in 1972 that, "It seems most reasonable to conclude that certain of the spiritual gifts active in the early church [i.e., the miraculous sign gifts] are no longer given to God's people,"[24] to contributing a book chapter entitled, "An Open but Cautious View" in 1996. He writes:

> There is no explicit biblical teaching that some spiritual gifts seen in the New Testament church did in fact cease at some point in church history. But neither does Scripture explicitly teach that all of the miraculous activity seen in the record of the New Testament church is intended to be normal throughout church history.[25]

As a result, Saucy's outlook toward the sign gifts became a cautious "both/and," not a hard "either/or." That is, my professor at Talbot, who went to be with the Lord in 2015, was no longer a cessationist.

Looking to Wage War?

So if anyone is looking to "wage war [against] . . . every pretension that sets itself against the knowledge of God" (2 Cor 10:3b, 5a NIV), it would be wise to do so against those who question the essentials of our faith, despite their clarity, than the nonessentials that are not as valuable and scripturally clear.

But its opposite is what has happened even though the conflict between the advocates of word over Spirit and vice versa is not "either/or" but "both/and." And while the target of their great polemics, the sign gifts, is a very important issue, it is not an essential doctrine. Nevertheless, this is where hard cessationism has come up very short. Its main architect—MacArthur—has condemned millions of Christ-confessing continuationists as not of the Holy Spirit, that is, not brothers and sisters in Christ, on account of disagreement over nonessential and not-as-weighty issues. That is an egregious error committed by this otherwise outstanding defender of the gospel.

This does not mean that no attempts should be made to correct an erring brother. In fact, Scripture exhorts us to do this; but, we are "not

24. Saucy, *Church in God's Program*, 136.
25. Saucy, "Open but Cautious View," 126.

[to] regard him as an enemy, but warn him as a brother" (2 Thess 3:15). This is wise counsel from the Lord that the *Strang Fire* crowd failed to heed. In the final chapter, I will briefly share how the Lord led me to the ministry of correction and reconciliation among warring pastors while serving in Mexico.

DISCUSSIONS TO FOLLOW IN THE FOLLOWING CHAPTERS

Earlier, while addressing general hermeneutics, we talked about different ways God framed biblical revelation (*the how* and *why* he did so). It was argued then that, along with general hermeneutics such as anthropomorphism and progressive revelation, the first type of antithetic revelation, in which both a thesis and its antithesis are held true, is one of those ways. The two encompassing questions arise at this point. The first is a matter of hermeneutics: What are the proper and improper ways to interpret antithetic revelation of the first type? The second is a matter of understanding God's heart: Why did the Lord give us such seemingly confusing and contradictory revelations in the first place (see chapter 11). Before we get to those questions, we need to first define the Radical Middle paradigm. Only then can we address those questions adequately.

QUESTIONS FOR REFLECTION & DISCUSSION

1. In your opinion what makes the Bible a not-so-easy book to understand?

2. Jesus came to give us peace. No, he came to give us a sword. Which one have you heard preached more frequently from the pulpit? Which one do you prefer? What does that say about us?

3. Do you think Jesus' remark, "The Father is greater than I," can affect the doctrine of the Trinity? What is your understanding of the Trinity?

4. What is your understanding of the relationship between faith and works?

5. Perhaps you discovered the antithetic nature of Scripture just now. How do you feel about it? Do you think it would be easy or hard to interpret these antithetic passages?

3

Logocentrism and the Radical Middle: How They Differ

CHAPTER 1 HIGHLIGHTED THE contentious relationship between continuationists, known for pursuing the Spirit while not always heeding the word; and cessationists who, while trying to uphold the historical doctrines of the Christian faith, have denied the validity of the sign gifts for today. This contentious relationship fractured the body of Christ, especially through the Strange Fire conference, by calling into question even the genuineness of the faith of Pentecostals and charismatics.

So what sets continuationists and cessationists apart? One obvious difference is over whether God continues to perform miracles even to this day. Would it be fair then to categorize cessationists as halfway naturalists for believing in the veracity of miracles recorded in Scripture, and yet denying the possibility of supernatural causation for today? Whether that charge is warranted is considered later. What is certain is that cessationists assert that their belief has nothing whatsoever to do with naturalism and everything to do with what Scripture teaches. They are confident that their exegesis on biblical passages pertaining to the sign gifts is correct, and such self-assurance stems from believing in the soundness of their hermeneutics. But that is precisely the problem. In actuality cessationists have unsound hermeneutics because they are either unwilling or unable to recognize that the question of the sign gifts is part of the antinomic nature of Scripture in which pairs of opposites (thesis and antithesis) are equally true and reasonable in themselves. Some continuationists make the same hermeneutical mistake by overstating the importance of speaking in tongues and claiming too much regarding healing.

In view of this, the goal of this chapter is to present the proper way to interpret antithetic revelation—the hermeneutics of the Radical Middle—in contrast to the improper manner—the hermeneutics of logocentrism. The first objective then is to introduce the concept of logocentrism and show how its hermeneutical orientation differs from the Radical Middle paradigm. Suffice it to say, if cessationists and some continuationists fail to see the difference between the two, their acrimonious relationship will not abate. The second objective is, after defining the Radical Middle paradigm, to indicate how the theologizing in the Radical Middle is found right in the pages of Scripture. A further demonstration will also show that several important theological discoveries that became part of the great historical doctrines of the Christian faith were the result of interpreting Scripture through the Radical Middle paradigm. In fact, it appears that many contemporary Christian thinkers are framing their thoughts in accordance with the Radical Middle paradigm as well. These discussions will not only show the necessity of the Radical Middle paradigm, but sharpen our understanding of it.

THE HERMENEUTICS OF LOGOCENTRISM

The apostle John, writing his gospel from the Greek city of Ephesus in the late first century AD, applied a familiar Greek word *logos* to Jesus, thereby denoting him as the Word incarnate (John 1:1, 14), who not only created the universe but rules over it (John 1:3; Eph 1:10).

The Essence of Logos

Long before John was inspired to make this connection, the essence of *logos*, which Heraclitus, a Greek philosopher from Ephesus, articulated in the sixth century BC, permeated the Hellenist mindset. Heraclitus, at first, observed what seemed obvious: "the universe, instead of standing still, is in continuous motion . . . Our bodies and minds are changing every moment, and our perceptions and ideas change with them."[1] But the fact that life was not complete chaos startled him. Heraclitus, therefore, reasoned that, according to Eva Brann in *The Logos of Heraclitus*:

1. Greer, *Brief History of the Western World*, 59.

the great *Logos* collects, discerns, and then brings the things that constitutes the world together; that is to say, working in the cosmos, the *[l]ogos* steers everything through everything and thus relates everything in a unity.[2]

It is, therefore, not hard to see why in the Greek mind, *logos* referred to the "originary source that is pure and undefiled . . . [that] not only gives meaning and purpose to all things but serves as the final referent point and touchstone against which all forms of *beauty* and truth can be measured and judged."[3]

Now, at this point, it is important to distinguish between *logos* as a proper noun and *logos* as a common noun. Once *logos* became a proper noun that refers to Christ (John 1:1), logocentrism would mean "Christocentric," which is both good and fitting since he is the originator and sustainer of all created things. But as a common noun, *logos* implies "a final center," and as such, the center can be occupied by any number of things: for the Enlightenment philosophers, it was reason (rationalist) or experience (empiricist); for the Muslims, it is the Koran, "the Mother of the Book" (Surah 13:39); for postmodernists, their center is that there is no center. Logocentrism, in this context, would mean that whatever occupies the center functions as the ultimate reference point. But, regardless of what or who occupies the center, logocentrism operates in the same manner: through binary opposition.

The Constitution of Logos

The key question is how *logos* emerges as the final reference point, the ultimate arbiter of truth and knowledge.

Oppositional Pairs

The first step in answering that question is recognizing the constitution of *logos*. Heraclitus postulated that *logos* consists of "pairs of opposites," that is, "intensely related pairs that are . . . starkly opposed in logical opposition."[4] Some examples given are "the surfeit-and-famine . . . wholes

2. Brann, *Logos of Heraclitus*, 50, 70.

3. Markos, *From Plato to Postmodernism*, 13.

4. Brann, *Logos of Heraclitus*, 74.

and not-wholes"[5]; "day and night and hot and cold."[6] On the surface, it is evident that the pairs do not relate to each other in "friendly mutual address but in antagonistic opposition . . . [They are held] "apart rather than together."[7] Meaning what?

"How are Heraclitean pairs actually related?" asks Brann.[8] "The *logos* brings [opposite] terms into relations to each other . . . relation that connects two terms in mutually determining juxtaposition."[9] Brann notes that Aristotle, who came several centuries after Heraclitus, misunderstood the connection of oppositional pairs as "mixing" and "blending" them, that is, "unitings by meldings."[10] "But," she says, "that is just what Heraclitus, the plain and radical, doesn't mean. Oppositions do not compose in sweetness and light," meaning their connection "is the balancing of opposites"[11]—it is not a synthesis—amid "tension . . . constantly generated between these pairs of opposites."[12]

This, then, is how Heraclitus came to "consider the *logos* to be a universal, cosmic law, according to which *all* things come into being, and which *all* the material elements of the universe are held in balance"[13] (italics mine). And it would take a special revelation given to the apostles John and Paul several centuries later for the world to see that this *logos* was none other than Jesus by whom "all things were created, in heaven and on earth, visible and invisible . . . and in him all things hold together" (Col 1:16a, 17b).

5. Ibid., 74.

6. Atkinson, *Philosophy Book,* 40.

7. Brann, *Heraclitus,* 72.

8. Ibid., 73.

9. Ibid., 11.

10. Ibid., 73.

11. Atkinson, *Philosophy Book,* 40.

12. Ibid., 40.

13. Ibid., 40.

Binary Opposition

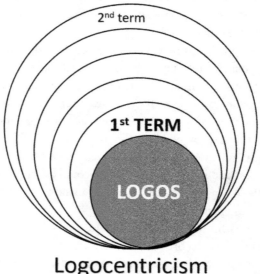

However, the way *logos* actually played out in the Western world, the *balancing* of opposites is not how it developed. Instead, binary opposition became the modus operandi of *logos* in which "the first term is privileged over the second and the second term is seen, in some way, as a falling away from the first: *form/imitation,* being/becoming, *presence/absence.*"[14] The first term is prioritized and preferred, the second term, devalued or even dismissed. It is a zero-sum game in which the first term's gain (i.e., perceived as more real and true) is the second term's loss (i.e., perceived less real and true).

When these operational characteristics of *logos* are rigidly and exhaustively followed, it constitutes "a metaphysical and theoretical orientation" called logocentrism, and it "has dominated Western thought since Plato"[15] as the final referent point. As a result, in Western logocentrism, whose center had long been occupied by part theism and part humanism, male had long been privileged over female, white over nonwhite, and intellect/knowledge over emotion/experience. As demonstrated later, the basic framework of systematic theology developed in the

---

14. Markos, *From Plato to Postmodernism,* 3.

15. Ibid., 13.

West—including cessationism—is logocentrism. This book presents the Radical Middle outlook as its alternative.

LOGOCENTRIC THEOLOGIZING

To conservative Christians, as heirs of Protestant Reformation rooted in "sola Scriptura," the originary source that is undefiled is God's word, and it occupies their center as the infallible canon through which all forms of truth are measured and judged. Utilizing the Bible as the final referent point, however, is not as easy as it seems, because many Scriptures are framed as pairs of opposing propositions that are reasonable in themselves but still appear contradictory, some raising more questions in our minds than others.

In the previous chapter, two terms are introduced to capture this scriptural reality: "antithesis," to denote thesis and antithesis in conflict, and "antinomy," to denote a contraction between two ostensibly true propositions. Another term is being introduced in this chapter—binary opposition—to show how the Western tradition has handled antithesis/antinomy: the privileging of one side over the other, a.k.a., logocentrism. So if this were a book on sociology we would be talking about racism and sexism; if this were a book on philosophy we would be talking about postmodernism and deconstructionism. But in this book, we are talking about biblical hermeneutics: whether we should continue to handle antinomic revelation—including Scriptures relevant to the sign gifts, in accordance to logocentricism—or change to the Radical Middle.

Truth be told, most of us do not necessarily have the cognitive category to recognize antithesis/antinomy in the Bible, because we assume that since every revelation that came from God is authoritative and absolute, only one proposition, one version, or one interpretation is valid, while all the rest is not as valid. So the King James Version is still revered by some as if it were the original; systematic theologians argue over why their system got it right; and we selectively read and study the Bible to ensure that our theology, the right theology, is left undisturbed. But, we saw in chapter 2 that the Scripture itself does not give us that option, because it is full of antithetic/antinomic propositions: Jesus equal to the Father/the Father greater than Jesus; God incited David/Satan incited David; divine sovereignty/human freewill, just to name a few. Obviously, the difficulty is in knowing to which Scripture we are to appeal in order to recognize what is true and reasonable with respect to a given issue, theological or otherwise, since Scripture presents both as valid.

A Proper Handling of Biblical Revelation

So in view of the antinomic and binary nature of Scripture, how should biblical revelation be handled (a matter of hermeneutics) when theologizing to produce doctrines that serve as the reference point? Should it be handled through the approach of both/and, that is, the balancing of opposites favored by Heraclitus? Or through the approach of either/or, that is, the zero-sum model of logocentrism? That depends on the type of binary opposition found in Scripture.

Handling of Non-antinomic Scriptures and the Radical Middle

As noted in chapter 2, not all biblical revelations are antinomic in nature—meaning, in a pair of opposite propositions, if one is true, then the other is necessarily false. Obviously, the truth needs to be privileged while its false opposite must be dismissed. For instance, while the proposition "Be holy" (1 Pet 1:16b) is privileged, since that is what God, who is holy, demands of us, its false opposite, "Let us do evil that good may result" (Rom 3:8b NIV) is discarded, because that reflects a false understanding of God's grace. As mentioned before, while the proposition "God . . . exists" (Heb 11:6b) is privileged, since without that *a priori* belief no one will come to God, its false opposite, "There is no God" (Ps 14:1b), is discarded because the denial of God's existence is what "the fools says in his heart" (Ps 14:1a).

This does not mean that disbelief in God serves no value, and perhaps for this reason Heraclitus would keep theism and atheism in balance. Philosophically, inasmuch as our awareness of and aversion to evil in the world points to the existence of moral law and the good it reveals, disbelief in God and its concomitant hopelessness can amplify the strength of its opposite—belief in God and its concomitant hope. That does not, of course, mean that Scripture privileges unholiness, evil, and atheism (as true and reasonable) in the same way their opposites—holiness, goodness, and theism—are privileged. As noted before, the Radical Middle paradigm of both/and would *not* apply to antithetic revelations in which the truthfulness of one proposition makes the other necessarily false; instead, this is a case for the approach of either/or.

Mishandling of Antinomic Scriptures and Systematic Theology

But, when Scripture presents pairs of opposite terms or propositions as equally true and valid (i.e., antinomic), both must be privileged, meaning kept in balance despite their seeming contradictory nature. This is the outlook of the Radical Middle.

In contrast, privileging one term (for instance, divine sovereignty) while devaluing the other (human free will) is to theologize according to the hermeneutics of logocentricism. And without a doubt, logocentricism is preferred by those who seek to theologize the Bible systematically under the rubric of one overarching or dominant theological outlook. In this regard, not much separates Calvinism from Arminianism, Reformed theology from Dispensationalism, and cessationism from continuationism. In chapter 1 are given examples of overarching outlooks such as the "sovereignty of God," "eternal security," (i.e., once saved, always saved), and "miracles only happened in the past." A dominant outlook itself is formed by way of privileging those Scriptures from which that outlook emerges, while ignoring or distorting other Scriptures that point to a different outlook.[16]

A typical outcome of the hermeneutics of logocentricism (i.e., privileging Scriptures while devaluing their opposites) is a theological system built on airtight, logical, and tidy arguments. But, as Keener notes, "while any 'logical argument' looks consistent from within the system that supports it, it will fail to persuade those outside the system because it depends on other elements within the system to support it."[17] In Calvinism, limited atonement is predicated upon unconditional election—the logic being that it is absurd to think that Jesus would die for the non-elect. In cessationism, the ceasing of sign gifts depends on the belief that miracles are not needed once the canon is complete (though no biblical text actually says this).

---

16. One obvious factor has a lot to do with exposure to a particular theology at the outset of one's faith journey. Once this theology is firmly in place, everything in the Bible is looked through rose-tinted spectacles. But, many also change their initial understanding of the Bible upon realizing their interpretive theology's weaknesses.

17. Keener, "Are Spiritual Gifts for Today?," 159.

But, there is one big problem with this hermeneutical approach: Scripture is not allowed to speak for itself. The aforementioned Reformed theologian, J. I. Packer, in his *Evangelism and the Sovereignty of God*, which tries to reconcile divine sovereignty and human responsibility, says:

> Our minds dislike antinomies. We like to tie up everything into neat intellectual parcels, with all appearance of mystery dispelled and no loose ends hanging out. Hence we are tempted to get rid of antinomies from our minds by illegitimate means: to suppress, or jettison, one truth in the supposed interests of the other, and for the sake of a tidier theology.[18]

Thus, as said earlier, it should surprise no one that most, if not all, systematic theologies, which dislike theological ambiguities, are logocentric, meaning Scriptures that lend support to one's theology are privileged, while those Scriptures that do not are devalued through ignoring or distorting them.

Occurrences of Logocentric Theologizing

So what does theologizing in accordance with the hermeneutics of logocentrism look like?

The Trinity

Consider the case of the Trinity. Which person in the Trinity is favored among the advocates of different systematic theologies? Among the promoters of Reformed theology, many of whom uphold unconditional election and double predestination, God the Father and his sovereignty are privileged over the Holy Spirit. The Reformed theology (to its credit) certainly talks a great deal about the regenerating work of the Spirit, but not too much is said about him after that. The Arminian theologian Roger E. Olson, while noting "Calvin's emphasis on the third person of the Trinity," comments that "too many Calvinists talk too little of the Holy Spirit."[19] N. T. Wright, in speaking of John Piper, a pastor known for his advocacy of Reformed tradition, says:

18. Packer, *Evangelism and the Sovereignty of God*, 25.
19. Witherington, "What Calvin Gets Right," 34.

John Piper, and the tradition he represents, have said that salvation is accomplished by the sovereign grace of God, operating through the death of Jesus Christ in our place and on our behalf, and appropriated through faith alone. Absolutely. I agree 100 percent . . . But there is something missing—or rather, some*one* missing. Where is the Holy Spirit?[20]

As for Pentecostals and charismatics, they so privilege the Holy Spirit, his gifts, and power that sometimes one wonders where is the gospel? I first observed this many years ago as a guest speaker at a youth retreat of a charismatic congregation in Oklahoma. It appeared to me that all the attendees spoke in tongues (very loudly). Thus, I found it very odd that almost everyone raised their hands to receive Christ as Savior after a gospel presentation was made to those few unbelievers I assumed were in attendance. By definition, these tongue-speakers were not only believers but had been baptized with the Holy Spirit, and yet they were not sure about their salvation. Even after being reminded that the gospel presentation was not for them, hardly anyone put their hands down. The same situation occurred later with another charismatic youth group. This clearly is not an optimal situation for spiritual growth when the gifts of the Spirit (regardless of which ones) are emphasized and practiced on a shaky doctrinal foundation.

As for the run-of-the-mill evangelicals, who are comfortable neither with the doctrines of election and predestination nor with the ministry of Holy Spirit, they tend to privilege Jesus the Savior (but not necessarily the Lord) and the gospel (but not necessarily its cost) by default.

Word and Spirit

Let's see now what happens when the matter of word and Spirit is theologized in accordance with logocentrism in which one is privileged over the other. Recall what was said in chapter 2: the relationship between word and Spirit has become antithetic only because cessationists and continuations have made it so; scripturally there is no warrant for it. That is to say, there is no Scripture that says, "Do not think that I have come to bring 'word' to the earth. I have not come to bring 'word,' but 'Spirit.'" Neither is its opposite found in the Bible. Instead, the believers are told

20. Wright, *Justification*, viii. This is an ironic comment about Piper since he is a continuationist.

to "be filled with the Spirit" (Eph 5:18b), as well as to love the Lord "with all your mind" (Matt 22:37b) and "with all your understanding" (Mark 12:33b).

Notwithstanding, cessationists privilege word, knowledge, and doctrine while devaluing Spirit, experience, and emotion. Knowing is privileged, while feeling is held in suspicion. Thus, Pentecostals and charismatics are dubbed as "feelers" at best, and "not of the Holy Spirit" at worst. Not to be outdone, continuationists invert this by privileging Spirit, experience, and emotion, while devaluing word, knowledge, and doctrine. I once heard a charismatic speaker say, "Let's get [the] 'word' over with so we can get to the ministry time." Instead of knowing the truth, some continuationists rather feel it. As already mentioned, seminary is purposefully mispronounced as "cemetery" to jab at what to them are spiritless cessationists[21], whose inability to speak in tongues points to their second-class status in the kingdom. Suffice it to say, in view of Christ's exhortation that "the true worshipers will worship the Father in spirit and truth," (John 4:23b), neither setting is optimal for producing authentic spiritual growth. (How the privileging of word over Spirt and vice versa actually affects our spiritual growth is discussed in the next chapter.)

THE THREE ESSENTIALS OF THE HERMENEUTICS OF THE RADICAL MIDDLE

While addressing the matter of logocentrism of either/or, much was already said about the hermeneutics of the Radical Middle of both/and, without which theologizing in the Radical Middle is not possible. Before presenting its three essentials, the following bears repeating: Scripture is full of antithetic (pairs of opposite propositions) and antinomic revelations (that are reasonable in themselves). If the hermeneutics of logocentrism of either/or is used to interpret them, its long-term effects are the loss of true biblical knowledge, the loss of grace which leads to disunity, and the loss of taking doctrine seriously (chapter 11). The hermeneutical approach that can avert these losses is the Radical Middle of both/and.

---

21. The privileging of the first term over the second in binary opposition is done in other ways. Liberal churches that have a low view of Scripture typically privilege social action (1 John 3:18) over the gospel. In contrast, conservative churches typically privilege the gospel over social actions. Most evangelical churches overwhelmingly privilege domestic ministry over foreign missions.

Refrain from "Marrying" a Systematic Theology

The first essential, without which the hermeneutics of the Radical Middle will not be embraced, is divesting oneself from interpreting the Bible from one dominant or overarching point of view, which is the basic orientation of systematic theology in general (e.g., the church and Israel are distinct; the sign gifts are unnecessary once the canon is complete, etc.). This, then, necessitates the privileging of Scriptures that lend support to one's preferred systematic theology while devaluing other Scriptures that do not. Obviously, those who are enamored with systematic theology are not likely to see any need for the Radical Middle of both/and; in fact, it may seem as nothing more than the moderates trying to keep everyone happy by giving into what each group wants. For instance, someone who believes that speaking in tongues still operates today, but it is not for everyone, may be deemed as a person without conviction, both to cessationists and to those continuationists who see speaking in tongues as *the* initial evidence of baptism in the Holy Spirit.

This is not to suggest that one should not learn systematic theology; in fact, the need for the Radical Middle is felt and the true appreciation for it will emerge after understanding each system, whether Reformed or dispensational, cessationism or continuationism—well enough to see what truly unites and separates them biblically. Upon realizing that our theological differences pale in comparison to our agreement on the essentials which unite us, the Radical Middle paradigm may be seen as a real and vital way of theologizing that actually allows Scripture to speak for itself.

Recognize the Validity of Inconvenient Scriptures

Second, once we are decommitted from rigidly reading the Bible from a particular standpoint, we become free to recognize the validity of all Scriptures relevant to a given issue, including those that are inconvenient to lend support to one's preferred theology. This of course is not conducive to producing a tidy, airtight theology, but the gain is well worth it. What is the gain? The true knowledge of God's word. It should be noted that while some may know their systematic theology well, they may not know the Bible itself as much. How so? It is because in systematizing the Bible from an overarching viewpoint, Scriptures that do not support that idea are necessarily ignored or distorted. After all, it was to the Sadducees, who "accepted only the written Torah and rejected all 'oral Torah,' i.e., the traditional interpretation of the Torah accepted by the Pharisees,"[22] that Jesus said, "You are in error because you do not know the Scriptures" (Matt 22:29a NIV). Not accepting the oral Torah was good but the Sadducees' denial of the existence of angels found all over the Pentateuch was not.[23] The Radical Middle paradigm of both/and allows its adherents to truly learn the Bible as it is because they owe no allegiance to any system to defend it at the cost of devaluing another part of Scripture.

Keep the Distinction, Avoid Synthesizing

Recall what Heraclitus said: "the balancing of opposites."[24] In the Radical Middle paradigm, this means that binary opposites, having been equally privileged, are brought to the center without being blended or synthesized. The distinctions between the pairs of opposites, for instance—divine sovereignty and human responsibility—are not only maintained, but are fully pursued, advocated, and obeyed. Regarding how this antinomic pair ought to be handled, Packer puts it this way:

> We shall try to take both doctrines perfectly seriously . . . We shall not oppose them to each other, for the Bible does not oppose them to each other. Nor shall we qualify, or modify, or water down, either of them in terms of the other, for this is not what the Bible does either. What the Bible does is to assert both truths side by side in the strongest and most unambiguous terms as two ultimate facts; this, therefore, is the position that we must take in our thinking.[25]

So then, what hermeneutical approach can reach such an exegetical outcome? Packer states:

> Use each within the limits of its own reference (i.e., the area delimited by the evidence from which the principle has been drawn). Note what connections exist between the two truths and their two frames of references, and teach yourself to think of reality in a way that provides for their *peaceful coexistence*,

---

22. Myers, *Eerdmans Bible Dictionary*, 902.

23. "For the Sadducees say that there is no resurrection, nor angel, nor spirit, but the Pharisees acknowledge them all" (Acts 23:8).

24. Atkinson, *Philosophy Book*, 40.

25. Packer, *Evangelism and the Sovereignty of God*, 35

remembering that reality itself has proved actually to contain them both. This is how antinomies must be handled ... in Scripture[26] (italics mine).

It appears that Packer's proposal to handle antinomic pairs is similar to that of Heraclitus, who held that "the *logos* ... connects two [opposite] terms in mutually determining juxtaposition."[27]

Both agree that opposite pairs must be equally privileged and connected.

The specifics of what this entails will be discussed in chapter 5. Suffice it to say, coexistence between two opposites—for instance, divine sovereignty and human responsibility—however peaceful it may appear on the outside, has tension within. So then, what should we do when attempts to uphold antinomy generate tension? Packer says, "Accept it for what it is, and learn to live with it"[28] and "recognize that here is a mystery which we cannot solve in this world."[29] No doubt a sense of uncertainty militates against a Western mindset that prefers a tidy system built on logic and reasoning, but that desire needs to be tempered if not altogether given up because the antinomic nature of Scripture renders that implausible, unless, that is, one resorts to the either/or hermeneutics of logocentrism.

THE UBIQUITOUS PRESENCE OF THE RADICAL MIDDLE

The fact is that the Radical Middle paradigm is not too hard to find. But, when we do not know what we are searching for, we not only miss out on something but are unaware that we have missed out! That certainly is the case with the Radical Middle because this paradigm of both/and has been around for some time, beginning with Scripture itself and continuing throughout church history when important theological discoveries were made. Furthermore, it appears that the Radical Middle paradigm of both/and has become quite popular among contemporary Christian thinkers of all spectrums. And upon examining these instances of the Radical Middle paradigm, it will become apparent the importance of, first, not

26. Ibid., 21.
27. Brann, *Logos of Heraclitus*, 11.
28. Packer, *Evangelism and the Sovereignty of God*, 21.
29. Ibid., 24.

committing rigidly to a systematic theology, second, recognizing the validity of Scriptures inconvenient to one's preferred theology, and third, avoiding the synthesis and biased choosing of antinomic Scriptures.

The Radical Middle Paradigm of Both/And in Scripture

One interesting example of the Radical Middle of both/and is Jesus' criticism of the Pharisees, who privileged one command of God while deprivileging the other. Jesus said to them (Matt 23:23 NIV): "Woe to you, teachers of the law and Pharisees, you hypocrites! You give a tenth of your spices—mint, dill and cumin. But you have neglected the more important matters of the law—justice, mercy and faithfulness. You should have practiced the latter, without neglecting the former." Objectively, giving tithe and being merciful are not an antithetic pair (tithing and not tithing is). But, the Pharisees had shown that they were capable of pairing up unrelated commands, such as helping parents and giving gifts to God (Mark 7:9–13), and then approaching it as if it were a matter of either/or, to their financial advantage. So, in this case, if a son, therefore, gave a gift to God, then, he did not have to do anything for his parents. (I am sure it did not work the other way around.)

In view of this, the Pharisees could have also formed an unlikely antithetic pair of tithing and mercy in which choosing one duty relieved them of the other responsibility. This is relevant to our discussion because, as said before, word and Spirit as an antithetic pair is man-made; there is no biblical warrant for it. But, like the Pharisees, we may be picking one or the other for reasons that have little or nothing to do with the Bible. Maybe cessationists do not want to admit that they are de facto naturalists. May be some continuationists are postmodernists who believe that anything goes, even beyond Scripture, in the spirit world. Nevertheless, Jesus tells the Pharisees to stop privileging the giving of tithe (which they did well) while devaluing justice, mercy, and faithfulness (which they did poorly); instead, the Pharisees are told to pursue both. I am certain that the Lord is saying the same to both cessationists and continuationists: Pursue both word and Spirit equally.

Now, let's consider two more examples of the Radical Middle found in Scripture.

Biblical Anthropology in the Radical Middle

The first matter has to do with anthropology. We begin with how the Old Testament Hebrews understood the constitution of a person by way of comparing it to how the Greeks in antiquity understood the same.

In short, the Greeks dichotomized humans into two distinctive parts: soul and body.

Subsequently, this dichotomy developed into a mind (soul)/body dualism that pitted one against the other. Nothing shows this dualism better than the stark contrast between the Epicureans, founded by Epicurus (341–270 BC), and the Stoics, founded by Zeno (340–265 BC). On the one hand, the focus of Epicurus was "to strive for personal happiness" by way of seeking "'passive' (quiet) pleasures . . . [such as] the pleasures of literature, recollection, and contemplation . . . and the enjoyment of nature."[30] But, once attaining pleasure became the primary means to personal happiness, it should come as no surprise that Epicurus's followers went from seeking cerebral pleasure to bodily pleasure. Privileging the body and the pleasure it sought, Epicureans became "linked with pleasures of the appetites . . . a connoisseur of fine food and drink"[31] as well as the "pursuit of sensual pleasures."[32] On the other hand, the Stoics, privileging what they saw as "a rational soul," emphasized the importance of reason as the governing principle through which humans ought to "striv[e] for *virtue*, rather than pleasure."[33] Evidently, dualism characterized the Greek anthropology in which one or the other was privileged but not both.

Contrarily, the Hebraic understanding of man's nature reflects a key aspect of the Radical Middle: both/and with a distinction. While many Christians see humans as made up of three distinctive parts—body, soul and spirit (a.k.a., trichotomy)—the Hebraic anthropology in antiquity, however, breaks from this in two major ways. First, to the Hebrews, soul and spirit did not "designate component parts" . . . [but] different aspects of human nature."[34] How so? Genesis 2:7 (KJV) states, "And the Lord God formed man of the dust of the ground, and breathed into his nostrils the breath of life; and man became a living soul [*nephesh*]." From this single

30. Greer, *Brief History of the Western World*, 103.

31. Ibid., 103.

32. Atkinson, *Philosophy Book*, 64.

33. Greer, *Brief History of the Western World*, 104.

34. Berkhof, *Systematic Theology*, 193.

act of God, came forth two major outcomes. First, the lifeless body of Adam became a "living being" or "soul" (KJV), after God breathed his Spirit (*ruach*) into him. This was also the moment when God "formed the spirit of man within him" (Zech 12:1). In light of this, Reformed theologian Louis Berkhof concluded with respect to the Hebrew terms *ruach* (spirit) and *nephesh* (soul): "A careful study of Scripture clearly shows that it uses the words interchangeably"[35]; "thus, it may be said that man *has* spirit, but *is* soul"[36] (italics his).

Second, whereas in Greek anthropology the body and soul are pitted against one another, "the Hebrew system of thought does not include the . . . opposition of the terms 'body' and 'soul.'"[37] Thus, as a corollary to not seeing body and soul in a binary opposition, neither body nor soul is privileged over against another.

Subsequently, the Hebraic anthropology, built on the belief that the creation of soul/spirit of man and the animation of lifeless *body* was executed by the same Spirit, captures two essentials of the Radical Middle (both/and with a distinction). First, both soul and body are equally privileged to make man whole; second, a distinction between the two is maintained even into eternity, whether in heaven (Rev 20:4; 1 Cor 15:42–44) or in hell (Matt 10:28). Whereas in Greek anthropology soul and body are detached entities independent of each other—becoming more pronounced in later docetism and Gnosticism—in the biblical anthropology of the Hebrews they are two distinctive yet integrated components of human nature. And in Christ, both soul/spirit and body "have been made holy" (Heb 10:10a NIV)—the believer's legal standing—and are being sanctified "from every defilement of body and spirit, bringing holiness to completion in the fear of God" (2 Cor 7:1b)—the believer's actual state.

Sovereignty of God and Human Responsibility in the Radical Middle

As for the next matter to be scrutinized, undoubtedly it has generated more polemics than any other theological matters: divine sovereignty and human responsibility. The foundational issue, of course, has to do

35. Ibid., 193.

36. Ibid., 194. The Hebrew word used in Genesis 2:7 is *neshâmâh*, meaning "a *puff*, i.e., *wind*, . . . *breath*." (Strong).

37. Vine et al., *Expository Dictionary of Biblical Words*, 238.

with the premise of God's election: Is it based on God's mysterious, pre-determined decree (espoused by Calvinism) or his foreknowledge (advocated by Arminianism)? Did Jesus die only for the elect or for the entire world? Can the non-elect be saved? Because Calvinists and Arminians typically view this matter through the lens of either/or, they have been feuding without much regard for each other's view.

Thus, this will surely come as a surprise to the diehard Calvinists and Arminians to find that Scripture equally privileges God's sovereignty and human responsibility (i.e., the exercise of human free will). Consider what the apostle Peter said to the Israelites on the day of Pentecost to explain how Jesus ended up being crucified. He said,

> Men of Israel, listen to these words: Jesus the Nazarene, a man attested to you by God with miracles and wonders and signs which God performed through Him in your midst, just as you yourselves know this Man, delivered over by the predetermined plan and foreknowledge of God, you nailed to a cross by the hands of godless men and put Him to death. (Acts 2:22–23 NASB).

Obviously, the crucifixion of Christ, as the essential component to God's redemptive plan (Gen 3:15), was unilaterally based on God's "predetermined plan." This indicates that this divine plan was not set in response to God having foreseen what men might do—it had nothing whatsoever to do with men's future actions. Therefore, since this is God's sovereign plan to redeem sinners, all glory that rightfully belongs to him should not be shared. Election, therefore, is based on God's predetermined decree.

Now, if Peter left it at that, then this would have been an either/or situation: either you believe that God unilaterally "works out everything for his own ends" (Prov 16:4b NIV), or you don't. But, this matter becomes complicated by the fact that the apostle immediately cites foreknowledge as another reason Jesus was delivered over to men to be crucified. The word "foreknowledge" (*prognōsei* in Greek) derives from a compound Greek word of *pro* (before, in front of) and *gnosis* (knowledge). Two implications arise from this: first, all that humans do, whether in the past, present or future, is taking place right before God's eyes; second: God, foreseeing their potential actions, would seal them as part of his predetermined plan. Accordingly, when God's foreknowledge is applied to salvation, it can be argued that "election is the result of God's having foreseen people's potential faith and that they would turn to him when they heard the gospel."[38] In response, Calvinists would recoil at that, seeing that God merely confirms men's decision to believe instead of that decision being the result of his prior electing grace.

While there is no doubt that this interpretation, when standing alone, is anthropocentric, once the same approach is applied to what humans do *against* God, it then becomes quite theocentric. That is to say, when a person's rejection of Christ is understood through God's foreknowledge, the same Calvinists would be free from the accusation that they make God out to be the author of sin, on account of their belief that God elects some to damnation. How so? God, foreseeing men's denial of Christ and the fact that they would turn against him, sealed their rejection as part of his predetermined plan. This is the reason Peter could pin the complicity of killing Jesus on men. Therefore, those who are hell bound deserve all the blame, since God merely honored their decisions to reject Jesus.

So here, Peter presents the theology of the Radical Middle in which both a thesis (God's predetermined plan, irrespective of what men will do) and its antithesis (God's plan based on his foreknowledge of what men will do) are presented as equally true. This theology is neither logical nor tidy to us, but it will keep at bay efforts "to assert man's responsibility in a way that excludes God from being sovereign, or to affirm God's sovereignty in a way that destroys the responsibility of man."[39] Thus, when this soteriological matter is theologized in the Radical Middle, we will sound a lot like Packer, who in a book chapter entitled "Divine Sovereignty and Human Responsibility" states:

> God's sovereignty and man's responsibility are taught side by side in the same Bible; sometimes, indeed, in the same text. Both are thus guaranteed to us by the same divine authority; both, therefore, are true. It follows that they must be held together, and not played off each other.[40]

Meaning what? Salvation is never the sole matter of sovereignty of God or human free will, but is of both—yet without losing sight of the fact that the redemptive plan, its execution by Christ, and appropriation through the Spirit comes from God, not man (Eph 1:4–5, 11).

38. Hammond, *In Understanding Be Men*, 88.
39. Packer, *Evangelism and the Sovereignty of God*, 25
40. Ibid., 22–23.

So can the non-elect be saved? Yes, because "we are . . . assured from Scripture that whatever man may find himself outside the sphere of the covenant of redemption has not had his chances of coming to Christ reduced one iota by God's election grace."[41] How so? In speaking of those Israelites not elected (Rom 11:7) who therefore "were broken off because of their unbelief" (Rom 11:20a) from, as it were, the "tree of life" (Rev 22:19b), Paul says, "And even they [i.e., those Israelites not elected], if they do not continue in their unbelief, will be grafted in, for God has the power to graft them in again" (Rom 11:23). Our logic says the non-elect cannot be saved, but Scripture says God has the power to do it, "for nothing will be impossible with God" (Luke 1:37).

Why then would God bother to elect people who are, therefore, assured of salvation, if the non-elect can be saved as well? For a possible answer, consider what John reveals: Jesus "ransomed people for God from every tribe and language and people and nation" (Rev 5:9b). It stands to reason then that, at the Marriage Supper of the Lamb, which is the spiritual consummation between Jesus and his bride the church (Rev 19:6–10), in order that "Christ might be presented with a redeemed church . . . as a supreme in the universe, God has ordained that at least some" from every nation "should be gathered out from the mass of men."[42] I would present this as election in the Radical Middle: the doctrine of election is upheld since it is biblical. "Everyone who calls on the name of the Lord will be saved" (Rom 10:13) is also espoused because it is just as biblical.

Theologizing in the Radical Middle in Church History

It is said that the canonicity of the Bible was waiting to be discovered, since those books that would eventually be recognized as Scripture had long been inspired by God, and not some pretext under which the early church compiled certain books to advance her political agenda.

The same can be said about true biblical theology: although it is articulated in the Bible, it took some time for the church to discover it and then fully express it. Now, while theologizing in the Radical Middle has not been commonly practiced throughout church history, several important theological discoveries were made as a result of churchmen

41. Hammond, *In Understanding Be Men*, 88.

42. Ibid., 88.

thinking in terms of both/and, thereby not caving into the binary opposition of either/or.

Christology in the Radical Middle

One major discovery from the application of both/and, later to be called "Radical Middle" with respect to theologizing, occurred in the area of Christology in the fifth century. Previously, the early church, while trying to understand the proper relationship between Christ's divinity and humanity—the three most important attempts being Apollinarism, Nestorianism, and Monophysitism (chapter 4)—always ended up synthesizing the two to the detriment of both natures. And it was not until the Council of Chalcedon in 451 that the church, through Leo I, was able to clearly articulate what Scripture teaches concerning the dual nature of Christ. Leo declared:

> Thus there was born true God in the entire and perfect nature of true man, complete in its own properties . . . He assumed the form of a servant without the stain of sin, making the human properties greater, but not detracting from the divine . . . Accordingly, he who made man, while he remained in the form of God, was himself made man in the form of a servant. Each nature preserves its own characteristics without diminution, so that the form of a servant does not detract from the form of God.[43]

This teaching—"Christology in the Radical Middle"—became the classical theology of the two natures constituted in the single person of Christ. This was not a Christ whose divinity was privileged over his humanity or vice versa. Neither was this Christ deemed as being 50 percent divine and 50 percent human. Instead, each nature is fully and completely privileged and constituted (i.e., 100 percent) in the single person of Jesus Christ. Therefore, while Christ, as fully human on earth, experienced hunger (Matt 4:2), thirst (John 4:7), and fatigue (John 4:6), he never ceased to be divine at any moment (Col 2:9).

---

43. Bettenson, *Documents of the Christian Church*, 50.

Justification in the Radical Middle

Another major discovery made from theologizing in the Radical Middle is the believer's standing before God. In fact, one of the best expressions of the Radical Middle was "what Luther and Calvin reproduced in the formula *simul iustus et peccator*. In other words, the believer is 'simultaneously justified and sinful.'"[44] This terse declaration equally privileges the continuous indwelling of sin in believers (Rom 7:17), as well as their legally justified state in Christ (Rom 5:1).

Subsequently, the awareness of indwelling sin counters the view of those who so privilege the justified state of the believer that they greatly minimize sin in a believer's life. Reflecting this view is Joseph Prince, the pastor of a megachurch in Singapore, who says, "His forgiveness should have no more consciousness of sin. Stop examining yourself and searching your heart for sin."[45] Among other outcomes, this belief in the hands of immature believers can easily turn into licentiousness (Jude 1:4). But, when this is reversed, that is, indwelling sin is privileged over justification, those believers with a sensitive conscience (particularly among the Arminians) may doubt their salvation every time they sin. During my early days as a young believer attending a Pentecostal congregation, I knew of a pastor who responded to the altar call every time it was offered. Finding it odd, when I asked him why he did so, his response was, "Because I am a sinner." Even though I did not know much Bible then, I thought his behavior was a result of some misunderstanding rather than humility.

In both cases, the one who privileges indwelling sin over justification and the other who does the exact opposite have one thing in common: the use of the hermeneutics of logocentrism of either/or to theologize. The results are unbiblical beliefs and practices that are unhealthy at best and dangerous at worst. As a remedy, the Radical Middle justification will challenge those who privilege the justified state over indwelling sin to repent, while assuaging the uneasy conscience of those who privilege indwelling sin over justification.

Since we are talking about justification, let me briefly comment on N. T. Wright's view. I see what he is saying, that Paul was countering the ethnocentrism of Jewish Christians whose insistence on circumcision, keeping the Sabbath, and dietary laws (a.k.a., the works of the law—*ergōn*

44. Horton, *Christ the Lord*, 51.
45. Prince, *Destined to Reign*, 187.

nomou) was alienating gentile Christians. Evidently, that is what went on at the church in Galatia (Gal 2:11–16; 5:2–6). But, I do not understand why that teaching has to come at the expense of seeing that "legalistic Jewish individuals . . . were attempting to earn their salvation through works-righteousness."[46] When both the rich young ruler (Matt 19:16–24) and an expert in the law (Luke 10:25–37) asked Jesus, "What shall I do to inherit eternal life?," they were thinking of moral laws—not murdering, stealing, and committing adultery—instead of circumcision, keep the Sabbath, and kosher laws. It can be said that they were wondering whether there were other moral laws to keep, thinking that that's how one attains eternal life. So, instead of seeing this matter as either the Jews trying to earn salvation through good works, or the Jews alienating gentile Christians through their ethnocentrism, why can't it be both, since they are equally taught in the Bible? Why do we have to make this an antithetic matter, then choose one view against the other, and then argue about our differences?

The Kingdom in the Radical Middle

Another key contribution made by theologizing in the Radical Middle is breaking the deadlock over whether God's kingdom has already been established on earth.

To the advocates of the Reformed theology, "the kingdom of God was founded by Christ at the time of his sojourn on earth, is operative in history now and is destined to be revealed in its fullness in the life to come [in heaven],"[47] not during the thousand-year reign of Christ (Rev 20:1–6) as dispensationalists believe. The purpose of the kingdom "is to redeem God's people from sin and from demonic powers, and finally to establish the new heavens and the new earth."[48] So the kingdom now is spiritual in nature, and to buttress that point, passages like Luke 17:20b–21 are cited: "[Jesus] answered them, 'The kingdom of God is not coming in ways that can be observed, nor will they say, "Look, here it is!" or "There!" for behold, the kingdom of God is in the midst of you.'" (See also Matt 12:28.)

Classical Dispensationalism would counter that position by stipulating the following: first, "the purpose of God is to establish a kingdom

---

46. Saucy and Gomez, "Justification and the New Perspective," 14.

47. Hoekema, "Amillennialism," 178.

48. Ibid., 178.

on the earth";[49] second, throughout the Old Testament, God promised this literal kingdom to the Israelites (2 Sam 7:12–15; 1 Chr 17:11–14) where they will be given "the place of priority among the nations"[50] (Isa 60:10–12); third, "the kingdom is only future,"[51] since the thousand-year reign of Christ described in Revelation 20:1–6, which will be the fulfillment of this promise made to Israel, has not happened yet. So they privilege those Scriptures indicating that the kingdom has not yet come. For instance, what Jesus said while he was hanging on the cross—"For I tell you that from now on I will not drink of the fruit of the vine until the kingdom of God comes" (Luke 22:18)—seems to indicate that the kingdom indeed has not come. (See also Luke 11:2.) What we have is yet another pair of opposites, and both the Reformed and dispensational-ist rely on the hermeneutics of logocentrism of either/or to justify their respective theologies.

Amid this conflict entered a third voice, that of the theologian George Ladd (Fuller Theological Seminary), who introduced the already/not yet framework to deal with this issue. The already/not yet framework is tantamount to the Radical Middle paradigm because Ladd refused to privilege one kingdom over the other; instead, he upheld the validity of a spiritual kingdom in the present and a literal kingdom on earth in the future (before the ushering in of the eternal state). He writes:

> Isolated verses can be quoted for most of the interpretations which can be found in our theological literature. The Kingdom is a present reality (Matt 12:28), and yet it is a future blessing (1 Cor 15:50). It is an inner spiritual redemptive blessing (Rom 14:17) which can be experienced only by way of the new birth (John 3:3), and yet will have to do with the government of the nations of the world (Rev 11:15). The Kingdom is a realm into which men enter now (Matt 21:31), and yet it is a realm into which they will enter tomorrow (Matt 8:11). It is at the same time a gift of God which will be bestowed by God in the future (Luke 12:32) and yet which must be received in the present (Mark 10:15)."[52]

Accordingly, God's kingdom as a spiritual entity has *already* been established in the hearts of believers when Jesus "destroy[ed] the one who

49. Hoyt, "Dispensational Premillennialism," 65.

50. Hoyt, *End Times*, 182.

51. Horton, *Christ the Lord*, 24.

52. Ladd, *Gospel of the Kingdom*, 18.

has the power of death—that is, the devil" (Heb 2:14b) through his cruci-fixion, resurrection, and ascension (Col 1:12–14; Matt 12:28). Certainly, the notion of God's kingdom already here makes the Reformed advocates happy. Then, this spiritual kingdom will fully be amplified when Christ returns to establish a literal kingdom on earth that lasts for a thousand years—this, then, is the *not yet* aspect of God's kingdom. While Ladd's belief in God's future kingdom on Earth will make dispensationalists happy, their reasoning for it differs. On the one hand, dispensationalists see the future kingdom as God keeping his promise made to Israel in the Old Testament; on the other hand, Ladd, not a dispensationalist, arrived at his conclusion by interpreting Revelation 20:1–6 literally: "Blessed and holy is the one who shares in the first resurrection! Over such the second death has no power, but they will be priests of God and of Christ, and they will reign with him for a thousand years" (Rev 20:6). And to those in the either/or crowd who want a tidier theology on the kingdom, Ladd will say, "Obviously no simple explanation can do justice to such a rich but diverse variety of teaching.[53]

The Radical Middle in the Writings of Contemporary Christian Thinkers

As said before,, when we do not know what the Radical Middle is, we not only miss out on it, but are unaware that we have missed out. My experi-ence has been that once we are acquainted with the Radical Middle and truly appreciate its both/and paradigm, we will readily notice it expressed in the writings of contemporary Christian thinkers of all theological per-suasions, even if the term Radical Middle is not used.

Christopher Wright and Missions

The first example is extracted from *The Mission of God's People: A Bibli-cal Theology of the Church's Mission,* written by Christopher J. J. Wright, an Old Testament scholar and current International Ministries Director of Langham Partnership International. In dealing with Ephesians 6:12, which states, "For we do not wrestle against flesh and blood, but against the rulers, against the authorities, against the cosmic powers over this present darkness, against the spiritual forces of evil in the heavenly

53. Ibid., 18.

places," Wright embraces the hermeneutics of the Radical Middle of both/ and. He writes:

> Personally, I reject two opposite extremes: those who 'demythologize' them as simply a cipher for human structures, political powers, economic forces, or social conventions; and those who view them as exclusively spiritual, demonic beings, with no connection to the world of political or economic powers and forces. It seems to me that both aspects are biblically valid.[54]

Not taking sides, he allows Ephesians 6:12 to speak for itself: on the one hand, institutional evil and injustice in the visible realm of society need to be addressed through practical activism (Isa 1:17; Mic 6:8); on the other hand, supernatural evil forces in the spiritual world, invisible to the naked eye, need to be addressed through spiritual warfare (Acts 16:18; Mark 9:29). In this way, both interpretations are equally privileged while maintaining their distinctions.

Shelly Rambo and Theology of Trauma

The next example of the Radical Middle found in contemporary writers comes from Shelly Rambo, professor of theology at Boston University. In her *Spirit and Trauma: A Theology of Remaining*, Rambo, seeing the need to present a more adequate Passion narrative for those suffering from trauma, writes about the importance of Holy Saturday, the middle day in the Passion story that is barely noticed. She feels that an almost exclusive focus on the victorious resurrection on Sunday does not speak to those who are still trapped on Saturday.

In many ways, Rambo is protesting the church's formulaic response that glosses over people's real pain (from Good Friday) that remains or returns (on Holy Saturday), no matter how many times they hear triumphant proclamations of redemption (on Easter Sunday).

And it is in her portrayal of the reality of Holy Saturday and the hope this day fosters that the outlook of the Radical Middle is expressed. As for the reality of this middle day where pain lingers, she writes, "Death is not an event that is concluded. Neither is life a victorious event that stands on the other side of death. Instead, trauma uncovers a middle to this narrative; it reveals a theological territory of remaining."[55] In other

---

54. Wright, *Mission of God's People*, 238.
55. Rambo, *Spirit and Trauma*, 16.

words, while *the force of death* from Friday lingers into Saturday, it is met by *the force of life* from Sunday. This is the Radical Middle of both/ and in which death and life, after having entered the middle day from opposite directions, exist in great tension. The question now is: Will the traumatized continue to remain in the middle day? "Is this death or life?" Rambo asks. Her ensuing response framed in the Radical Middle imparts hope: "It seems to be both. It is old and new, laden with death but moving toward life, turning nothing into something."[56]

So what is Rambo really after by pulling death and life toward the middle day? First, she wants the church to acknowledge that pain is still formidable for the traumatized even after redemption; therefore, the triumphalism of Sunday ought to be moderated by empathy and compassion. At the same time, she wants the traumatized to recognize the power of Easter Sunday that pulls them toward the light; the hopelessness of Friday is ebbing away by hope in the resurrected Christ. In view of this, Rambo's approach toward healing the traumatized can be called "The Passion Story in the Radical Middle."

Kevin DeYoung and New Heavens and a New Earth

As the final example, consider how Kevin DeYoung, a popular Reformed pastor and coauthor of *What is the Mission of the Church?*, responds to the question of "How much continuity will there be between the old earth and the new one?"[57] On the one hand, Jesus' declaration, "Heaven and earth will pass away, but my words will not pass away" (Matt 24:35), seems to favor discontinuity—meaning, nothing in the present world will be part of the "new heavens and a new earth" (Isa 65:17b). On the other hand, the apostle Paul's statement in Romans 8:21–22 indicates that there may be some continuity after all: "That the creation itself will be set free from its bondage to corruption and obtain the freedom of the glory of the children of God. For we know that the whole creation has been groaning together in the pains of childbirth until now."

So how does DeYoung try to resolve this antimony? First, he understands that this question has been "answered with great confidence by people on both sides of the issue,"[58] that is, between those who privi-

---

56. Ibid., 56.

57. DeYoung and Gilbert, *What is the Mission?*, 213.

58. Ibid., 213.

lege passages that teach "substantial continuity" and those who privilege passages that present "radical discontinuity." Feeling the tension between the two, he states:

> There's simply no way to read the entire Bible and come away thinking that there is no continuity between this world and the next, and there's no way to read it and think that it will be seamlessly continuous either . . . The image of creation, *restored, freed,* and *released* from bondage is quite a different image from that of it "passing away." And yet they are both taught in the Bible, and therefore they are both true. But how? How can the world both "pass away" and at the same time be "set free from its bondage to decay?"[59]

Referring to this type of textual situation in the Bible, the following terms have been used: antithesis, antinomy, pairs of opposites, and binary opposition. One way to handle them is through the hermeneutics of logocentrism of either/or, which is good for advocating a particular position but not necessarily for imparting true biblical knowledge. For that, the hermeneutics of the Radical Middle of both/and is needed.

And DeYoung opts for the Radical Middle by refusing to choose a side—that is, he does not privilege Scriptures that support one position while ignoring other passages that do not; rather, he simply allows the Bible to speak for itself, even if the conclusion is not as tidy as some would like. He says:

> It's important that we don't lean so far in one direction that we undercut the other. We should not so emphasize continuity that we wind up denying that there will be a cataclysmic end to this age and even to the present heavens and earth . . . On the other hand, we also should not so emphasize *dis*continuity that we wind up saying that this world does not matter. Scripture tells us that there is in fact continuity of some kind between this world and the next; the cataclysm is not absolute . . . Too often the discussion just bounces back and forth between strong assertions of extremes—Continuity! Discontinuity!—without a sober acknowledgement that the Bible in fact teaches both.[60]

What DeYoung does here is a picture-perfect demonstration of how to theologize in the Radical Middle: refusing to take a side, considering

59. Ibid., 213, 216.
60. Ibid., 216, 219.

all the relevant passages, even if they are antithetic to each other, and drawing the two emphases to the center and equally privileging them.

I hope that the Radical Middle paradigm has been adequately explained as a necessity to properly interpret antinomies in the Bible. As a concept and approach, it was utilized by biblical writers as well as by theologians throughout the ages, and is being employed even now by modern authors. Before attempts are made to interpret the eight pairs of antinomic Scriptures according to the hermeneutics of the Radical Middle in chapter 5, the next chapter deals with several improper ways of handling antinomic revelation in accordance with logocentrism.

QUESTIONS FOR REFLECTION & DISCUSSION

1. Why do we prefer to privilege one doctrine or mandate over against another? What has been your own experience?

2. What was the approach taken by Leo and Luther toward theologizing? What can you learn from it? What is Joseph Prince's approach? Why wouldn't that be part of the Radical Middle?

3. In what sense does the apostle Peter's sermon recorded in Acts 2:22–23 capture the Radical Middle? Should that affect one's stance on Calvinism or Arminianism? If so, how?

4. In what sense does the Christology of Leo I capture the Radical Middle? Does it make sense to human logic? What should that mean to us?

5. How does Luther's Radical Middle understanding of the believer's position before God counter those who believe that we don't need to confess our sins anymore because of the finished work of Christ?

4

The Interpretation of Antithetic/Antinomic Revelation According to the Hermeneutics of Logocentrism

I HAVE SAID THAT whereas the meaning of biblical texts in general, particularly those pertaining to essential doctrinal matters, is clear, such is not always the case because, as Peter said of Paul's letters, there are "some things in them that are hard to understand" (2 Pet 3:16b). While I am not sure whether Peter was thinking of antinomic Scriptures when he wrote that, the ubiquitous presence of an apparent "contradiction between two seemingly true statements," as the *Merriam-Webster Desk Dictionary* defines it, in the Bible certainly makes it harder to understand. This of course poses a big challenge to those who want what Packer calls "a tidier theology,"[1] or what I call an airtight theology.

The issue then boils down to how to properly handle pairs of opposite Scriptures that are equally true. Packer has observed, as mentioned earlier, that many are "tempted to get rid of antinomies from our minds by illegitimate means: to suppress, or jettison, one truth in the supposed interests of the other."[2] This is generally done in two ways. The most popular approach, often favored by the ardent advocates of respective systematic theologies, is choosing sides and then ignoring or distorting Scriptures that do not lend support for their sides chosen. The other is the

1. Packer, *Evangelism and the Sovereignty of God*, 25.
2. Ibid., 25.

synthetic approach advocated by Ellul (see chapter 2). Neither of these approaches, however, corresponds to the hermeneutics of the Radical Middle, and as a result, fails to capture the authorial intent behind why God may have framed many of his revelations antithetically, instead of in a straightforward manner.

The goal of chapter 4 is to prepare the readers for chapters 6–10 that will delve into whether the sign gifts are for today. To do that, several issues foreign to the matter of word and Spirit are discussed here to show that the conflicts between cessationists and continuationists and the hermeneutical approaches used to neutralize each other's theology are not unique.

From this goal stem two objectives: first, to show the improper hermeneutics of logocentrism in handling antithetic revelation, which is how cessationists and some continuationists typically handle Scriptures relevant to the sign gifts; and second, to distinguish between the hermeneutics of logocentrism and the hermeneutics of the Radical Middle that will be used to examine Scriptures related to the sign gifts.

THE HERMENEUTICS OF LOGOCENTRISM: IGNORING INCONVENIENT SCRIPTURES

Recall that given pairs of opposites, logocentrism privileges the first term while dismissing the second. Thus, when logocentrism is applied to Scripture, it results in choosing sides between those passages that favor one's preferred theology over those that do not. (I call these inconvenient Scriptures.)[3] This approach is either/or, not both/and. So what happens to these inconvenient Scriptures? They are either ignored or their meanings are distorted to fit the preferred or privileged theology. When this happens, its outcomes are two-fold: first, any theology that disagrees with the privileged theology is discredited as unbiblical or not biblical enough; and second, a middle ground where two opposing groups can dialogue disappears, since the group operating out of logocentrism does not view the opposite group as having any merit to consider. And this logocentric tendency is not something modern theologians have invented; we see its clearest expression in 1 John in the form of docetism.

3. It seems to me that preferring one theology over another has a lot to do with exposure to a particular theology at the outset of one's faith journey. Once this theology is firmly in place, everything in the Bible is viewed through that outlook. However, many also turn from their initial understanding of the Bible upon realizing its weaknesses.

Logocentric Theologizing of the Docetics

Docetism, deriving "from the Greek verb 'to seem or appear,'"[4] was the precursor to Gnosticism that arose in the mid-second century AD, and it was on the apostle John's mind when he penned 1 John in the late first century. The apostle, having lived in the Hellenist city of Ephesus during his later years, well understood that the Greeks, as alluded to in chapter 3, dichotomized humans into two distinctive parts—soul and body—which then developed into a mind (soul)/body dualism that pitted one against the other.

Privileging the Spirit

Influenced heavily by this Greek dualism, docetists privileged "spirit" as the first term (i.e., closest to the original source—God) and "flesh" as the second (i.e., falling away from God). Naturally, when speculating about the nature of Christ, they rejected the second term, flesh, while privileging the first term, spirit. In so doing, they completely denied that Jesus came in the flesh and held that he was entirely of the spirit; that is, "Christ's human body was a phantasm, and . . . his sufferings and death were mere appearance."[5] Evidently, they favored Scriptures like Romans 8:9, 1 Peter 1:11, and Philippians 1:19 that speak of Jesus as "the Spirit of Christ."

Ignoring Inconvenient Scriptures

Now, by the late first century, churches had access to Paul's Epistles for a while, such as his letter to the church in Colossae (written in AD 60), in which he clearly states, "For in Christ all the fullness of Deity lives in bodily form" (Col 2:9). The docetists, however, completely ignored that Jesus had come in the flesh. So to combat this heresy, the apostle John renounced the docetists in the strongest of terms: "Every spirit that confesses that Jesus Christ has come in the flesh is from God; and every spirit that does not confess Jesus is not from God; this is the spirit of the antichrist" (1 John 4:2–3). Docetism was extremely radical, but it was not the Radical Middle.

4. Wright, "What the First Christians Believed," 109.
5. Bettenson, *Documents of the Christian Church*, 35.

Logocentric Theologizing by Reformed and Dispensationalism Groups

The way the docetists argued to defend their compromised Christology back in the first century is similar to how many theologians defend their ecclesiology (i.e., the study of church). As alluded to in chapter 1, to many laities, the relationship between Israel and the church seems unimportant and irrelevant; but no single issue affects the interpretation of the Bible more so than this.

Different Ecclesiologies

The discussion on the relationship between Israel and the church ought to begin with noting different definitions of the church between the Reformed and Dispensationalism. According to Reformed theologian Louis Berkhof, "the church . . . as . . . *the community of believers* . . . existed from the beginning of the old dispensation right down to the present time and will continue to exist on earth until the end of the world"[6] (italics mine).

Disagreeing with this view, dispensationalist theologian Charles Ryrie, after characterizing the church as "the indwelling presence of Christ in the members of [the body of Christ],"[7] states that because "on the day of Pentecost men were first placed in the body of Christ . . . the church could not have begun until Pentecost, and it had to begin on that day."[8] So the difference between these two systematic theologies is this: for the Reformed, the church, as a community of believers chosen by grace (Rom 11:5), existed in the Old Testament; for the dispensationalists, the church, as the body of Christ indwelt by the Spirit, did not begin until Pentecost, when the Spirit entered human heart for the first time (John 7:39; 2 Cor 1:22).

This ecclesiastical difference, then, affects the relationship between Israel and the church.

The Reformed posits that the church is the true Israel; therefore, the church is the one that fulfills the promises God made to Israel in the Old Testament. Classical Dispensationalism[9] counters this by saying that

---

6. Berkhof, *Systematic Theology,* 571.

7. Ryrie, *Dispensationalism Today,* 135.

8. Ibid., 137.

9. The so-called "Progressive Dispensationalism" takes a more nuanced approach

the church is distinct from Israel; therefore, the church does not fulfill the promises God made to Israel in the Old Testament, but Israel will. Consider an example in Exodus where God seems to promise the nation of Israel that if they "obey [God's voice] and keep [his] covenant . . . [they] shall be to [God] a kingdom of priests and a holy nation" (Exod 19:5a, 6a). The Reformists believe that this promise has already been fulfilled in the church, the true Israel, since the apostle Peter says to the New Testament believers, "You are . . . a royal priesthood, a holy nation" (1 Pet 2:9a). Disagreeing with this, classical dispensationalists believe that the nation of Israel will fulfill this promise of priesthood during the thousand-year reign of Christ on earth (Rev 20:1–6).

And the difference over the church/Israel distinction affects how the following eschatological matters are viewed: the rapture of the church (the Reformed: no rapture; Dispensationalism: yes, there will be rapture)[10] and the thousand-year reign of Christ on earth (a.k.a., millennial kingdom) before the ushering in of the eternal state (the Reformed: no; Dispensationalism: yes).

Ignoring Inconvenient Scriptures

Among the more ardent supporters of these theological outlooks, this is strictly a matter of either/or; there is no middle ground: either the church is Israel, or the church is not Israel. They are separate entities.

So how would dispensationalist Charles Ryrie interpret Romans 9:25? Here, Paul, in speaking to the Roman Christians, many of whom were gentiles, writes: "Even us [including Paul], whom he also called, not only from the Jews but also from the gentiles? As he says in Hosea: "I will call them 'my people' who are not my people; and I will call her 'my loved one' who is not my loved one . . ." Notice what Paul does with the promise given to Israel in Hosea (written in the eighth century BC): he applies the promise of, "I will call them 'my people' who are not my people" and "I will call her 'my loved one' who is not my loved one," to the church. Paul is, in effect, saying that the promises made to Israel in the Old Testament

---

that allows the church and Israel to coexist in the millennial kingdom as the unified people of God.

10. Dispensationalism sees the rapture as the necessary means to remove the church out of the world in order that God may reinstate the program (i.e., the 70th week in Daniel 9:24–27) for the nation of Israel that had been suspended (Rom 11:25).

are now being fulfilled, as said earlier, by the church. This is the Reformed position.

So how would Ryrie, who does not believe that the church existed in the Old Testament, respond? Curiously, he does not deal with Roman 9:25 in his influential book, *Dispensationalism Today*. In fact, the book's Scripture index does not list key passages in Romans, such as 2:28–29 ("a Jew is one inwardly, and circumcision is a matter of the heart, by the Spirit") and 11:1–5 ("so too at the present time there is a remnant, chosen by grace"), that deal with the church and Israel matter. Could it be because these Scriptures give credence to the view that the church is one and the same as the true Israel?

Now, let's consider Romans 11:25–26a (NASB) in which Paul seems to distinguish Israel from the church. Here Paul says,

> For I do not want you, brethren, to be uninformed of this mystery—so that you will not be wise in your own estimation—that a partial hardening has happened to Israel until the fullness of the gentiles has come in; and so all Israel will be saved.

Note that "fullness of the gentiles" refers to the church. So if Israel is one and the same as the church, this verse would read, "A partial hardening has happened to the church until the fullness of the church has come in." This, of course, makes no sense. Thus, Robert Saucy, who remained a dispensationalist until his passing, commented:

> Paul's prayer for "Israel" (Rom 10:1; cf. 11:1) and his references to Israel throughout the discussion of God's program in Romans 9–11 concerns his "kinsmen according to the flesh" (Rom 9:3). If "Israel" [in Romans 11:25] were a reference to the church, the reference to Israel's "blindness in part . . . until the fulness of the gentiles be come in" (Rom 11:25) would be meaningless.[11]

This is to say, Romans 11:25 indicates that the church and Israel are separate entities. This distinction is clear enough so that Reformed theologian R. C. Sproul even admitted that by the term "Israel," "the apostle has ethnic Jews in mind . . . The fact that he mentions gentiles as a distinct group in the same passage further confirms this view."[12] This would imply that the church and Israel are not one and the same, which is problematic to the Reformed. Regardless, the aforementioned Reformed theologian

---

11. Saucy, *Church in God's Program*, 70–71.
12. Sproul, "Israel's Temporary Hardening," para. 1.

Louis Berkhof still insisted that Israel in Romans 11:25 does not refer to ethnic Jews (i.e., the nation of Israel), but "the spiritual Israel"[13]—meaning, Christians who happen to be Jews, or, as he puts it, "[God's] elect remnant out of the Jews during the entire new dispensation."[14] He believes this way because his reading of the Bible would not allow for the restoration of Israel as a nation comprised of ethnic Jews. Writing before Israel became a nation in 1948, he had said, "It is very doubtful . . . whether Scripture warrants the expectation that Israel will finally be re-established as a nation [in the Holy Land], and will as a nation turn to the Lord."[15] In fact, he says that dispensationalists "have exploited this scriptural teaching [Romans 11:25–29] for their particular purpose"[16]—the same charge, I might add, dispensationalists can easily make against the Reformed.

The Radical Middle Ecclesiology of Both/And

In the ecclesiology of logocentrism of either/or, either the church is Israel, or they are separate entities; but these two antinomic propositions cannot be biblically true at the same time. So what would it take to hold onto logocentric ecclesiology? It would take "jettison[ing] one truth in the supposed interests of the other . . . for the sake of a tidier" Dispensationalism or Reformed theology.[17] The entire Bible is, then, not allowed to speak for itself—but not so in the Radical Middle of both/and.

I find it odd that many theologians cannot simultaneously uphold that the Bible sometimes presents the church and the true Israel as one and the same, while recognizing that sometimes the church and the nation of Israel are seen as distinctive entities. Thus it stands to reason that the church fulfills many of the promises made in the Old Testament. Another example is the promise of wolf and lamb feeding together (Isa 65:25a)—a powerful image of two natural enemies in reconciliation. Perhaps it can be said that this promise is fulfilled in the church where longtime antagonists Jews and Greeks "are all one in Christ Jesus" (Gal 3:28).

13. Berkhof, *Theology*, 699.

14. Ibid., 699.

15. Ibid., 699.

16. Ibid., 699.

17. Packer, *Evangelism and the Sovereignty of God*, 25.

At the same time, certain promises are reserved for Abraham's phys-ical descendants (through Isaac) to fulfill, such as the latter-day blessing promised in Romans 11:25–26.

It is also odd that many theologians have a difficult time accepting that the church, as a remnant chosen by grace (Rom 11:5), existed in the Old Testament (Acts 7:38),[18] but the church of the New Testament is much better since "it is founded on better promises" (Heb 8:6) and "a bet-ter covenant" (Heb 7:22). For one thing, "the Spirit had not been given" (John 7:39b) "in our hearts as a guarantee" (2 Cor 1:22b) until Pentecost. Probably that is the reason "many prophets and kings desired to see what [the people of the New Testament] see, and did not see it, and to hear what [they] hear, and did not hear it" (Luke 10:24).

THE HERMENEUTICS OF LOGOCENTRISM: DISTORTING THE MEANING

In the logocentric hermeneutics of either/or, even more common than ignoring inconvenient Scripture is distorting the obvious meaning of the text to make it fit into one's preferred theology. This, of course, is what often happens when cessationists and continuationists vehemently argue against one another in an all-or-nothing manner. In this section, we will examine two examples of distorting inconvenient Scriptures—1 John 2:2 and James 2:14–17—to point out what to avoid when interpreting antithetic/antinomic Scriptures, particularly those pertaining to the sign gifts.

Choosing Limited Atonement Over Unlimited Atonement (1 John 2:2)

The first example is to see whether the clear meaning of 1 John 2:2, which says, "He is the propitiation for our sins, and not for ours only but also for the sins of the whole world," supports the doctrine of limited atone-ment (i.e., Christ died only for the elect) of Reformed theology (Calvin-ism). Note that even if the finding suggests that it does not, it does not

---

18. Stephen refers to the Israelites in the wilderness as "the church" (*ekklesia*). Acts 7:38a reads, "This is he, that was in the church in the wilderness with the angel which spake to him in the mount Sinai, and with our fathers . . ."

necessarily mean that limited atonement is unbiblical, since other Scriptures may lend credence to that doctrine (Acts 13:48; John 6:37).

A problem is that, to justify this or any other preferred doctrine, the clear meaning of those Scriptures that seem to support this opposite view is replaced with a forced interpretation. This sort of hermeneutic is well illustrated by how Sproul interprets 1 John 2:2 in trying to make it fit with limited atonement.

Despite Seeing the Obvious

Interestingly, Sproul clearly recognizes the potential hazard of this passage to limited atonement. He comments as follows:

> On the surface this text seems to demolish limited atonement, saying explicitly that Christ is the propitiation of the sins for the "whole world." The whole world is set in contrast with "our." We must ask, What does *our* mean here, and what does *whole world* mean here? *Our* could refer to Christians as distinguished from non-Christians, believers as opposed to nonbelievers. If this interpretation is correct, then Christ is a propitiation not only for Christian believers, but for everybody in the world.[19] (italics his)

But Sproul, theologizing out of the either/or mode of logocentrism, cannot concede the third point of Calvinism's TULIP, because unlimited atonement would mean, for him, the diminishing significance of election that affects other doctrines related to election.[20] For instance, if indeed "everyone who calls on the name of the Lord will be saved" (Rom 10:13), since Jesus died "for the sins of the whole world," then it stands to reason that unconditional election is rendered meaningless, and the glory is taken away from God.

Distorting the Obvious

To avoid this rather natural interpretation of 1 John 2:2, this esteemed Reformed theologian suddenly introduces an issue that is not part of the authorial intent of 1 John. Now, most scholars would agree that one

19. Sproul, *What is Reformed Theology?*, 176.

20. Total Depravity, Unconditional Election, Irresistible Grace, and Perseverance of Saints..

reason John wrote this epistle was "to warn against incipient heretical doctrine, which denied either the real deity or the real humanity of Christ."[21] However, Sproul injects a foreign meaning to 1 John 2:2 when he comments:

> *Our* [in "he is the propitiation for *our* sins"] could refer specifically to Jewish believers. One of the central questions of the church's earliest formative period was this: Who is to be included in the New Covenant community? The New Testament labors the point that the body of Christ includes not only ethnic Jews, but Samaritans and gentiles.[22]

So Sproul would read 1 John 2:2a as, "He is the propitiation for the sins of the Jewish believers."

What Sproul says here is, of course, true; the issue, however, is whether 1 John actually addresses this matter. It does not appear to be so. First, the phrase "Jewish believers" or anything to do with Israel, is not mentioned in 1 John. Second, Paul, not John, is the one who addresses the Jewish-gentile conflict in the early church as early as AD 49 (Gal 3:28[23]); John wrote 1 John between AD 90–95.[24] Regardless, Sproul drops a major Pauline concern in the middle of a Johannine epistle, which, as mentioned earlier, addresses the threats of the docetists who denied Christ's humanity. (By the way, this shows the advantage of biblical theology over systematic.)

Making Light of the Bible

As for 1 John 2:2b, which says, "He is the propitiation . . . for the sins of the whole world," Sproul reinterprets the phrase "the whole world" to mean something different as well. He says:

> Ample evidence indicates that the term *world* in the New Testament often refers to neither the entire globe nor to all persons living on earth. For example, we read this in Luke: ". . . it came to pass in those days *that* a decree went out from Caesar Augustus that all the world should be registered" (Luke 2:1). We know

21. De Young, "1–3 John," 1177.

22. Sproul, *What is Reformed Theology?*, 176–77.

23. "There is neither Jew nor Greek, there is neither slave nor free man, there is neither male nor female; for you are all one in Christ Jesus" (Gal 3:28 NASB).

24. De Young, "1–3 John," 1177.

> this census did not include the inhabitants of China or South America, so "all the world" does not refer to all people in the entire world. The usage of *world* in this manner is widespread in Scripture.[25] (italics his)

To assert that 1 John 2:2b does not mean the entire world on account of a Roman census that only counted people living in the Roman Empire seems quite dubious. After all, no national or empire-wide census is literally worldwide in scope. This seems like comparing apples and oranges. Wouldn't John 3:16a, which says, "For God so loved the world," be a more fitting cross reference for 1 John 2:2b? Unless election is read into *the world* in John 3:16a, as some Calvinists do, the natural meaning of both passages is the *whole entire world*.

Furthermore, the effort to maintain an airtight five-point Calvinism at all costs as Sproul does here often produces the unintended effect of making a travesty of the Bible. First, note that although Sproul does not actually say, "part of the world," that is a fair rendering since he insists that "all the world does not refer to all people in the entire world." Second, note this: the Greek word *cosmos* (world) is used seventeen times in 1 John. Therefore, is Sproul willing to interpret *cosmos* used elsewhere in 1 John as "part of the world?" For instance, since 1 John 2:15 says, "Do not love the *world* or anything in the *world*," is he willing to read that as, "Do not love *part* of the *world* or anything in *part* of the world?" Should 1 John 3:13 be read, "Do not be surprised, my brothers, if *part* of the *world* hate you?" Third, note that "the whole world" in 1 John 2:2b comes from the Greek phrase *holou tou cosmou*, and John uses the same phrase in 1 John 5:19, when he writes, "We know that we are from God, and the whole world [*ho cosmos holos*] lies in the power of the evil one." So should that verse be read as, "We know that we are of God, and that *part* of the world lies in *the power of* the evil one?" I am sure Sproul would not do that—meaning, he makes a special plea regarding the usage of *holou tou cosmou* in 1 John 2:2. To avoid saying that Jesus died for the sins of the whole world, he has 1 John 2:2 say: "He himself is the propitiation for the sins of *the Jewish believers*; and not for the sins of *the Jewish believers only*, but also for the sins of *part of the* world." I am quite sure that disinterested readers would find this odd interpretation quite contrived, and this logocentric approach to privilege one's preferred doctrine at all costs quite disconcerting.

25. Sproul, *What is Reformed Theology?*, 177.

Choosing the View that a Dead Faith can Still Save (James 2:14–17)

Another example of distorting the obvious meaning of the text to maintain one's favorite theology is how the advocates of free grace thoroughly disconnect faith from works to guarantee eternal security—that is, "once saved, always saved." One inherent problem with this doctrine is how to account for those, who after making a profession of faith in Christ, stop believing later. Obviously, "once saved, always saved" loses its meaning if a condition is attached like, "as long as you believe and walk in your faith."

Consider the example of Bart Ehrman, who had chaired the department of religious studies at the University of North Carolina, Chapel Hill. He admits to having been *born again* in his teen years; in fact, he is a graduate of Moody Bible Institute and Wheaton College, two flagship conservative Christian institutions that likely adhere to some version of eternal security. But now, Ehrman is a self-proclaimed "happy agnostic" who no longer believes and is a leading critic against the Christian faith.[26] Is he still saved?[27]

Safeguarding the Doctrine of Eternal Security

Free grace advocates have resolved this problem by detaching saving faith from what happens thereafter—meaning, once a profession of faith is made, what that person does afterward (including apostasy) is irrelevant. Robert Wilkin, a leading proponent of free grace, writes, "Jesus guarantees eternal life to all who come to faith in Him, even if they later stop believing in Him for eternal life."[28] Lordship salvation led by, yes, MacArthur, opposes free grace by stressing, first, the importance of producing good works to verify one's salvation, and second, how "faith is not complete unless it is obedient."[29] Now, it is not that free grace does not offer anything valuable; it does. One beneficial aspect to soteriology is that it keeps unfair pressure off of people to produce good works *fast*

---

26. Burge, "Lapsed Evangelical Critic," 26.

27. Ehrman is reintroduced in the final chapter because I find his reasoning for leaving the faith relevant to why cessationists theologize the way they do.

28. Wilkin, *Confident in Christ*, 185.

29. Horton, *Christ the Lord*, 36.

in order to showcase their salvation, thus deflecting unwarranted criticism. And it isn't that lordship salvation is entirely right; for it can border on salvation by works.[30] But, much like the way cessationists and continuationists have argued, particularly since 2013 when *Strange Fire* was published, the advocates of these two systems, free grace and lordship salvation, have been fighting tooth and nail, claiming each other's gospel as false and unbiblical. Thus, Wilkin, the abovementioned proponent of free grace, says, "If a person believes the gospel and is then led astray by lordship salvation, he or she is still a Christian, albeit one who no longer believes the gospel."[31] That sounds like what MacArthur says about continuationists in *Strange Fire*: "The gospel that is driving [their growth] is not the true gospel, and the spirit behind them is not the Holy Spirit."[32] Soon, everyone will be believing a false gospel in someone's eyes.

THE WAY WE THEOLOGIZE

Distorting the Obvious

In view of such soteriological thinking, what do the free grace adherents do with passages like James 2:14–17, which says:

> What good is it, my brothers, if someone says he has faith but does not have works? Can that faith save him? If a brother or sister is poorly clothed and lacking in daily food, and one of you says to them, "Go in peace, be warmed and filled," without giving them the things needed for the body, what good is that? So also faith by itself, if it does not have works, is dead.

30. Regarding MacArthur's soteriology ("Disobedience is unbelief"), Reformed theologian Michael Horton comments, "Faith produces obedience, but to suggest that faith is obedience is to confuse justification with sanctification." Ibid., 36.

31. Wilkin, *Confident in Christ*, 185.

32. MacArthur, *Strange Fire*, xvii.

The faith in question here is a dead faith (nonworking faith), characterized by not having produced good works (i.e., obedience). So, according to James, does the absence of works in one's life indicate that that person never possessed a saving faith (therefore, he is still headed to hell)? Or despite that he is still going to heaven but, in the meantime, God will punish him (including death) for a life of disobedience? That is to ask: What does "can that [dead] faith save him" in James 2:14b mean? James's answer is an emphatic no, but what is the question? Saved from what? Is it, "Can a non-working faith 'deliver[us] from hell'"[33]—meaning, even though I have no works and I may no longer believe, I am still going to heaven? That's not the right question, according to Zane Hodges who writes, "[James] is not discussing salvation from hell!"[34] Instead, the apostle is saying that a nonworking faith cannot "save our lives from the deadly consequences of sin"[35] while on Earth, but "these dangers do not include hell"[36]—meaning, he is still going to heaven despite having a dead faith.

This is yet another example of protecting a doctrine that one favors—in this case, "once saved, always saved, even if the person no longer believes"—by way of distorting the obvious. The context of James 2:14–26 is salvation; that is, the apostle is concerned not only about being justified before God, which, according to Romans 3:28b, is by "faith apart from works of the law," but being "justified" before men. Thus, when James says, "You see that a person is justified by works and not by faith alone" (Jas 2:24), "he is speaking of," as commentators David Steel and Curtin Thomas assert, "*a Christian being justified before men by his works*, whereas Paul in Romans 3:28 is speaking of a *sinner being justified before God apart from his works*"[37] (italics theirs).

Making Light of the Bible

In the same way that Sproul makes light of 1 John 2:2 (by saying that *holou tou cosmou* does not mean the entire world but part of the world), Hodges does the same with James 2:18–20, which says,

33. Hodges, *Gospel Under Siege*, 26.
34. Ibid., 30.
35. Ibid., 30.
36. Ibid., 38.
37. Steele and Thomas, *Romans,* 124.

> But someone will say, "You have faith and I have works." Show
> me your faith apart from your works, and I will show you my
> faith by my works. You believe that God is one; you do well. Even
> the demons believe—and shudder! Do you want to be shown,
> you foolish person, that faith apart from works is useless?

Obviously, to James, the faith that demons have in God represents faith apart from works that is both dead and useless to save them from going to hell. But, if Hodges's view was correct (that a dead faith that produces no fruits can still save), then that would mean that demons, whose faith in God produces no good works, are not in danger of hell; rather, they are merely punished for bearing no fruits on the earth, but in the end will make it to heaven. No one in their right mind would say that (including Hodges),[38] but it seems to be the logical conclusion to the distorted interpretation of James 2:14–17, which stems from privileging the role faith plays in our justification before God while dismissing the role works plays to justify us before man. This is another version of logocentric soteriology.

Why Synthetic Soteriology Fails

Does the Bible teach limited atonement or unlimited atonement? Is eternal security biblical or unbiblical (meaning one can lose salvation)? If we are honest with ourselves, we would admit that each of these pairs of opposites can be supported by several passages in the Bible. These issues may appear clear-cut to their respective advocates, but they are antinomies—that is, pairs of opposites that are in themselves biblically valid. But the fact that their respective advocates claim their position as the true, biblical view means only one thing: parts of God's word are either ignored or their meanings distorted. Being made oblivious to what they do to Scripture by their commitment to the logocentrism of either/or, they embody no tension—that is, feeling some degree of uncertainty over the rightness of their theology. This inevitably produces competing airtight theologies that lend themselves to the kind of argumentativeness that eventually turns into divisiveness. The feud between two groups

---

38. Hodges makes a special plea (it's "a reduction to absurdity," *Gospel Under Siege*, 21.) to avoid implying that demons can go to heaven, based on his belief that James 2:19 is said by an imaginary objector, not the apostle James himself. I disagree.

committed to logocentric pneumatology—cessationists and a segment within continuationists—has followed this pattern to a T.

In contrast, the Radical Middle equally privileges and upholds both pairs of opposites, thesis and its antithesis—sometimes in great tension—while "recogniz[ing] that here is a mystery which we cannot expect to solve in this world."[39] We still must try to understand (chapter 5), but with humility, love, and unity; otherwise, we will become too certain of our understanding of antinomies and begin to look down on others for not being biblical enough. Having said this, there is yet another hermeneutical approach—the synthetic approach—that appears to resemble the hermeneutics of the Radical Middle but ultimately is not the same.

THE HERMENEUTICS OF SYNTHESIZING EQUALLY TRUE OPPOSITES

Recall how Jacques Ellul views interpreting the Bible: "We have to recognize that everything in revelation is formulated in antithetical fashion (in a dialectical way from certain standpoints) . . . There is no 'either/or,' only 'both/and.' We find this on every level."[40] Much of what Ellul refers to is the type of revelation in the Bible represented by the eight pairs of opposites introduced in chapter 2 (e.g., "I have not come to bring peace, but a sword"—Matt 10:34b). Let me add a couple more: "hate [your] own father and mother" (Luke 14:26b)/"honor your father and your mother" (Mark 7:10a); "I do not permit a woman to teach . . . a man" (1 Tim 2:12a)/"Priscilla and Aquila . . . explained to [Apollos] the way of God more accurately" (Acts 18:26b). Notice that Priscilla taught a man.

To the question of how we should, then, approach antithetic Scripture hermeneutically, Ellul states, "[Revelation] unites two contrary truths that are truth only as they come together. I say advisedly that *everything* that the Bible presents takes this form."[41] What Ellul seeks is a synthesis, but does the Radical Middle synthesize as well?

---

39. Packer, *Evangelism and the Sovereignty of God*, 24.

40. Ellul, *Subversion of Christianity*, 43–44.

41. Ibid., 43–44.

The Hegelian Approach

Evidently, what Ellul had in mind is the dialectical approach of the nineteenth-century German philosopher Friedrich Hegel. Christian philosopher Francis Schaeffer summarizes Hegel's approach in the following manner:

> I have a new idea. From now on let us think in this way; instead of thinking in terms of cause and effect, what we really have is a thesis, and opposite is an antithesis, and the answer to their relationship is not in the horizontal movement of cause and effect, but the answer is always "synthesis."[42]

This synthesis, then, becomes the new thesis, which in time will be challenged by its antithesis, at which point, a new synthesis emerges. This cyclical process, then, repeats itself over and over, and what is held as truth at the moment evolves, seeking to be more rational as it progresses upward. Truth, therefore, is not fixed, but always changing.

Ultimately, Ellul's suggestion of fusing two contrary truths as the way to discover the real truth of Scripture does more harm than good. How so? By synthesizing an equally true thesis and its antithesis, it weakens the essence (or purpose) of both. This certainly is not the approach of the Radical Middle paradigm in which an equally true thesis and its antithesis are centered as distinctive entities without fusing the two. Discovering "what connections exist between the two [antithetic] truths"[43] is certainly within the purview of the Radical Middle, but not synthesizing the two. At this point, it would be of great benefit to consider some examples of Ellul's synthetic approach. Further explanations will then be provided.

Synthesizing an Equally True Thesis and Antithesis in Soteriology

First, consider a clear example of what can be dubbed as "synthetic theologizing" (i.e., mixing two equally true doctrines) that plagued the Galatian church to its great detriment.

---

42. Schaeffer, *God Who is There*, 20.
43. Packer, *Evangelism and the Sovereignty of God*, 21.

The Galatian Synthesis

For those Jews who became Christians, accepting the thesis that faith in Christ is necessary for salvation apparently was not too difficult; though, evidently, it was not sufficient for some of them. Luke writes, "But some men came down from Judea and were teaching the brothers [in Antioch], 'Unless you are circumcised according to the custom of Moses, you cannot be saved'" (Acts 15:1). Of course, to the Israelites, the rite of circumcision was a tremendous blessing, since it was the sign that the Lord, after choosing them, would establish an everlasting covenant with Israel (Gen 17:9–10). But since circumcision was instituted after God had already justified Abraham on account of his faith (Rom 4:10), it is not essential to how a person gets saved. The apostle Paul makes this point abundantly clear when he writes, "[Abraham] received the sign of circumcision as a seal of the righteousness that he had by faith while he was still uncircumcised" (Rom 4:11). But, some Jewish Christians in Galatia, instead of maintaining the distinction between faith and circumcision, synthesized the two to the point of corrupting both.

Why the Soteriological Synthesis Failed

Now, if works are viewed as the evidence of faith (Jas 2:14), it is a positive antithesis to faith, but when faith and works are blended, their respective distinctions are lost. So in Galatia, once circumcision (works) was deemed as a necessary condition for salvation, it became a negative antithesis that corrupted the salvific doctrine of "the righteous shall live by faith" (Rom 1:17b).

Having opted for salvation by works, "every man who accept[ed] circumcision . . . [now was] obligated to keep the whole law" (Gal 5:3). Obviously, these people did not realize that it was an all-or-nothing deal. So once faith and works were synthesized, it became "a different gospel" (Gal 1:6b).

Synthesizing an Equally True Thesis and Antithesis in Christology

Now, let's examine how the early church dealt with the binary nature of Christ. Scripture says that Christ is both divine and human at the same time. Obviously, divinity and humanity are antithetical to each other.

In the early church, one question on many people's mind was this: How much of Jesus is divine and how much is human? The first group to take a stab at this question was the aforementioned docetists in the late first century. To them Jesus was 100 percent divine (that is, Spirit) and zero percent human, since they refused to believe that Jesus had come in the flesh (1 John 4:2–3).

Later, several ecumenical councils were held in the fourth and fifth centuries to discuss, among other matters, this essential christological issue. And the early church theologians, in effect, used the Hegelian approach to understand the relationship between the divinity and humanity of Christ.

The Synthesis of Apollinaris

After the docetists came the Laodicean Bishop Apollinaris, who tried to synthesize the two binary natures of Christ. He conceived of the humanity of Jesus as "consisting of body, soul, and spirit, and sought the solution of the problem of the two natures in Christ in the theory that the Logos [i.e., divinity] took the place of the human *pnuema* (spirit),"[44] meaning, Jesus no longer had the spirit of man. In Apollinarianism, Christ's humanity was not discarded, which is what docetism did, but it was no longer true that Jesus was "born in the likeness of men" (Phil 2:7b) in its entirety, since his human spirit was replaced by *logos*. The Council of Constantinople, held in AD 381, rejected Apollinarianism because it "denied the true and proper humanity of Jesus Christ"[45] in such a way that he was not "made like his brothers in every respect" (Heb 2:17a). If I were to put a number on it, it was as if Jesus was only 75 percent human and 25 percent divine.

The Synthesis of Nestorius

Then came Nestorius, the patriarch of Constantinople. From afar, it seems as if his Christology resembles the Radical Middle, because it distinguishes between the divine and human nature of Christ, while equally valuing them. Furthermore, "instead of blending the two natures into a single self-consciousness, Nestorianism places them alongside of each

44. Berkhof, *History of Christian Doctrines*, 102.

45. Ibid., 102.

other"[46] so that "the two natures are also two persons."[47] Perhaps realizing the abstractness of this concept, Nestorius used the institution of marriage to further explain it. He saw the union of Christ's two natures as if it were the "union of husband and wife, who become 'one flesh' while remaining two separate natures and persons."[48] But, it is at this point Nestorianism, in effect, becomes synthetic, because the analogy of marital bond implies the blending of two natures (50 percent humanity and 50 percent divinity, if you will) to become whole. Perhaps, this Christology makes more sense to the rational mind.

However, whereas the synthetic union of two persons in a matrimony is fitting to explain the mystery of the relationship between Christ and the church (Eph 5:31–33), it does little to explain what is called "the hypostatic union of the two natures in the Person of Christ."[49] This is to say, while we are not entirely sure how the hypostatic union came about, the Council of Ephesus in AD 431 reached a conclusion that it was not like the union of husband and wife, and thus Nestorianism was rejected.

Perhaps the mistake of Nestorius was trying to make sense of something that really should have been left as a mystery. But like many systematic theologians who try to build an airtight system that explains everything logically, Nestorius tried to create a rational Christology devoid of any mystery and tension; in the end, it greatly weakened the unified personhood of Jesus consisting of the two natures.

The Synthesis of Eutyches

Then came Eutyches, a presbyter in Constantinople, who taught that the human and divine natures of Christ were so fused or synthesized that it resulted in a third "singular" nature (a.k.a., Monophysitism). Eutyches's understanding can be described as Christ being 100 percent divine and 100 percent human but without distinction, or zero percent divine and zero percent human. Eutyches commented, "I admit that our Lord was of two natures before the union, but after the union one nature."[50] This

46. Ibid., 105.

47. Ibid., 104–5.

48. Bettenson, *Documents of the Christian Church*, 46. Bettenson notes that "Nestorius seems to have learned this doctrine from his master, Theodore of Mopsuestia, who illustrated the union by the union of husband and wife . . ."

49. Holloman, "Theology II," III-13.

50. Ibid., 49.

Monophysitism was denied at the Council of Chalcedon in 451, because it effectively produced a third nature that was neither fully divine nor fully human.

Why Synthetic Christology Fails

So why did these attempts fail? While these teachings were sincere efforts to find the most adequate understanding of the two natures of Christ, each failed because they attempted to synthesize, to varying degrees, the divinity and humanity of Christ, which ironically, ended up damaging the essence of both. But, as mentioned in chapter 3, it was Leo I who, at the Council of Chalcedon in AD 451, succinctly expressed what Scripture says about the dual nature of Christ:

> Thus there was born true God in the entire and perfect nature of true man, complete in its own properties . . . Each nature preserves its own characteristics without diminution, so that the form of a servant does not detract from the form of God.[51]

This is the Radical Middle Christology: each nature is fully and completely privileged and constituted (i.e., 100 percent) in the single person of Jesus Christ.

THE HERMENEUTICS OF SYNTHESIZING A TRUE THESIS AND ITS FALSE ANTITHESIS

Now, let's switch over to a different category: What happens when a thesis, which is true, is synthesized with its false antithesis? For instance, whereas Scripture posits that God created the universe (Heb 11:3), nowhere does the Bible say its opposite—an eternal universe—is true as well. As firmly stated in chapter 3, the Radical Middle paradigm of both/and does not apply to this type of antithesis in which the correctness of one proposition necessarily means the falsity of its opposite. This is strictly a matter of either/or; nevertheless, it has not stopped many from trying to synthesize truly contradictory opposites, resulting in the disastrous outcome—namely anthropocentric synthesis—of corrupting the theocentric truth itself.

---

51. Ibid., 50.

Synthesizing Special Creation and Evolution

For instance, the corruption of truth is precisely what has happened as a result of Christians seeking to synthesize the Genesis account of the origin of men with evolutionism.[52] The key biblical thesis is that humans are the result of God's special creation with purpose (Eph 2:10), irrespective of whether this happened 6,000 to 10,000 years ago, as advocates of young earth insist, or much earlier in time (as implied by the adherents of Intelligent Design).[53] Its antithesis posits that humans are the result of undirected and unguided evolutionary processes (no purpose).

Synthesis: Theistic Evolution

When these two competing claims are synthesized, the outcome is theistic evolution, which posits that "God guided the evolutionary process and that Adam and Eve were animals 'ensouled' by God."[54] This synthetic outlook inevitably triggers a low view of the Bible, since it requires ignoring key Scriptures that do not support the evolutionary scheme of things. For example, death, without which natural selection is improbable, becomes a default reality without sin having to enter the world and introduce death as its result (Rom 5:12). Once a key truth is compromised, it does not stop there. Now, "a vocal group of theistic evolutionists . . . insist that God did not even guide the evolutionary process, that the Fall never occurred, and that Adam, Eve, and the Garden of Eden are only myth or metaphors."[55]

52. Since evolution does not and cannot answer the question of how life evolved from inorganic matters, it should be seen for what it is: an explanation for the diversity of life on earth. Dawkins admits that "the origin of life . . . lies outside the reach of [Darwin's] crane, because natural selection cannot proceed without it." Dawkins, *God Delusion*, 168.

53. William Lane Craig states, "The Bible thus teaches that the universe had a beginning. It does not teach that this beginning was recent. That is a mistaken inference based on adding up the life spans of various Old Testament figures." Craig, "Tough Questions about Science," 54.

54. Bloom, "Theistic Evolution Isn't Fit for Survival," 28.

55. Ibid., 28.

A Lethal Result

For many, this synthetic trajectory leads to atheistic evolution, which, to those who commit to that course, is the end of the dialectical process with respect to the matter of origins. New Atheist and former Oxford biologist Richard Dawkins, who grew up Anglican, says that if someone were to ask him, "'Has your knowledge of evolution influenced you in the direction of being an atheist?' [he] would have to answer yes,"[56] adding, "Darwin made it possible to be an intellectually fulfilled atheist."[57]

The late Cornell historian of science William Provine, who gave up his faith in high school after discovering evolution, quips, "Evolution is the greatest engine of atheism ever invented."[58] As for purpose, whereas belief in God's special creation gives humans intrinsic worth and purpose, atheistic evolution fosters an outlook of hopelessness and purposelessness. Provine frankly admits that

> there are no gods, no purposes, and no goal-directed forces of any kind. There is no life after death. When I die, I am absolutely certain that I am going to be dead. That's the end of me. There is no ultimate foundation for ethics, no ultimate meaning in life, and no free will for humans, either.[59]

Now, neither Provine nor Dawkins are adherents of theistic evolution, which they disdain (the latter more so than the former). Their views are cited to show that the ultimate destination of theistic evolution, an anthropocentric synthesis of an essential truth and its false antithesis, can be, for many, atheistic evolution (Dawkins agrees), which is the corruption of truth itself with the disastrous outcome of purposelessness and hopelessness.

Synthesizing the Exclusivity of Christ and Universalism

Another instance of synthesizing a true thesis with its false antithesis is fusing the exclusivity of Christ for salvation (John 14:6; Act 4:12)[60] with

56. Dawkins, *God Delusion*, 93.

57. Frankowski, *Expelled*.

58. M., "Is Intelligent Design 'Apologetics?'" lines 14–15.

59. Provine, "Darwinism," para. 56.

60. "And there is salvation in no one else; for there is no other name under heaven that has been given among men by which we must be saved" (Acts 4:12 NASB).

its postmodern antithesis—all religions lead to the same God. When these diametrically opposed beliefs are synthesized, it turns into what Carlton Pearson, once a very influential Pentecostal minister, calls "the gospel of inclusion," meaning everyone in the world is already saved because Jesus died for the sins of the world. He says:

> Christ's crucifixion and death on the Calvary accomplished its purpose of reconciling all mankind to God . . . The message man needs to hear, then, is not that he simply has a suggested opportunity for salvation, but that through Christ he has, in fact, already been redeemed to God and that he may enjoy the blessings that are already his through Christ.[61]

Pearson's "gospel of inclusion" is the synthesis of universalism with the substitutionary death of Christ to declare that everyone in the world is already saved in Christ without having to make personal faith commitment. Pearson's universalism may feel different than the run-of-the-mill universalism based on moral light or religious pluralism, but the result, however, is the corruption of the gospel, which Paul calls "a different gospel—which is really no gospel at all" (Gal 1:6b–7a NIV).

Synthesizing Christianity and Islam

The latest example of fusing two disparate beliefs to form a synthesis is the so-called "Chrislam." With respect to Abraham, the biblical thesis is that he is the father of faith and only "those who believe [Jesus] are children of Abraham" (Gal 3:7b NIV). As for Islam, since it is a movement to return to the monotheistic religion of Abraham, the fusion of Christianity and Islam appears to be warranted. Thus, an advocate of Chrislam writes,

> Since when are Muslims non-believers? Muslims do not need converting, because Christians and Muslims believe in and worship the same God. Why can't we recognize this simple fact and worship together in harmony?[62]

However, this synthetic approach completely ignores one fundamental difference between the two faiths. On the one hand, the belief in the Son for the Christian faith is central to salvation, for the apostle John declares, "Whoever has the Son has life; whoever does not have the Son

---

61. Taylor, "Heresy Charge Torpedoes Pastor's Political Debut," 19.

62. "Evangelism Antagonism," 32.

of God does not have life" (1 John 5:12). However, Islam denies the son-
ship of Jesus, saying, "Say: Allah is One, the Eternal God. He begot none,
nor was He begotten. None is equal to Him" (Sura 112); "Allah forbid
that He should have a son" (Sura 4:171). Instead, Jesus is the second most
important prophet, a notch below the prophet Mohammed. In so doing,
Islam discards the foundational basis of the Christian faith, namely that
"Jesus is the Christ, the Son of God" (John 20:31b). Ultimately, this synthesis will lead to taking neither Islam nor Christianity seriously, since
whatever substantial differences exist between the two faiths are deemed
insignificant.[63]

Lessons Learned from the Failure of Synthesizing Truth and Untruth

So then, what can be learned from these and other efforts to synthesize
biblical truth with its false antithesis?

First, attempts by some evangelicals—perhaps to stay culturally
relevant—to fuse unbridgeable binary oppositions stem not from what
theologian Carl Henry (who "pioneered the renewing of the evangelical
mind"[64] a generation ago) described as "the uneasy conscience"[65] of those
trying to live out "the Christian's dual citizenship"[66] amid "crucial problems confronting the modern mind."[67] Rather, the root of such unwarranted synthesis comes from a deep insecurity and desire to be liked and
respected by mainstream society. Today's evangelicals, better educated
than their predecessors, are troubled by comments from secular liber-

---

63. Merely using the word *Isai*, an Arabic name for Jesus, should not be grounds
for accusing someone of upholding Chrislam. In cross-cultural communication, the
use of native terms is always recommended instead of introducing foreign words. Islam is unique in that, unlike other world religions, its holy book contains numerous
references to biblical personage like Moses and Abraham. There is still much debate
among Arabic Christians about the use of Allah (which is used in the Arabic Bible) as
a reference to the God of the Bible, since some characteristics attributed to Allah in
the Koran are not congruent with the God of the Bible (e.g., "Allah does not love the
unbelievers"—Sura 3:57b). But, as long as the debate is still taking place and each side
has good arguments, it is not fair to accuse someone of practicing Chrislam for calling
Jesus *Isai*, especially to build a bridge with Muslims (1 Cor 9:20).

64. Spring, "Carl F. H. Henry Dies," 20.

65. Henry, *Uneasy Conscience of Modern Fundamentalism*, xviii.

66. Spring, "Carl F. H. Henry Dies," 20.

67. Henry, *Uneasy Conscience of Modern Fundamentalism*, xviii.

als who continue to question their intellectual ability, as well as cultural sensitivity. Once, reporter Michael Weisskopf, writing in the Washington Post, "quipped that Christian conservatives were 'largely poor, uneducated and easy to command.'"[68] New Atheist Sam Harris, in *The End of Faith*, states that religious beliefs "should not survive an elementary school education."[69]

In view of this, the second lesson is this: those who try to uphold God's timeless truth in a secular and pluralistic society should remember these words of Christ: "If the world hates you, know that it has hated me before it hated you" (John 15:18). This realization, therefore, ought to put the conflict between cessationists and continuationists in its proper perspective. It is hard enough that the world hates those who refuse to synthesize the truth of God with its false antithesis derived from secularism or pluralism. It makes hardly any sense, therefore, that those who agree on the essentials of faith should "hate" each other over, of all things, spiritual gifts, an important but nonessential matter.

THE HERMENEUTICS OF LOGOCENTRISM ON WORD AND SPIRIT: ITS EFFECT ON SPIRITUAL GROWTH

Thus far, we have seen several examples of the hermeneutics of logocentrism that ignore or distort the obvious meaning of those Scriptures which are inconvenient to one's preferred theology. We also saw how biblical truth is weakened when an equally true thesis and its antithesis are synthesized, as well as how truth is corrupted when a biblical thesis is fused with its false antithesis. This is nothing short of "tamper[ing] with God's word" (2 Cor 4:2b).

As indicated at the outset, the discussion presented in this chapter over issues not directly related to the tension between word and Spirit is to prepare the readers for chapters 6–10, which will discuss the scriptural validity of the sign gifts: tongues, prophecy, apostleship, and healing. What is presented in the remainder of this chapter concerns another dimension to the word and Spirit dichotomy: its effect on our spiritual growth.

---

68. Shepherd, "For the 'Poor, Uneducated,'" lines 1–2.

69. Harris, *End of Faith*, 25.

The Truth behind Binary Opposition Between Word and Spirit

In chapter 3 it was said that binary opposition between word and Spirit is a man-made conflict. As demonstrated here, it is the result of incorrect exegesis based on the improper hermeneutics of logocentrism. Now whether word or Spirit is privileged, it has implications for what activities (e.g., Bible study, praying, praise and worship, etc.) are pursued to promote spiritual growth at the individual level. Because certain activities are prioritized, perhaps at the exclusion others, it diminishes God's power through his word (Heb 4:12) and Spirit (Acts 1:8) to effect transformative changes in those of us who are in desperate need of them.

The Outcome of Privileging Knowledge

First, consider what may ensue when the attainment of biblical knowledge is privileged, while ignoring or minimizing what the Spirit brings, such as fervent emotion (1 Thess 5:19) and unscripted/spontaneous moments (1 Cor 14:30).[70] It may puff up the mind (1 Cor 8:1), which will certainly lead to spiritual impoverishment. Alister McGrath, currently Andreas Idreos Professor of Science and Religion at Oxford University, seeing that the root of Western Christianity rests on "a deepened understanding of the basics of Christian teachings and a deeper knowledge of the biblical works,"[71] also recognizes its downside. He says,

> This demand to read, learn, and understand has undoubtedly been helpful in many ways. For a start, it leads to better-informed Christians with a much better grasp of the basic Christian beliefs. Yet in another way, it had led to spiritual impoverishment."[72]

---

70. I have been in two worship services in which a powerful time of praise and worship left no room for preaching. This is not normative, but it can happen, and when it does, we should let the Spirit take over. I am also thinking of situations in which people can freely share what the Lord did for them or a fresh biblical insight. The Baptist church I attended in Mexico always offered a time of sharing ("open mike") during Sunday services for this very purpose. The congregants were instructed beforehand what was expected of them (edifying the body, reasonable length, etc.).

71. McGrath, *The Journey*, 14.

72. Ibid., 14–15.

Confessions of a Doctoral Student

This reminds me of an email I received in 2013 from John, a young Reformed seminarian whom I mentioned in chapter 1, who spoke at my church's retreat some 15 years earlier along with a flaming Pentecostal. By this time, after having attained a PhD in Old Testament studies, John had been teaching at a Reformed seminary for some time. In this email however, he admits how the exposure to cessationism during his seminary days gradually enervated his spirituality. He says:

> But during my years at Westminster, I was taught a strict cessationist position with respect to the spiritual gifts. Although I didn't believe what I was taught, it began to filter into my thinking and practice . . . As an ardent Calvinist (I think you can recall . . . that I was fairly gung-ho about Covenant Theology and Calvinism), I began to develop a critical spirit which eventually worked itself out in the way I lived . . . I was a struggling Christian who was reading a lot about the Bible (and a lot of liberal critical theories for my doctoral courses), but not really getting to know the Bible or the God who inspired it. I mean I did believe, pray and go to church regularly, but I was not growing as a Christian, and I was not able to resist temptation as effectively as I did before, and I would be prone to losing my temper and just be "in the flesh" . . . I like to compare that spiritual season of my life to a dried-up raisin in contrast to a plump, juicy grape.[73]

Imagine that you were John's pastor during the time while he was undergoing these struggles and pursuing his doctorate. How would you have counseled him? Would you tell him to read more Scriptures? Study more theology? Listen to more expository sermons? Undertaking these types of spiritual activities that feed the mind certainly help, but their efficacy increasingly diminishes when that alone is stressed. Along with that, what this doctoral student desperately needed was to pursue the Spirit, which he himself came to see. In the same email he writes, "I now have a hunger for the things of the Holy Spirit and desire the gifts of tongues and to prophesy . . . I have fervently sought the work of the Holy Spirit in my life."[74]

73. John, email to author, January 12, 2013 (cited with John's permission).
74. Ibid.

Historical Outcome when the Spirit is Suppressed

The fact that John, with multiple degrees in theology and now being a veteran seminary professor, turned to the ministry of the Spirit has been the exception rather than the rule.

Consider reactions by learned men to the First Great Awakening, a series of great revival movements that broke out in northeast America in the eighteenth century. Suffice it to say, the established churches in colonial America were not used to seeing what typically occurred in these meetings where the Spirit moved powerfully for it was a movement to "awaken . . . people to a deeper, more experiential knowledge of Christian faith."[75]

Historian Kenneth Latourette describes it this way:

> Much excitement and many emotional disturbances accompanied the revival . . . There were screaming, laughing, trances, visions, and convulsions . . . The Great Awakening emphasized the importance of individual decision, tended to nurture the belief that the Christian should be able to tell the day and the hour of his conversion, and to encourage each Christian to seek to win his non-Christian or only nominally Christian fellows.[76]

So how did the learned men of the day respond to the Great Awakening that had its share of "emotional disturbances"[77] and "disruptive activities?"[78] Perhaps, as harbingers of modern cessationists, "many disliked the intensity and emotionalism of the revival and opposed it"[79] as religious excitement among the uncontrolled and uneducated:

> Both clergy and laity, who were alienated by the emotional excesses, were angered by the denunciations of the more ardent . . . preachers, and held onto the cold, rational approach to religion which was beginning characteristics of what was dubbed the Age of Reason [Deism]. "New Lights" and "Old Lights" in Presbyterian and Congregational churches often separated into distinct units. The "Old Lights" were critical of what they deemed the lack of education of the "New Light" clergy.[80]

75. Walker, *History of the Christian Church*, 465.

76. Latourette, *History of Christianity*, 960.

77. Ibid., 960.

78. Walker, *History of the Christian Church*, 466.

79. Ibid., 465.

80. Latourette, *History of Christianity*, 960.

Subsequently, "this schism led eventually to the development of an orthodox group and a liberal group. Out of the latter the Unitarian group [that denies all major doctrines of the historic faith], which split off New England Congregationalism, emerged early in the nineteenth century."[81]

But like John, there were many exceptions to the rule, such as the great theologian Jonathan Edwards (1703–1758), who "believed that the Awakening was a genuine work of grace, expressing itself in both mental and physical excitement."[82] But, eventually, he "was forced out of his parish in Northampton (1750),"[83] some fifteen years after "the Great Awakening broke out [there] under the preaching of . . . Edwards.[84]

In view of this historical development, the opposition to the works of the Spirit can be summed up in two ways: First, because of intense emotional and physical responses occurring in these revival meetings, many respectable Christians of that era found it easy to privilege intellect over emotion, restraint over vulnerability. Second, to those who eventually turned to Unitarianism and liberalism, the "messy" works of the Spirit was the nudge they needed to reject the faith rooted in revelation, which increasingly became an embarrassment to their budding intellect, and opt for something more respectable. What does this show? The more we accumulate knowledge, biblical or otherwise, the more we need the works of the Spirit to stay humble and true to God's word. As for cessationists and continuationists, while the latter may err on emphasizing too much manifestations, the danger of the former is stifling the Spirit himself.

The Outcome of Privileging the Spirit

But the danger of pursuing the Spirit and all that comes with it, without much regard for biblical knowledge and doctrine, is just as real. The apostle Paul warns that such faith is susceptible to being "tossed to and fro by the waves and carried about by every wind of doctrine, by human cunning, by craftiness in deceitful schemes" (Eph 4:14). That seems to be precisely what happened following the Second Great Awakening that "swept the Middle Atlantic states, the South, and the frontier" during the

81. Cairns, *Christianity through the Centuries*, 402.

82. Sainsbury, "Jonathan Edwards," 438.

83. Latourette, *History of Christianity*, 960

84. Ibid., 959.

early-to-mid nineteenth century.[85] Renowned apologist J. P. Moreland notes that

> thousands of people were "converted" to Christ by revivalist preaching, but they had no real intellectual grasp of Christian teaching. As a result, two of the three major American cults began in the Burned Over District among the unstable, untaught "converts": Mormonism (1830) and the Jehovah's Witnesses (1884).[86]

For these reasons both word and Spirit must be equally privileged and pursued instead of set against each other. While John probably never heard of the Radical Middle before writing his email to me in 2013, I could not help but notice how he nailed it. He writes:

> Don't take me wrong, I do believe in sound hermeneutics; I take the Bible literally, but it cannot be fully understood only with grammatical-historical method. Human-centered approaches will never reveal what the Holy Spirit intended in His word since his words are spiritually discerned.[87]

That is the Radical Middle of word and Spirit!

SYNTHESIZING WORD AND SPIRIT

It should also be noted that word and Spirit should not be synthesized. Meaning what?

Not One and the Same

In a manner of speaking, the spiritual benefits of studying Scripture come from studying God's word and not necessarily from singing praises or praying in tongues. Conversely, the spiritual benefits of praising God or praying come from praising or praying, respectively, and not necessarily from studying the Bible. The point is that pursuing one's favorite spiritual activity to the exclusion of all others is not the proper way to achieve spiritual growth. Obviously, studying the Bible in seminaries is preferred over praying, clearly out of necessity. But for those who think that this is

85. Walker, *History of the Christian Church*, 508.

86. Moreland, *Love Your God*, 23.

87. John, email to author, January 12, 2013.

optimal, they are, in effect, fusing word and Spirit, as if they render the same effect (they do not). Consider the matter of temptation. No one can overcome it every time we are tempted, but if we succumb to it regularly, it will surely stunt our spiritual growth. So how can we overcome temptations? We see two main strategies Jesus uses in Matthew: first, Jesus overcame the temptation of the devil through knowledge of God's word and the declaration of it (Matt 4:4)[88]; second, Jesus told the disciples to "pray that [they] may not enter into temptation" (Matt 26:41a).

What do you prefer? Word? Doctrine? Knowledge? If so, then, when an erudite like Paul, who was educated by Gamaliel (Acts 22:3), "a teacher of the law held in honor by all the people" (Acts 5:34b), says, "'knowledge' puffs up, but love builds up" (1 Cor 8:1b), we should heed his words. Why? Because the same outcome of being puffed up awaits those who seek knowledge without pursuing the Spirit and all that it entails, such as being vulnerable before the Lord, which often manifests through emotions or being rebuked by the "Spirit of truth" (John 16:12). And it is when contributions made by word and Spirit are integrated that individual believers can reach an optimal spiritual state. Therefore, activities concomitant to pursing word and Spirit, respectively, should be kept distinct, even as they are pursued in tandem.

Hearing from God through the Spirit

Some Christians might take umbrage at what I am about to share since, to them, it is unbiblical to hold that God still speaks to his people. I will have more to say on this matter in chapter 8 about prophecy. For now, this chapter ends with what it means to me personally that word and Spirit work in tandem to produce necessary changes in our lives.

Finishing a PhD Dissertation for Spiritual Dummies

I was pursuing a PhD at Fuller in the 1990s, but on the cusp of completing the program I ran into a major roadblock: my doctoral mentor, Dr. Charles Kraft, refused to read my 600-page dissertation because yes, it was too long! Upon being told to reduce it in half, I did not know what to do because every sentence seemed so precious and vital. I thought

---

88. "It is written, 'Man shall not live by bread alone, but by every word that comes from the mouth of God.'"

that if Dr. Kraft only read it, then he would recognize the greatness of my dissertation (that's how spiritual dummies think). Feeling frustrated and helpless, I went before the Lord to pray about what to do. Perhaps I was thinking that if I prayed hard and long, God would change Dr. Kraft's mind. That did not happen. What did happen was this: during a quiet moment while I was praying, I heard these words spoken clearly into my heart: "It is not that good." I immediately took that to mean, "Humble yoursel[f] before the Lord" (Jas 4:10a). This is Spirit and word working in tandem. What happened to me that day was what Jesus said the Spirit will do when he comes: "The Helper, the Holy Spirit, whom the Father will send in my name, he will teach you all things and bring to your remembrance all that I have said to you" (John 14:26). After the Spirit reminded me of the word that I needed to hear, I began to see that my dissertation was not all that good. So I got a "pair of scissors" and began the process of whittling it down to 360 pages, after which it was submitted to the delight of my mentor who eventually approved it. Perhaps this is what 1 Peter 5:6 (NIV) had in mind: "Humble yourselves, therefore, under God's mighty hand, that he may lift you up in due time."

Spiritual Growth

So I left Fuller with a degree on one hand and an important spiritual lesson, in word and Spirit, on the other—humility may not be sufficient to complete a doctoral program, but it is absolutely necessary. The same can be said about spiritual growth. Without humility, while we may say all the right spiritual-sounding things (e.g. "apart from Christ I can do nothing"), our actual mode of operation is self-reliance (2 Cor 1:9) and self-aggrandizement (Luke 18:11). And living daily amid that awareness, however clumsy it may look, is essential to how I would define spirituality: "Walk[ing] in the same way in which [Jesus] walked" (1 John 2:6).

In chapter 5, before examining several major arguments of cessationism and continuationism over the sign gifts in chapters 6–10, attempts are made to interpret the eight pairs of antithetic/antinomic Scriptures presented in chapter 2 through the hermeneutics of the Radical Middle. This should prepare us for discussions on many hermeneutical issues related to the sign gifts.

QUESTIONS FOR REFLECTION & DISCUSSION

1. Are you surprised by highly trained theologians picking and choosing their favorite verses to back up their theology, while ignoring inconvenient Scriptures or distorting the obvious meaning of the text? Why do you believe they do that? How can we avoid doing that?

2. We all have issues with our attitudes from time to time. What types of attitudes are inappropriate, especially for those who desire to embody the Radical Middle?

3. Why do some people reject the work of the Spirit in general? What's the fear?

4. What are some issues that are troubling you because your beliefs based on the Bible conflict with those held by the world? Are you struggling to hold on to your beliefs? What did you learn about synthesizing a thesis that is true with its false antithesis?

5. Why is it so necessary to hold to word while not letting go of Spirit, and vice versa? What has been your experience? Do you prefer one over the other?

5

The Interpretation of Antithetic/ Antinomic Revelation According to the Hermeneutics of the Radical Middle

IN CHAPTER 2, EIGHT pairs of opposite Scriptures were introduced. One example is "In me you may have peace," which Jesus says in John 16:33b, but elsewhere he says the exact opposite: "I did not come to bring peace, but a sword" (Matt 10:34b NIV). To capture conflicting revelations of this sort, several terms have been used: "antithetic," to denote their contradictory nature; "binary opposition," to call attention to their opposite meanings; "antinomy" to point out an ostensible contradiction between two apparent truths that are reasonable and valid in themselves. The fact is that the Bible is replete with pairs of Scriptures in binary opposition that are antithetic yet antinomic.

As discussed in previous chapters, the Radical Middle of both/and, not the logocentrism of either/or, is the most optimal hermeneutical approach to handle antithetic/antinomic Scriptures. This approach avoids ignoring or distorting Scriptures that do not lend support to one's favorite theology. It also avoids synthesizing two contrary truths, as Ellul suggests, in the hope that the real truth would emerge only as they come together. Instead, the hermeneutics of the Radical Middle recognizes the validity of both pairs of antithetic Scriptures without synthesizing them even if the result may not fit neatly into one's preferred and preconceived theology. For many of us, particularly those who are enamored with airtight theology, this is not an ideal situation. But the worst thing to do is to force the Bible to fit our system, or as J. I. Packer puts it, "Nor is there any way to get rid of [antinomy], save by falsifying the very facts that led us to it."[1]

GUIDING PRINCIPLES FOR THE HERMENEUTICS OF THE RADICAL MIDDLE

Now, what Packer says should not be seen as a sign of giving up on interpreting antinomic Scriptures; in fact, he provides a general guideline as to how to properly handle them. He says:

> Refuse to regard the apparent inconsistency as real; . . . think of the two principles as, not rival alternatives, but, in some way . . . complementary to each other. Be careful, therefore, not to set at loggerheads, nor to make deductions from either that would cut across the other . . . Use each within the limits of its own reference (*i.e.,* the area delimited by the evidence from which the principle has been drawn). Note what connections exist between the two truths and their two frames of references, and teach yourself to think of reality in a way that provides for their peaceful coexistence, remembering that reality itself has proved actually to contain them both. This is how antinomies must be handled . . . in Scripture.[2]

Using this as a guide, we will now discuss briefly some hermeneutical principles essential for the proper handling of antinomic Scriptures under the rubric of the Radical Middle.

Within the Limits of its Own Reference

First, note what Packer means by "within the limits of its own reference" and "the area delimited by the evidence." It simply means that biblical meaning is shaped more by context than anything else. In the hermeneutics of the Radical Middle there are four types of context, identified by Bernard Ramm in his *Protestant Biblical Interpretation*, that are factored into the process of interpretation:

> The [first] context of any verse is the entire Scripture. This is what is meant by "Scripture interprets Scripture" . . . The second

1. Packer, *Evangelism and the Sovereignty of God*, 21.
2. Ibid., 21.

context of any passage is the Testament it is in—Old or New.
Each Testament has unique features of its own [e.g., the Old being "a shadow of the good things to come instead of the true
form of these realities" found in the New—Heb 10:1] . . . The
third context is the particular book in which the passage occurs
[e.g., the context of *Galatians*: defending justification by faith
against adding works—circumcision in this case—to it] . . . The
fourth context of any passage is the materials immediately before it, and, immediately after it.[3]

Now, while all contextual considerations are important to extract
the intended meaning of texts, the context of the entire Scripture is particularly more relevant to the hermeneutics of the Radical Middle. What
this context implies, according to Ramm, is that "all of the relevant material on a given subject [is] to be collected together so that that the pattern
of divine revelation concerning that subject would be apparent"[4] (a.k.a.,
the analogy of faith). Whereas systematic theology settles for a logical
pattern based on selective Scriptures (while depriviliging the inconvenient ones), the Radical Middle theology listens to all relevant and often
antinomic Scriptures on a given matter, even if the pattern that stems
from them is not so tidy.

Obviously, the consideration of these four contexts demands a
broad knowledge of the Bible; it will also consume more time because
there is more biblical data to consider. Scriptural knowledge and time
commitment are all the more required of the Radical Middle because
interpreting pairs of Scriptures that appear contradictory is rarely easy
and simple to resolve quickly.

Connections Between Two Frames of Reference

Second, what is helpful for finding connections which exist between
pairs of antinomic scriptures is cross-reference; and of the three types
of cross-references identified by Ramm, the so-called "conceptual cross-
reference" is more pertinent to the hermeneutics of the Radical Middle
than others. "A conceptual cross-reference means that there is a verse or
passage in one book of Holy Scripture that has the identical substance

3. Ramm, *Protestant Biblical Interpretation*, 138–39.
4. Ibid., 56.

or content of another part of Scripture even though there is no use of common words."[5]

For instance, in Hebrews 12:14, which says, "Strive for peace with everyone, and for the holiness without which no one will see the Lord," the word "salt" is not found. Nevertheless, Mark 9:50, which uses that word, may be a good conceptual cross-reference for Hebrews 12:14, since both passages deal with being at peace with people and not losing credible witness for God. This verse says, "Salt is good, but if the salt has lost its saltiness, how will you make it salty again? Have salt in yourselves, and be at peace with one another." Matthew 5:13 is helpful to explain Hebrews 12:14 as well since what it says—that salt that has lost its saltiness is "no longer good for anything" and therefore is "trampled by men" (NIV)—conceptually ties in with no one seeing the Lord when holiness (i.e., figuratively, saltiness) is absent, thereby becoming an ineffective witness for Christ.

As seen through this brief demonstration, conceptual cross-reference ensures that no random verses are used to produce artificial interpretations, particularly with respect to antithetic/antinomic texts.

Before proceeding, let me reiterate the purpose of the following section. In chapters 6–10, the interpretation of Scriptures relevant to the sign gifts by hard cessationism and flawed versions of continuationism will be examined in accordance with the hermeneutics of the Radical Middle of both/and. But first, the latter will be applied to the eight pairs of antinomic Scriptures presented in chapter 2 to seek "their peaceful coexistence,"[6] obviously with some tension in them, as a way to set the framework for the discussion to follow.

DID JESUS COME TO BRING PEACE OR A SWORD?

The first three of the eight pairs presented here have to do with seemingly contradictory statements Jesus made about his earthly ministry. The first of these issues is whether Christ came to bring peace or a sword.

---

5. Ibid., 141. The other two types of cross references are: first, *real* "verbal cross reference" which is a "parallelism of words or expression where the content or the idea is the same"; and second, "parallel cross reference," situations where "two or more books of the Holy Scriptures describe essentially the same events." Ibid., 141–42.

6. Packer, *Evangelism and the Sovereignty of God*, 21.

Antithetic Scriptures

On the one hand, Jesus says, "I have said these things to you, that in me you may have peace" (John 16:33a); "Peace I leave with you; my peace I give to you" (John 14:27a). The apostle Paul says that "[Jesus] himself is our peace" (Eph 2:14a). On the other hand, Jesus says, "Do you think that I have come to give peace on earth? No, I tell you, but rather division" (Luke 12:51). Elsewhere he says, "Do not think that I have come to bring peace to the earth. I have not come to bring peace, but a sword" (Matt 10:34).

Proper Hermeneutical Procedure

The first step in handling these antithetic passages is to avoid choosing one revelation ("I bring peace") over and against the other ("I bring a sword") and vice versa. Instead, we accept both the thesis (peace) and its antithesis (a sword) without synthesizing their respective meanings. So then, what may be a plausible explanation that enables us to accept these seemingly antinomic statements of Jesus?

Accepting the Thesis: Jesus Came to Give Peace

First, we accept the premise that Christ came to give peace, but in what sense? Upon examining the context of the entire Bible, it stands to reason that prior to the coming of Christ, the sin of Adam (Rom 5:12) had long separated a holy God from humans who were objects of his wrath. Jesus says, "Whoever does not obey the Son shall not see life, but the wrath of God remains on him" (John 3:36b); the apostle Paul adds, "We . . . were by nature children of wrath, like the rest of mankind" (Eph 2:3b). However, "God . . . through Christ reconciled us to himself (2 Cor 5:18b) because Jesus became "the propitiation for our sins" (1 John 2:2). Thus, "hav[ing] been justified by faith, we have peace with God through our Lord Jesus Christ" (Rom 5:1). Peace with God then speaks of the forensic aspect of our salvation: "There is therefore now no condemnation for those who are in Christ Jesus" (Rom 8:1).

Accepting its Antithesis: Jesus Came to Give a Sword (i.e., Divide)

At the same time, we must also accept its antithesis that Christ certainly came to give us peace with God, but "not as the world gives" (John 14:27b), which is based on an abundance of worldly possessions (Luke 12:15). Therefore, "I bring a sword" signifies that Jesus intends to afflict those who, despite not having God at the center, have a false sense of peace and security. For instance, to the Jewish returnees from Persia living comfortably in their "paneled houses" (Hag 1:4) while being dis- obedient in not rebuilding the ruined temple, God said, "You looked for much, and behold, it came to little. And when you brought it home, I blew it away. Why? . . . because of my house that lies in ruins, while each of you busies himself with his own house" (Hag 1:9). In this way, a false sense of peace was rudely broken up by God.

Then, the imperative to center our lives on God's will carries over to family matters, which is the context of Matthew 10:34 ("not . . . peace, but a sword"). Matthews 10:35–38 reads as follows:

> For I have come to set a man against his father, and a daughter against her mother, and a daughter-in-law against her mother- in-law. And a person's enemies will be those of his own house- hold. Whoever loves father or mother more than me is not worthy of me, and whoever loves son or daughter more than me is not worthy of me. And whoever does not take his cross and follow me is not worthy of me.

This rather uncomfortable teaching speaks of the possibility that a family may be divided when one of its members decides to obey God out of his love for him, despite the objections of the rest of the family. For instance, the family of Jesus was divided over him, even to the point of "seiz[ing] him, for they were saying, 'He is out of his mind'" (Mark 3:21). In fact, Jesus' brothers, in addition to not believing in him (John 7:5), thought that he was performing miracles to "show [himself] to the world" (John 7:4b)—meaning, seeking glory and fame for himself. So when one breaks away from doing the will of man (including that of par- ents) to serve God's will, it could mean a divided family (that, in time, may be mended as others in the family accept God's will as well). I believe the usage of the word "sword" in Luke 2:35b by Simeon, who foretells to Mary, "A sword will pierce through your own soul," and by Jesus in Mat- thew 10:34, is a *real* verbal as well as conceptual cross-reference since, in both cases, it denotes the cost to the family when one of its members obeys God's will.

Peaceful Coexistence with Tension in the Radical Middle

So how can these two opposite truths (i.e., Jesus came to give peace as well as a sword) exist peacefully—meaning, both are equally privileged while being connected? This can only happen when this pair of antithetic Scriptures that seem to pit peace against sword/division is interpreted through the hermeneutics of the Radical Middle of both/and without synthesizing them.

Thus, it can be said that since "for our sake [God] made [Christ] to be sin who knew no sin, so that in him we might become the righteousness of God" (2 Cor 5:21) and "have peace with God" (Rom 5:1b), he expects us to "seek first the kingdom of God and his righteousness" (Matt 6:33a), even if it means incurring a loss, whether material or familial.

DID JESUS COME TO JUDGE OR NOT JUDGE?

The second antithetic pair of Scriptures considered here is what Jesus said about his mission on Earth.

Antithetic Scriptures

On the one hand, Jesus says, "For judgment I came into this world, that those who do not see may see, and those who see may become blind" (John 9:39). But elsewhere, Jesus makes a polar opposite statement about judging, "If anyone hears my words and does not keep them, I do not judge him; for I did not come to judge the world but to save the world" (John 12:47). The question boils down to this: In what sense did Jesus come to judge or not judge?

Proper Hermeneutical Procedure

Again, the first step in dealing with these opposite Scriptures is to avoid privileging one revelation ("For judgment I came") over and against the other ("I did not come to judge") and vice versa. Instead, we accept both the thesis (not judge) and its antithesis (judge) without synthesizing their respective meanings. Is there a reasonable explanation that can lead to accepting these seemingly contradictory statements of Jesus?

Accepting the Thesis: He Came to Judge

First, the context of John 9 indicates that it was to the Pharisees, the religious leaders of the Jews "who were confident of their own righteousness" (Luke 18:9a NIV), that Jesus directed his warning that he came to judge those who claim to see so that they may become blind. The claim "to see" alludes to the Pharisees' confidence that they knew Scripture and the law better than anyone else. Once, the Pharisees said to those sympathetic to Christ's teaching, "Have any of the authorities or the Pharisees believed in him? But this crowd that does not know the law is accursed" (John 7:48–49). The Pharisees, having been offended by Jesus' assertion, rhetorically asked, "Are we also blind?" (John 9:40b). In response, Jesus said, "If you were blind, you would have no guilt; but now that you say, 'We see,' your guilt remains" (John 9:41).

What does this all mean? The Pharisees, "who trusted in themselves that they were righteous, and treated others with contempt" (Luke 18:9), also looked down on Jesus, even more since he "ha[d] never studied" (John 7:15b). As a result, this pride made them spiritually blind, rendering them unable and unwilling to recognize and submit to the very Messiah that Scripture, which they diligently studied, testified to (John 5:39).

Thus, Jesus did not really judge the Pharisees so much as the Pharisees judged themselves by "refus[ing] to come to [Christ] that [they] may have life" (John 5:40). In this manner, John 9:39 ("For judgment I came into this world, that . . . those who see may become blind") resonates with James 4:6a that says, "God opposes the proud."

Accepting the Antithesis: He Did Not Come to Judge

On the other hand, Christ "did not come to judge the world but to save the world" (John 12:47b), and elsewhere he declares, "For the Son of Man came to seek and to save the lost" (Luke 19:10). Now, part of the hermeneutical process is raising good questions after observing the text. So here I would ask: How can sinners be saved unless their sins are judged and condemned first after which the substitutionary death of Christ is offered as the atoning sacrifice for sin? The fact is "whoever does not believe is condemned already" (John 3:18b) and "the wrath of God remains on him" (John 3:36b); thus, Jesus does not need to judge them now. But the judgment will come later, for "the one who rejects [Christ] and does not receive [his] words has a judge; the word that [Christ] ha[s] spoken will judge him on the last day" (John 12:48).

Peaceful Coexistence with Tension in the Radical Middle

How then can these two opposite truths (i.e., Jesus came to judge as well as not judge) exist peacefully—meaning, both are equally privileged and connected? Perhaps Luke 18:14 serves a good conceptual cross-reference. Referring to the tax collector who "beat his breast, saying, 'God, be merciful to me, a sinner'" (Luke 18:13b), Jesus says, "I tell you, this man went down to his house justified, rather than the other [a proud Pharisee]. For everyone who exalts himself will be humbled, but the one who humbles himself will be exalted" (Luke 18:14). So, if you are proud, then God will oppose you; if you are humble, then God will give you grace (1 Pet 5:6). In this manner, Jesus' statements that he came to judge the world as well as not judge but save it are neither contradictory nor inconsistent. In their respective contexts, these antinomic statements are reasonable and valid.

IS JESUS EQUAL TO THE FATHER OR IS THE FATHER GREATER THAN JESUS?

The third seemingly contradictory statement of Jesus examined here undoubtedly presents a significant theological challenge to the doctrine of the Trinity and the nature of Christ.

Antithetic Scriptures

On the one hand, Jesus "was even calling God his own Father, making himself equal with God," (John 5:18b) adding, "I and the Father are one" (John 10:30). But the Lord seemingly contradicts himself when he says the exact opposite in John 14:28: "If you loved me, you would have rejoiced, because I am going to the Father, for the Father is greater than I."

Proper Hermeneutical Procedure

So in what sense are the statements Jesus makes about himself an ostensible contradiction? The historical doctrine regarding the relationship between God the Father and Jesus the Son has been the Creed of Nicaea promulgated in AD 325:

> We believe in one God . . . and in one Lord Jesus Christ, the Son of God, *begotten of the Father*, only-begotten, *that is, of the substance of the Father*, God of God, Light of Light, *true God of true God, begotten not made, of one substance with the Father*, through whom all things were made . . .[7] (italics his).

This creed leaves no doubt that the Son and the Father, both sharing the same divine substance, are absolutely equal in every aspect. But, the statement "the Father is greater than I" makes Jesus inferior to the Father. It would seem fair to speculate, therefore, how these two opposing ideas can be true at the same time even though Jesus said them. This is a hard antinomy that requires a serious study of word.

Here, the temptation, as Packer notes, is "to suppress . . . one truth in the supposed interests of the other . . . for the sake of a tidier theology"[8]— this is the hermeneutics of the logocentrism of either/or. When we give into this temptation, we privilege Scriptures that agree with our theology while not paying much attention to other texts that seem to question it. So in this instance, while trinitarians would lean on "I am equal to God," anti-trinitarians, Jehovah's Witnesses, would favor "the Father is greater than I." This certainly can result in a tidier Christology, but it comes at the expense of ignoring Scriptures. The most difficult approach is the hermeneutics of the Radical Middle that first accepts the validity of both claims, and second, seeks to discover what correlations exist between these two truths that appear to be in binary opposition.

Accepting the Thesis: Jesus is Equal to God

First, we accept the thesis that Jesus is equal to God, which means that the Father and the Son have existed from eternity (John 1:1) and share the same exact divine substance (*homoousios*) instead of similar substance (*homoiousios*). And at no time during his stay on earth did Jesus fail to

---

7. Bettenson, *Documents of the Christian Church*, 25.

8. Packer, *Evangelism and the Sovereignty of God*, 25.

share the same divine substance of the Father, for the apostle Paul declares, "In [Christ] the whole fullness of deity dwells bodily" (Col 2:9). The writer of Hebrews, in agreement with the apostle, says that "he is the radiance of the glory of God and the exact imprint of his nature" (Heb 1:3). Thus, Christ could confidently assert that "whoever has seen me has seen the Father" (John 14:9b). Evidently, these biblical texts validate the full divinity of Christ expressed through Jesus' claim, "I and the Father are one" (John 10:30).

Accepting its Antithesis: The Father is Greater than Jesus

So then, how are we to understand the statement "the Father is greater than I" (John 14:28b)? While it is evident that commentators agree as to what this verse does *not* mean, namely, "the creaturely subordination of the Son to the Father . . . [who] was greater in power or in divinity,"[9] they are not as certain about its actual meaning. According to the contributors to *Hard Sayings of the Bible*, which include Walter C. Kaiser Jr. and F. F. Bruce, it may be a reference to "the Father exist[ing] in heaven in complete power and glory, while Jesus was then living on earth in relative humility and obscurity," or to "Godhead [in which] the one designated 'father' ha[ving] greater authority . . . over the one designated 'son.'"[10] In the Radical Middle, both are recognized as viable interpretations, as Kaiser and Bruce have done. Of course, believers are free to uphold the view that makes more biblical sense to them; and they can certainly persuade others to see the strength of the view they hold, but without "quarrel[ling] about words, which does no good, but only ruins the hearers" (2 Tim 2:14b), which then can lead to disunity. So whereas the interpretation of the father having more authority makes sense to Kaiser and Bruce, the temporary self-abnegation of Jesus while on Earth makes more biblical sense to me. And the following is my attempt to point to the strength of this view.

A Temporary Self-Abnegation of Jesus

I begin this interpretation with conceptual cross-references in which the Father is depicted as being greater than the Son in some respects. First,

9. Tasker, *Gospel According to St. John*, 173.
10. Kaiser Jr. et al., *Hard Sayings of the Bible*, 504.

consider what Christ said to the Father the night before the crucifixion: "And now, Father, glorify me in your presence with the glory that I had with you before the world existed" (John 17:5). This indicates that Jesus had renounced the glory he shared with the Father while on Earth. Second, part of his omniscience was given up as well because Christ chose not to know when he would return, saying, "But concerning that day or that hour, no one knows, not even the angels in heaven, nor the Son, but only the Father" (Mark 13:32). In addition, since Christ was subject to hunger, thirst, and fatigue, he had renounced part of his omnipotence while living as fully human (and divine). What this suggests is that Jesus voluntarily gave up certain attributes, not the divine essence, to come in the flesh.

This bears out in the Greek as well when "the Father is greater than I" of John 14:28b is contrasted with Jesus is "made so much better than the angels" of Hebrews 1:4b (KJV). In John's passage, the Greek word *meizōn* is translated as "greater," while in the Hebrews passage, the Greek word *kreittōn* is rendered as "better." Based on this the renowned cult expert Walter Martin says (in response to the Jehovah's Witnesses who believe in a created Jesus inferior to Jehovah):

> Paralleling these two comparisons . . . one startling fact immediately attracts attention. In the fourteenth chapter of John, as the Son of man who had emptied himself of his prerogatives of deity (Phil 2:8–11), and taken upon himself the form of a slave, the Lord Jesus Christ could truthfully say, "My Father is greater than I," greater being a *quantitative* term descriptive of *position* and certainly in no sense of the context could it be construed as a comparison of nature of quality. In the first chapter of Hebrews, however, the comparison made there between the Lord Jesus Christ and angels is clearly one of nature. The Greek *kreittōn* being a term descriptive of quality; Christ was *qualitatively* better than the angels because he was their Creator (Col 1:16–17), and as such, he existed before all things . . . [11]

But Jesus took back all his glory and attributes once he returned to heaven to resume his place "at the right hand of God" (Acts 7:55b). That is why the disciples "would have rejoiced, because [Christ was] going to the Father" (John 14:28b).

---

11. Martin and Klann, *Jehovah of the Watchtower*, 163.

Peaceful Coexistence (with Tension) in the Radical Middle

Hopefully, it is clear that when the seemingly contradictory statements of Jesus regarding his relation to the Father are interpreted in accordance with the hermeneutics of the Radical Middle of both/and, the result is the upholding of two separate yet related teachings. Jesus was, is, and always will be fully God. Nevertheless, he suspended some of his divine attributes to come in the flesh in order to bear "our sins in his body on the tree, that we might die to sin and live to righteousness" (1 Pet 2:24a). In addition, because Jesus "has been tempted as we are, yet without sin" (Heb 4:15b), we can "with confidence draw near to the throne of grace, that we may receive mercy and find grace to help in time of need" (Heb 4:16).

WHO INCITED DAVID TO TAKE THE CENSUS? GOD OR SATAN?

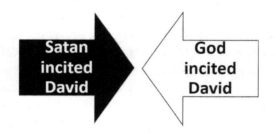

The next set of three issues derive from the Old Testament. The first is the very issue that began this book: Who incited David to take a census of Israel that later led to God's judgment against the king?

Antithetic Scriptures

On the one hand, the writer of 2 Samuel says that it was God who caused the bad census: "Again the anger of the Lord was kindled against Israel, and he incited David against them, saying, 'Go, number Israel and Judah'" (2 Sam 24:1). On the other hand, the Chronicler states that it was "Satan [who] rose up against Israel and incited David to take a census of Israel" (1 Chr 21:1). Obviously, both verses cannot be right: if one is right, then the other is necessarily wrong. However, we do not have that option unless we are willing to declare that either the writer of 2 Samuel or the Chronicler made a mistake.

Proper Hermeneutical Procedure

It is evident that resolving this issue to whatever degree of satisfaction appears formidable; thus, we may be tempted to ignore one or the other passage. But in the hermeneutics of the Radical Middle, both claims in binary opposition are privileged—meaning, they are both accepted as true. What should we do then with this antinomy?

Finding a Useful Hermeneutical Angle

Again, there is no one right way of approaching this matter. And that is one reason hermeneutics is often called "science" as well as "art." For instance, narratives can be read from the standpoint of someone other than the main protagonist; more nuanced observations can produce better questions. As for me, the first step toward interpreting this pair of opposite passages is to see what Scripture says about people bent on disobeying God, since that is what David seemed to have done (a point I will elaborate on later). Paul describes such people as ones who "refused to love the truth and so be saved" (2 Thess 2:10b) and "exchanged the truth about God for a lie" (Rom 1:25a). Paul warns those in Thessalonica who behaved like this, "Therefore God sends them a strong delusion, so that they may believe what is false" (2 Thess 2:11); he also says to the Romans caught up in a similar situation, "For this reason God gave them up to dishonorable passions . . . and . . . a debased mind to do what ought not to be done" (Rom 1:26a, 1:28b). Evidently, when people choose to live in rebellion against God, he may allow them to go from bad to worse.

Does God Tempt Us to Do Evil?

When Paul reveals that God is willing to let disobedient people to become more morally worse, it brings up the matter of whether God tempts us to do evil. If there was any uncertainty about this matter in the Old Testament, it is cleared up in the New when the apostle James writes:

> Let no one say when he is tempted, "I am being tempted by God," for God cannot be tempted with evil, and he himself tempts no one. But each person is tempted when he is lured and enticed by his own desire. Then desire when it has conceived gives birth to sin, and sin when it is fully grown brings forth death. (Jas 1:13–15)

Accordingly, at no time is God an active agent of temptation or delusion, for he does not tempt anyone. But when a person is "lured and enticed by his own desire" to the point of "bring[ing] forth death," (meaning, he persists in unrepentant sin) this can lead to the suspension of God's "hedge around him" (Job 1:10a), as seen in Job's life (although, in his case, this removal was not due to his sin—Job 1:8). Thus, God's allowing the unrepentant to further morally decline is the result of the devil, who "prowls around like a roaring lion, seeking someone to devour" (1 Pet 5:8b), having free rein on the spiritually recalcitrant, but still under the orchestration of the Lord (Job 1:12).

Consider the case involving a group of false prophets through whom God allowed a lying spirit to entice King Ahab, the evilest king of Israel, to engage in an ill-advised war. It was God's will that Ahab die in that battle, for the Lord said:

> "Who will entice Ahab, that he may go up and fall at Ramoth-gilead?" And one said one thing, and another said another. Then a spirit came forward and stood before the Lord, saying, "I will entice him." And the Lord said to him, "By what means?" And he said, "I will go out, and will be a lying spirit in the mouth of all his prophets." And he said, "You are to entice him, and you shall succeed; go out and do so." Now therefore behold, the Lord has put a lying spirit in the mouth of all these your prophets; the Lord has declared disaster for you (1 Kgs 22:20–23).

Note that prior to this war that would lead to Ahab's death, this vile king actually had repented, which pleased God to no end (1 Kgs 21:27–29b[12]); however, Ahab's repentance did not last, which brought on "a fearful expectation of judgment" (Heb 10:27a).

---

12. "And when Ahab heard those words, he tore his clothes and put sackcloth on his flesh and fasted and lay in sackcloth and went about dejectedly. And the word of the Lord came to Elijah the Tishbite, saying, 'Have you seen how Ahab has humbled himself before me?'"

It was Both God and Satan, but How So?

The preceding discussion puts us in a better place to understand how both God and Satan are said to have incited David to take the census.

It should first be recognized that David, who wrote Psalm 20:7—"Some trust in chariots and some in horses, but we trust in the name of the LORD our God"—knew better than to put his trust in the strength of his army over placing trust in God. Even Joab, David's general, who was not known for deep faith (2 Sam 3:39, 20:10), thought that the census-taking was "repulsive" (1 Chr 21:6). He said to David, "Why does my lord want to do this? Why should he bring guilt on Israel" (1 Chr 21:3b NIV)? It is possible that, as David was being tempted, God used Joab to "provide the way of escape, that [he] may be able to endure it" (1 Cor 10:13b). "But the king's word prevailed against Joab" (1 Chr 21:4a)—meaning, David was "lured and enticed by his own desire" to the point of "bring[ing] forth death" (Jas 1:14b, 15b).

We can now explain, according to the hermeneutics of the Radical Middle, why the names "God" and "Satan" are used interchangeably in 2 Samuel 24:1 and 1 Chronicles 21:1. The question is this: In what sense did God incite David to take this census, which showed that David relied on his own strength and not God's? It was because the king refused and suppressed the truth that God lifted his protection from him, thereby leaving David at the mercy of Satan who deceived the king with a spirit of delusion. Satan is the one who actually incited David; its entire orchestration, however, was set up and executed by God in response to David's spiritual obstinacy.

Peaceful Coexistence (with Tension) in the Radical Middle

This is probably one of the hardest teachings for us to accept: that God even uses Satan to carry out his purposes. This is something most believers would rather not hear; but, there is no denying that Scripture teaches it. And a pair opposite Scriptures—2 Samuel 24:1 and 1 Chronicles 21:1—presents an apt opportunity to discover Satan's role when interpreted through the hermeneutics of the Radical Middle of both/and. Peaceful coexistence between these two antithetic passages stems from knowing that (1) God is not Satan, (2) God is greater than Satan in power and authority (no dualism), and (3) Satan's attack is still under God's sovereign control.

DID MOSES FEAR PHARAOH OR NOT?

The next pair of antithetic passages deal with what really happened the day after Moses killed an Egyptian who was beating a fellow Hebrew.

Antithetic Scriptures

On the one hand, Exodus 2:14 says, "Moses was afraid, and thought, 'Surely the thing is known.' When Pharaoh heard of it, he sought to kill Moses. But Moses fled from Pharaoh and stayed in the land of Midian." (Exod 2:14b–15a). Stephen, when recounting this event in a speech that led to his death, says the same: "Moses fled" (Acts 7:29a). But the writer of Hebrews says exactly the opposite: "By faith [Moses] left Egypt, not being afraid of the anger of the king, for he endured as seeing him who is invisible" (Heb 11:27). So which is it? Was Moses afraid of Pharaoh as he himself admitted, or was he not afraid of the king of Egypt as the writer of Hebrews asserts?

Proper Hermeneutical Procedure

The first thing that needs to be clarified is whether this is a truly antithetic situation, since Moses left Egypt on two different occasions. Hebrews 11:27–28 reads: "By faith he left Egypt, not being afraid of the anger of the king, for he endured as seeing him who is invisible. By faith he kept the Passover and sprinkled the blood, so that the Destroyer of the firstborn might not touch them." Some may wonder whether the Hebrews version refers to Moses leading the nation of Israel out into the wilderness, not when he escaped to Midian after killing an Egyptian. If that were the case, "it would then not be in chronological order with vs. 28" since the Passover happened just before the exodus.[13] In fact, this would be the only thing unchronological in Hebrews 11:1–31—a section which is otherwise entirely chronological. So it is very probable that the Hebrews version refers to the time when Moses hurriedly left Egypt after Pharaoh discovered that he had killed an Egyptian. Once the antithetic nature of the two versions is confirmed, the next step is to consider the context of Hebrews 10 that precedes 11.

13. Dennis, *ESV Study Bible*, 2381.

The Context of Hebrews 10

The context of Hebrews 10 is the new covenant, which is summarized in Hebrews 10:17–18: "'I will remember their sins and their lawless deeds no more.' Where there is forgiveness of these, there is no longer any offering for sin." Suffice it to say, God is very gracious in how he remembers things, which is reflected in the retelling of Moses' departure from Egypt, first told in Exodus 2:11–15, by the writer of Hebrews. To that end, consider Hebrews 11:24–27, a very gracious recounting of Exodus 2:11–15 in which Moses is seen fleeing from Pharaoh in fear:

> By faith Moses, when he was grown up, refused to be called the son of Pharaoh's daughter, choosing rather to be mistreated with the people of God than to enjoy the fleeting pleasures of sin. He considered the reproach of Christ greater wealth than the treasures of Egypt, for he was looking to the reward. By faith he left Egypt, not being afraid of the anger of the king, for he endured as seeing him who is invisible.

Therefore, it stands to reason that while Moses was indeed afraid and fled, God in Christ graciously remembered that event as leaving Egypt by faith, perhaps taking into account that he came to an Israelite's defense out of his belief "that God was giving [Israel] salvation by his hand" (Acts 7:25b). Since Moses, in doing so, ended up losing all his wealth and privilege (by inadvertently killing an oppressive Egyptian), God in his infinite grace reinterpreted that (i.e., the rescuing but not necessarily the killing) as Moses "regard[ing] disgrace for the sake of Christ as of greater value than the treasures of Egypt" (Heb 11:26 NIV).

Peaceful Coexistence (with Tension) in the Radical Middle

As is evident here, when the two opposing texts regarding Moses' departure from Egypt are processed through the Radical Middle of both/and, the frailty of man's best effort (the Exodus version) and God's gracious evaluation of our works in Christ (the Hebrews version) are equally privileged. Suppressing one or the other version of what happened on that fateful day, whether out of ignorance or laziness, diminishes the blessings obtainable through the hermeneutics of the Radical Middle.

DID GOD KEEP THE PROMISE
MADE TO ABRAHAM OR NOT?

The sixth issue is whether God kept his promise made to Abraham.

Antithetic Scriptures

The irony is that the same Hebrews writer says yes and no to this question. He says in Hebrews 6:15, "And thus Abraham, having patiently waited, obtained the promise." But in two places in Hebrews he says, in effect, no, not yet. Hebrews 11:13a says, "These [including Abraham] all died in faith, not having received the things promised"; Hebrews 11:39–40 states, "And all these [again, including Abraham], though commended through their faith, did not receive what was promised, since God had provided something better for us, that apart from us they should not be made perfect." So did God keep the promise made to Abraham or not?

Given the two choices, most Christians would prefer Hebrews 6:15 since it appeals to our desire to enjoy God's blessings here and now. But, privileging Hebrews 6:15 while ignoring Hebrews 11:13, 39–40 is to practice the hermeneutics of logocentrism of either/or that discards one truth in favor of the other. In doing so, we may hear what we like but we are not really learning the Bible. So how would the hermeneutics of the Radical Middle explain this antithetic situation in which it is said that Abraham received and did not receive what God had promised him?

Proper Hermeneutical Procedure

Since these passages are about a promise, a logical question to raise is: Exactly what did God promise Abraham?

At a time when Abraham was neither rich nor had a son, "the Lord said to Abram . . . 'Lift up your eyes and look from the place where you are, northward and southward and eastward and westward, for all the land that you see I will give to you and to your offspring forever" (Gen 13:14–15). Evidently, a vast land was promised. In the next verse, God added, "I will make your offspring as the dust of the earth, so that if one can count the dust of the earth, your offspring also can be counted" (Gen 13:16). In addition to land, generations of descendants were promised to Abraham as well.

Accepting the Thesis: How Abraham Obtained the Promise

So in what sense did Abraham obtain God's promise of land and off-spring? First, it can be reasoned that the land promise was partially fulfilled during Abraham's lifetime, since he and his wife were buried in Hebron (Gen 23:19, 25:10), a city that would one day be part of the promised land occupied by Israel, his descendants.[14] Second, as for the promise of offspring, this too was partially fulfilled since Abraham had a son, Isaac, who was going to be the grandfather to the Twelve tribes of Israel. Obviously, Abraham did not expect to see a nation full of his descendants during his lifetime; he probably died happy, believing that God had kept the promise.

Accepting the Antithesis: How Abraham Did Not Receive What Was Promised

Now, to consider in what sense Abraham did not receive what was prom-ised, it is important to distinguish the context between the Old Testament ("a shadow of the good things to come"—Heb 10:1b) and the New ("the good things" that have come).

Spiritually, Abraham was looking for heaven; "For he was looking forward to the city that has foundations, whose designer and builder is God" (Heb 11:10). But, during the Old Testament period, no one could enter heaven because Christ had not yet died "for the sins of the whole world" (1 John 2:2b). And after having done so, Christ was the first to enter heaven (Heb 9:24).[15] This means that Abraham had to wait *some-where* before he received the promise of heaven. It has been speculated that he, along with other Old Testament saints, descended into a place called *sheol* (often translated as "grave")[16] to wait for Christ's eventual vic-tory over sin and death.

In addition, the promise of, "I will make your offspring like the dust of the earth," will be fully fulfilled through Abraham's spiritual children,

14. Genesis 23:2a says, "Sarah died at Kiriath-arba (that is, Hebron) in the land of Canaan." And later, "there Abraham was buried, with Sarah his wife" (Gen 25:10b).

15. "For Christ has entered, not into holy places made with hands, which are cop-ies of the true things, but into heaven itself"

16. If "Sheol" is referred to as "Abraham's bosom" (KJV) in the story of the rich man and Lazarus (Luke 16:19–31), then it is the home of both the righteous and the unrighteous but whose dwellings are separated by an unbridgeable chasm.

also known as "the children of the promise" (Rom 9:8b), for Paul states, "Those who believe are children of Abraham" (Gal 3:7 NIV). The fulfillment of the promise of spiritual children also had to wait until Christ came, died, and was resurrected.

Peaceful Coexistence (with Tension) in the Radical Middle

Let me reiterate what the issue is before proceeding. On the one hand, Hebrews 6:15 says that Abraham "obtained the promise" God made to him during his lifetime. On the other hand, Hebrews 11:13, 39–40 says the just the opposite, that Abraham died, "not having received the things promised" (Heb 11:13b).

Eventually, God fully fulfilled every promise made to Abraham, probably in a way he did not expect, but only after Christ died for the sins of the world. So when these antithetic/antinomic passages are interpreted through the hermeneutics of the Radical Middle of both/and, its outcome is a pertinent message to two types of believers. First, to the prosperous Western Christians to whom death is an interruption, since their heaven is on Earth, the message is that they need to heed Hebrews 11:13, 39–40 and realize better things wait for us in heaven. Second, to those who are so heavenly minded that it is said that they are no earthly good, they need to heed Hebrews 6:15 and realize a life well-lived in the here and now matters to God who blesses us with many of his promises kept in the present. In this way a peaceful coexistence (with tension) is established between life on Earth and hope of heaven.

ARE BELIEVERS ALIENS AND STRANGERS OR NOT?

We now consider the remaining two pairs of antithetic Scriptures from the eight presented in chapter 2; these come from the writings of the apostle Paul and Peter. The first of these is whether believers are aliens and strangers in the world.[17] What does that even mean?

---

17. The two Greek words used in 1 Peter 2:11, *paroikos* and *parepidēmos*, are translated "aliens" and "strangers," respectively, while *xenos* and *parepidēmos* in Hebrews 11:13 are translated the same in the NIV (this makes no sense; "translated the same?"). Ephesians 2:19 has the combination of *xenos* and *paroikos* but is translated the same in the ESV: "strangers" and "aliens."

Antithetic Scriptures

On the one hand, the apostle Peter declares, "Dear friends, I urge you, as aliens and strangers in the world, to abstain from sinful desires, which war against your soul" (1 Pet 2:11 NIV). The Hebrews writer echoes the same sentiment, referring to those living by faith in God as "aliens and strangers on earth" (Heb 11:13b NIV). On the other hand, the apostle Paul, in his Epistle to the Ephesians, says the exact opposite of Peter's thought. He says to both gentile and Jewish believers, "For through him we both have access in one Spirit to the Father. So then you are no longer strangers and aliens, but you are fellow citizens with the saints and members of the household of God" (Eph 2:18–19). So which is it: Are we aliens or strangers or are we not?

Proper Hermeneutical Procedure

Again, the first hermeneutical step is to privilege both claims as true and valid despite their differences.

Accepting the Thesis: Yes, We are Aliens and Strangers

Now, upon closer examination of 1 Peter 2:11 and Ephesians 2:18–19, it becomes evident that their context is different. While Peter ("aliens and strangers") addresses what our relationship *ought* to be with the world, Paul ("no longer strangers and aliens") deals with what our relationship *is* with God.

So, as far as "lov[ing] the world or the things in the world" (1 John 2:16)—such as money, sex, and power—is concerned, believers are "not of the world" (John 17:14b), meaning they are to live as aliens and strangers in the world. To the Hebrew writer, living like "aliens and strangers on earth" (Heb 11:13) means "regard[ing] disgrace for the sake of Christ as of greater value than the treasures of [this world], because [a believer is] looking ahead to his reward" (Heb 11:26 NIV). Thus, the reason for living like aliens and strangers on earth is to advance the cause of Christ, and the motivation is to receive eternal rewards instead of settling for temporary pleasure.

Accepting the Antithesis: No, We are Not Aliens and Strangers

But, in what sense are believers no longer aliens and strangers to God while they live on Earth? This is another matter related to the different contexts found in the Old and New Testaments. That is to say, without proper background of the Old Testament, what Paul says here cannot really be appreciated. During the Old Testament days, the curtain of the Tabernacle separating the Holy of Holies from the Holy Place signified the separation of God and humans. In that sense the Israelites (representing the entire humanity) were aliens and strangers to God. But when the curtain of the temple was torn in two at the moment of Christ's atoning death, this meant that "the new and living way" was "opened for us through the curtain, that is, through his flesh" (Heb 10:20). Subsequently, "now . . . [we] have come to know God, or rather to be known by God" (Gal 4:9a); that is, we "are no longer strangers and aliens, but . . . members of the household of God" (Eph 2:19).

Peaceful Coexistence (with Tension) in the Radical Middle

In conclusion, by seeing these antithetic passages through the hermeneutics of the Radical Middle, we are made aware that while believers are to be aliens and strangers to the sinful ways of the world, they are no longer aliens and strangers to God because he knows them in Christ. The peaceful coexistence between the two opposite texts is found in 2 Corinthians 5:20, which says, "We are ambassadors for Christ, God making his appeal through us. We implore you on behalf of Christ, be reconciled to God." So believers, though aliens and strangers to the world, still need to engage with the world as Christ's ambassadors so that the world may no longer be aliens and stranger to God in Christ.

ARE GOOD WORKS NEEDED FOR SALVATION OR NOT?

Now, we have reached the final pair of antithetic/antinomic revelation introduced in chapter 2: the relationship between faith and works as it affects salvation. Obviously, this is a doctrinal matter weightier than arguments over spiritual gifts between cessationists and continuationists.

Antithetic Scriptures

More to the point, the question is what role good works play in our salvation. It appears that Paul and James are on opposite ends of the salvific spectrum. Paul says that salvation is "not a result of works, so that no one may boast" (Eph 2:9). On the contrary, James, insisting that "faith apart from works is useless" (Jas 2:20b), says that "a person is justified by works and not by faith alone" (Jas 2:24). This appears to be an insolvable quandary.

Proper Hermeneutical Procedure

After we are saved, what affects matters related to salvation more than anything else is our desire for its assurance: How do I know I am truly saved? How can I stay saved? And we demand precise, airtight answers to these questions because salvation is just too important of a matter, we feel, to leave to ambiguity, and even worse, chance. Having said that, the first thing to do as part of proper hermeneutical procedure is to check those concerns at the door, and then read Scripture and allow it to speak to us.

Accepting the Thesis: Salvation by Faith Alone

Once we do that, we will all agree with the apostle Paul who says, "For by grace you have been saved through faith. And this is not your own doing; it is the gift of God" (Eph 2:8). Elsewhere the apostle says that "to the one who does not work but believes in him who justifies the ungodly, his faith is counted as righteousness" (Rom 4:5). However, "salvation by faith alone" is easily misunderstood, as evidenced by the likes of free grace teaching that assures salvation even to those who renounce their faith after believing at first—this sort of teaching completely disregards what James has to say on salvation.

Accepting the Antithesis: Faith that is Not Alone

As already discussed in chapter 4, when James says, "I will show you my faith by my works" (Jas 2:18b), he is merely echoing Jesus' teaching that "by their fruit you will recognize them" (Matt 7:20 NIV). In the soteriology of the Radical Middle, the importance of both faith and works is upheld while maintaining the distinction with respect to their roles in salvation.

Martin Luther, who left the Catholic Church and became the progenitor of the Protestant Reformation, once declared, "We are saved by faith alone but not by faith that is alone." Fast forward 500 years to 2007: Francis Beckwith, then-president of Evangelical Theological Society, did the reverse of Martin Luther: He left the Protestant faith to join the Roman Catholic Church. In speaking of why he made the switch, Beckwith states:

> The Catholic Church frames the Christian life as one in which you must exercise virtue—not because virtue saves you, but because that's the way God's grace gets manifested. As an evangelical, even when I talked about sanctification and wanted to practice it, it seemed as if I didn't have a good enough incentive to do so. Now there's a kind of theological framework, and it doesn't say my salvation depends on me, but it says my virtue counts for something. It's important to allow the grace of God to be exercised through your actions.[18]

Evidently, Beckwith felt that the part in Luther's declaration that says "but not by faith that is alone" has long been omitted from the Protestant faith. But that is precisely James's point: we are saved by faith alone but our works (i.e., fruits, changes), produced in time (Luke 13:8), verify before men whether we are truly saved. The so-called faith that does not produce any change may indicate that that person was never saved, which is the Reformed view (1 John 2:19), or lost salvation, which is the Arminian view (2 Pet 2:20–22; Heb 6:4–6). While systematic theologians may argue intensely over which one is biblical, the Radical Middle understands the issue, may take a position, and even contend for it, but never to the point of compromising the unity in Christ.

Peaceful Coexistence (with Tension) in the Radical Middle

In the Radical Middle, therefore, on the one side is found justified by faith alone before God, and on the other side, justified by works before man. Is this understanding precise enough to satisfy those who seek peace of mind over matters of salvation through airtight definitions and slogans

18. Beckwith, "Q&A," para. 4.

("Once saved, always saved")? Probably not, but we should "not go be-yond what is written" (1 Cor 4:6b). This is as much of an assurance as the word gives us, but there is an additional way through which we may know we are saved. This assurance comes from the Spirit, for Paul writes, "The Spirit himself bears witness with our spirit that we are children of God" (Rom 8:16).

THE SIGNIFICANCE OF CHAPTER 5 FOR THE DISCUSSION ON THE SIGN GIFTS

As this chapter comes to end and the discussion on the sign gifts is about to start, some readers might have felt that the matters addressed in chap-ter 5 have little to do with the conflict between cessationists and continu-ationists, the tension between word and Spirit. I beg to differ.

Spirit Also

The previous section ended with Romans 8:16, which presents the Holy Spirit as bearing witness with our spirit to tell us that we are children of God. If truth be told, many cessationists would feel that this verse sounds too subjective for us to be certain of what the Spirit allegedly said. It could simply be a self-realization when someone says, "The Spirit told me that I am a child of God." While such a possibility exists, the truth is that many Christians have neglected becoming acquainted with the ministry of the Spirit, and as a result, feel uncomfortable in discussing God speaking to them through the Spirit (see chapter 8). And that is also why, to many cessationists, whether the sign gifts still operate today is a settled mat-ter because they privilege the role the word plays, without giving much thought to the role the Spirit plays in spiritual growth and ministry.

One contributing factor to the depriviledging of the Spirit is that, as addressed in chapter 1, cessationists have long felt that continuationists are neither willing nor able to properly interpret God's word; as a result, their pneumatology has fallen on deaf ears. Historically, renewal move-ments, typically initiated among those on the periphery (as was the case with the Pentecostal movement), are long on "Spirit's fire" (1 Thess 5:19b NIV) and short on a balanced theology. But as these movements become matured or institutionalized, for better or worse, their theology catches up to the erudition of those who occupy the center.

Word Also

So to those cessationists who question the willingness of continuationists to "correctly handle[] the word of truth" (2 Tim 2:15b NIV) and uphold the great doctrines of our faith, I hope my small effort to interpret antinomic Scriptures with sound hermeneutics (for the most part, I would hope) shows that their mistrust of continuationists is not valid today as it was, perhaps, fifty years ago. It is not valid for Reformed charismatics today; it is not valid for the Assemblies of God pastors in Mexico whom I taught for seven years (including Greek); and it is not valid for the pastors of Acts Ministries International. So, I say to my cessationist friends, discard any preconceived bias against continuationists and consider their exegetical work on the ministry of the Holy Spirit.

The Three Tenets of the Radical Middle Paradigm

Now, in view of the three essentials of the hermeneutics of the Radical Middle discussed in chapter 3 (54–57), the following three tenets can be extracted from the way antinomic Scriptures have been interpreted. First, when God's word presents a thesis and its antithesis as being equally true, the Radical Middle pursues, discovers, and advocates their respective meanings wholeheartedly and in tension. Second, to do that, the Radical Middle avoids privileging those Scriptures that support preferred positions while ignoring or distorting those that may lead to a different conclusion. Third, the Radical Middle theology is based on all relevant passages, even if they appear antithetic, and the conclusion is not affected by one's preferred systematic theology.

Now, we are ready to apply these principles in addressing whether the sign gifts are still in operation today. This is to say, we must examine all the pertinent Scriptures that speak of the gifts of tongues, prophecy, apostleship, and healing.

QUESTIONS FOR REFLECTION & DISCUSSION

1. What is the goal of hermeneutics? What do we want to avoid (Gal 1:7; 2 Cor 4:2)?

2. What type of sermon or teaching do you personally prefer and why? In light of what Paul told Pastor Timothy in 2 Timothy 2:15, what do you think mattered to the apostle the most?

3. In view of Hebrews 2:1, which says, "Therefore we must pay much closer attention to what we have heard, lest we drift away from it," how can we improve our receptivity of sermons and teachings we hear?

4. Have you ever experienced "sword"—meaning, rupturing in your relationship with the members of your family because of your commitment to serve God despite their objections?

5. Are you ready to study God's word more faithfully and seriously? How has this chapter challenged you in that regard?

6

The Gift of Tongues in the Radical Middle: A Hermeneutical Response to Hard Cessationism

BEFORE PROCEEDING, PLEASE NOTE the gist of this chapter and the next. This chapter consists of two parts: first, a general response to the standard cessationist arguments against miraculous gifts for today; and second, a hermeneutical response to hard cessationism with respect to the gift of tongues. Chapter 7 is a hermeneutical response to flawed versions of continuationism regarding this gift.

A GENERAL RESPONSE TO THE STANDARD CESSATIONIST ARGUMENTS

It was shown in chapter 1 that the term "Radical Middle" emerged out of the contentious debate between cessationists, who hold that the sign gifts are no longer operating today, and Pentecostals and charismatics, who vehemently disagree. Suffice it to say, no one who believes in the cessation of the gift of tongues, prophecy, healing, and apostleship can embrace a ministry in which word and Spirit are equally valued and pursued. The first prerequisite, therefore, for accepting the Radical Middle paradigm is to provide a rational basis for disagreeing with cessationism in general and hard cessationism in particular.

Cessationism at its Root

We start this discussion with the cessationist view that the sign gifts, such as tongues and prophecy, have ceased in the apostolic age after the completion of the Biblical canon, the logic being that without the completed canon, miracles were needed to authenticate the divine origin of messages proclaimed by the apostles. Hebrews 2:3–4 is frequently used to validate this assertion:

> How shall we escape if we neglect such a great salvation? It was declared at first by the Lord, and it was attested to us by those who heard, while God also bore witness by signs and wonders and various miracles and by gifts of the Holy Spirit distributed according to his will.

Evidently, this divine authentication of the apostolic message is what seems to have happened in Iconium (in today's Turkey) during the first missionary trip by Paul and Barnabas (AD 46–48). Luke, the author of the book of Acts, writes, "So they remained for a long time, speaking boldly for the Lord, who bore witness to the word of his grace, granting signs and wonders to be done by their hands" (Acts 14:3).

Now, while there is no question that miracles can immediately validate the messenger and his message, nothing in Scripture says that this verification function of miracles necessarily rules out miracles. After all, more signs and wonders were performed by the prophets Elijah and Elisha than were done by prophets in any other period in the Old Testament, with the exception of the Mosaic period of deliverance. And the miracles were permitted, not because the Israelites did not have a completed canon, referring to Torah and other books recognized as authorities, but more likely because they failed to heed them. Therefore, the view that miracles were only permitted because Scripture had not been completed is a rather weak argument for cessationism.[1]

So why do cessationists believe this way? In particular, what does this anti-miracle stance reveal about the advocates of two theological systems born and bred in Western Europe—namely Reformed theology and Dispensationalism—who make up the bulk of cessationists?

---

1. For a detailed discussion on this matter, see Jack Deere's "Were there Only Three Periods?," 209–24.

A Child of the Enlightenment

First, it shows that despite their long-running theological feud over eccle-siology (the study of the church) and eschatology (the study of the end times), Reformed theology and Dispensationalism are joined at the hip; that is, both are heavily influenced by the core of Enlightenment natu-ralism, a belief that all that exists is in the physical world, rather than scriptural supernaturalism. Alister McGrath writes:

> Western Christianity has been deeply affected by a particular way of thinking, a way of thinking that has seriously limited our grasp of our faith and apprehension of its wonder. Many call it "the Enlightenment"—the period in Western culture that began about 1750 and placed enormous emphasis on the power of hu-man reason. Reason could explain everything.[2]

For cessationists, their Enlightenment-inspired theology would in-clude miracles in the category of phenomena ruled out by reason.

That is not to say that they are all sympathetic to the likes of Da-vid Hume, the eighteenth-century Scottish empiricist who "argued that miracles contradicted the laws of nature, and were therefore improb-able," since they do believe that the miracles recorded in Scripture actu-ally happened.[3] The irony is that while cessationists would rebuff those questioning the validity of biblical miracles, such as Thomas Jefferson who "wrote a version of the Four Gospels from which he removed all references to 'fantastic' events, retaining only the ethical content of Jesus' teaching,"[4] they proffer the same resistance against continuationists for believing that God still preforms miracles today. So when it comes to miracles happening in modern times, cessationists are, in effect, in agree-ment with Hume's naturalism. What separates them is that while Hume's outlook stems from his commitment to naturalism, cessationists, who reject naturalism, insist that their rejection of the sign gifts is biblical, not realizing that they use improper hermeneutics to make that claim.

---

2. McGrath, *Journey*, 14.

3. Brown, *Philosophy & the Christian Faith*, 69.

4. Postman, *Amusing Ourselves to Death*, 53.

Inordinately Western-centric

Furthermore, cessationists seem to be oblivious to larger implications arising from the reality of Bible translation in the world. According to the Wycliffe Bible Translators, "at least 1.5 billion people do not have the full Bible in their first language. More than 110 million do not have a single verse of Scripture . . . [and] approximately 1,600 languages still need a Bible translation project to begin."[5] So if the purpose of the sign gifts prior to the completion of the New Testament was to confirm the gospel and authenticate God's messengers prior to the completion of the canon, then should not we be open to the possibility of miracles, particularly the sign gifts, when millions of people are without a Bible in their own tongues? To say no because we in the West have the Bible in multiple versions is nothing short of displaying our Western bias against the rest of the world.

Broad-Brush Bias

Another cessationist argument that shows careless thinking and unfair characterization is the assertion that speaking in tongues is a mere human reaction—a behavior that is psychologically induced and not prompted by the Holy Spirit. This type of characterization is the epitome of painting with a broad brush in a way that is completely unfair. So what is meant by "psychologically induced?" John MacArthur explains it this way:

> Another basic reason for the growth of tongues is the need for acceptance and security. People need to be in the "in group." They want to be among the ones who "have it," and they cringe at the thought of being among the have-nots who are on the outside looking in. It is very satisfying to be in the charismatic movement . . . It makes many people feel like they are somebody, like they belong to something, like they have something others do not have.[6]

While this may be true in some cases, can this explanation alone account for hundreds of millions of tongue speakers throughout the world? Many people have received the gift of tongues in such a spontaneous

---

5. Wycliffe, "Why Bible Translation?," para. 7.
6. MacArthur, *Charismatic Chaos*, 297–98.

manner that they neither had much prior knowledge of it nor had much time to ponder its social implications.

Consider my own conversion experience. In 1981, I found myself praying alone around midnight by the altar of a church that I visited two days earlier. As I was confessing my sin and expressing faith in Christ to become a believer, the pastor of the church whom I barely knew came to me, and, after laying his hand on my head, said, "The Lord already gave you tongues, *speak*." Immediately, I spoke in tongues. Since I had my eyes closed and, by this time, others were around me praying (quite loudly), I was unaware of what the pastor was doing. In fact, neither speaking in tongues nor acceptance by those who did was ever on my mind that night; believing in Jesus was.

When Will the Sign Gifts Disappear? (A General Response)

Now, before getting into the specifics of the current validity of the sign gifts, we will begin with a general question, namely, "Did some gifts come with an expiration date?" Cessationists would certainly say yes, but how would the apostle Paul respond, given what he writes in 1 Corinthians 1:4–8?

> I give thanks to my God always for you because of the grace of
> God that was given you in Christ Jesus, that in every way you
> were enriched in him in all speech and all knowledge—even as
> the testimony about Christ was confirmed among you—so that
> you are not lacking in any gift, as you wait for the revealing of
> our Lord Jesus Christ, who will sustain you to the end, guiltless
> in the day of our Lord Jesus Christ.

Of all the churches planted by the apostle, the church in Corinth was unique in that this congregation was best known for robust manifestations of the gifts of the Spirit. Although Paul had to correct the Corinthians for their abusive practice of the gift of prophecy and tongues in particular (1 Cor 14), they nonetheless possessed these sign gifts.

Whereas cessationists insist that these sign gifts have long disappeared, Paul himself made no such assertion in the quoted passage—to assume so is to inject something foreign into the text. The meaning of this passage appears to be two-fold: first, God had enriched the Corinthian church through the impartation of spiritual gifts, including the sign gifts; second, these spiritual gifts were given to keep the church firm and holy until the second coming of Christ. An obvious implication is that these gifts will no longer be needed once Christ returns. It stands to reason, therefore, that since Christ has not yet returned, these spiritual gifts, whose aim was to keep the Corinthian believers firm and holy in the first century, will continue to do the same for today's church.

While I hardly expect my explanation to be convincing for cessationists to accept continuationism, the following discussion is specifically in response to the claim that there is only one type of tongues, which disappeared in the first century. I will make an argument that Scripture seems to present two types of tongues, and when the hermeneutics of the Radical Middle of both/and is applied to all passages relevant to this matter, the two types will indeed emerge, in which case both ought to be embraced as biblical manifestations. Having said this, I am reminded of what Robert Saucy, a fair-minded professor who taught me at Talbot, said: "The nature and function of the gift of tongues are not easily determined from Scripture."[7] So if my argument in favor of two types of tongues sounds too airtight, remind me to practice what I preach.

HARD CESSATIONISM AGAINST THE GIFT OF TONGUES

Probably no one has spoken more vociferously against tongues than John MacArthur, whose primary arguments are based on his understanding of two scriptural passages in 1 Corinthians: chapter 13:8–12, which deals with when the gift of tongues may expire; and chapter 14:2, which holds the key to whether Scripture warrants one or two types of tongues. First articulated in *The Charismatics* (1978)—the first of his trilogy against continuationists—MacArthur's position has remained unchanged in succeeding publications (*Charismatic Chaos*, 1992; *Strange Fire*, 2013).

Gibberish Spoken in Corinth

In *The Charismatics*, MacArthur does not deny that there are two types of tongues based on his understanding of 1 Corinthians 14:2a, which reads: "For one who speaks in a tongue speaks not to men but to God" (*ŏuk anthrōpois lalei alla theō*). Regarding this verse, MacArthur states that,

---

7. Saucy, "Open but Cautious View," 131.

> Paul's comment in 1 Corinthians 14:2 is not a commendation to
> the Corinthians; he was using satire. It is also possible from the
> Greek, because of the absence of the definite article, to translate
> the term for God as "a god"—referring to a pagan deity.[8]

Dionysius, the Greek god of wine, and Cybele, the goddess of fertility, are then mentioned as possible identities of this pagan deity. Accordingly, the tongues spoken by the Corinthians were "counterfeit pagan gibberish (unintelligible speech)," not real languages.[9]

Either Tongues Are Real Languages or Else They are Not from God

So for MacArthur, there is only one legitimate gift of tongues, which, based on Acts 2, has to be a real, known language. Concerning this point, he writes:

> The Greek word used in this passage is *glōssa*, the normative
> Greek word for "language." Many within the charismatic move-
> ment today claim that the gift of tongues is a "private prayer
> language," ecstatic uttering in a language known only to God.
> But here in Acts 2 it is clear that the disciples were speaking in a
> *known* language.[10] (italics his)

The other kind, the counterfeit pagan gibberish spoken by the Corinthians back then and the psychologically induced gibberish spoken by continuationists today, is the illegitimate type of tongue for MacArthur.

In this fashion, cessationism turns the issue of tongues into a second type of antithetic revelation in which, if the thesis is right, then its antithesis is necessarily false. Accordingly, either tongues from God are always real languages, or if they are not, then they are not from God.

A Change in MacArthur's View

Now those who read *Strange Fire* may be led to believe that MacArthur later changed his mind on what type of tongues the Corinthians spoke. He writes, "Since the gift of tongues consisted of authentic foreign languages on the day of Pentecost, then the same was true for the believers in

8. MacArthur, *Charismatics*, 161.

9. Ibid., 159.

10. Ibid., 158.

Corinth."[11] Further reading of the book, however, indicates that MacArthur's view has remained the same except for one change. His 1978 book says that "the counterfeit pagan gibberish . . . was being used by *many* of the Corinthian believers instead of the true gift of languages"[12] (italics mine). In *Strange Fire*, MacArthur writes that "*some* within the Corinthian congregation had even begun to mimic the unintelligible utterances of the Greco-Roman mystery religions, sounding much like those within the contemporary charismatic movement"[13] (italics mine). The implication of this change from *many* to *some* will be discussed shortly.

MacArthur's Justification

So how does Pastor MacArthur justify his interpretation that some Corinthians were babbling in pagan gibberish? In *The Charismatics*, MacArthur gives two arguments from Greek grammar to back his conclusion. Already mentioned is his translation of *lalei alla theō* as "but speak to a god" instead of "but speak to God." He also adds that whenever Paul uses the Greek word *glōssa* ("tongue") in the singular, as he does in 1 Corinthians 14:2, "he was referring to the counterfeit pagan gibberish . . . Whenever Paul wanted to refer to the real gift of tongues, he used the plural" (*glōssai*, meaning "tongues").[14]

In *Charismatic Chaos*, these two Greek arguments are placed in the endnote[15]; in *Strange Fire* the conclusion is retained (as noted earlier), but not the supporting arguments based on Greek. Perhaps MacArthur feels no reason to include them, believing that he has convincingly justified his position in his prior works.

However, it is important to realize that MacArthur's only scriptural support in favor of his interpretation of Corinthians hinges on his translation of *lalei alla theō* (1 Cor 14:2) and the singular/plural argument over *glōssa/glōssai* (tongue/tongues). Now realize this: even if MacArthur's arguments are proven to be invalid, that does not change his assertion that the tongues spoken in Corinth by some were not real languages—I agree, they were not. But it will mean that what was spoken in Corinth was a gift

---

11. MacArthur, *Strange Fire*, 141.

12. MacArthur, *Charismatics*, 159.

13. MacArthur, *Strange Fire*, 147.

14. MacArthur, *Charismatics*, 159–60.

15. MacArthur, *Charismatic Chaos*, 387–88.

of tongues that was different from the linguistic tongues spoken at Pentecost. We will return to this point after considering whether biblical Greek grammar warrants MacArthur's interpretation of 1 Corinthians 14.

EXAMINING THE VIEW THAT THE CORINTHIANS SPOKE COUNTERFEIT PAGAN GIBBERISH

Before proceeding, two comments need to be made about the credibility of MacArthur's research and his aptitude in biblical Greek. In 2006, Dr. Warren Larson, then-director of Muslim Studies at Columbia International University, after reviewing MacArthur's *Terrorism, Jihad, and the Bible*, commented, "This book fails for generalities, inaccuracies, and weak research."[16] That description, I believe, can also extend to MacArthur's trilogy against Pentecostals and charismatics, particularly when he relies on Greek to debunk today's tongues. As for his experience with Greek, he is admittedly not a Greek expert, having only had seminary-level training in Koine Greek. All this to say, the credibility of conclusions drawn from his or my understanding of biblical Greek hinges on citing proper authority on this ancient language, which MacArthur does not have when making the abovementioned arguments based on Greek.

Supporting Argument Based on *Theō* in 1 Corinthians 14:2

First, regarding *lalei alla theō* in 1 Corinthians 14:2, what is astounding is the price MacArthur is willing to pay to defend cessationism at all costs. By saying that this Greek phrase could be referring to a pagan deity, which no Bible translation does, he is introducing a radically dangerous hermeneutic. After all, "God" and "a god" are not synonymous.

Making the Same Mistake Made by the Jehovah's Witnesses

One way to show MacArthur's overreaching is to note the similarity between his understanding of 1 Corinthians 14:2 and the Jehovah's Witnesses' translation of the last part of John 1:1 in Greek: *theos ēn ho logos* ("the Word was God"). Note that the definite article (*ho*) is not placed before *theos*, the Greek word for God, just like in 1 Corinthians 14:2 where

---

16. Larson, "Unveiling the Truth about Islam," 39.

the definite article (*tō*) is absent before the same word *theō*. Keep in mind that although *theos* and *theō*, and *ho* and *tō*, respectively, appear different, they are the same word.[17] It should also be noted that the comparison between the absence of the definite article in John 1:1 and 1 Corinthians 14:2 is adequate mainly because MacArthur employs the exact same argument used by the Jehovah's Witnesses to render the same conclusion (a god). Having said that (and if you do not understand the following clarification, it is totally okay), parts in both passages relevant to this discussion are constructed differently in a grammatical sense: whereas *theō* without the definitive article in 1 Corinthians 14:2 functions as an indirect object, *theos* at the end of John 1:1 is part of what is called "predicative nominative." Meaning what? See the footnote for an explanation.[18]

Now to truly appreciate the Jehovah's Witnesses translation, note what they believe about Jesus: "The word, or Logos is 'god,' a mighty god, the 'beginning of the Creation' of Jehovah."[19] Meaning what, exactly? Jesus, having been created by Jehovah, is inferior to him. So how do the Jehovah's Witnesses translate the last part of John 1:1? As "a god," which is how MacArthur prefers to translate 1 Corinthians 14:2. The New World Translation of the Jehovah's Witnesses reads thusly, "the word was a god," which, according to the aforementioned cult expert Walter Martin, "is both incorrect grammar and poor Greek."[20] Martin probably would have made the same comment about MacArthur's handling of 1 Corinthians 14:2.

17. In Greek, nouns, adjectives, and articles are inflected in accordance to person, number, gender, and case.

18. While the Jehovah's Witnesses have no ground to translate *theos* without the definite articles as "a god," *theō* without the definite article can be translated as "a god." While the context determines whether it is God or a god, it appears that, based on how the same construction is translated in eight other passages (discussed later), *theō* without the definite articles in the New Testament always refers to God, not a god. In the case of 1 Corinthians 14, it is evident that the context does not allow *theō* without the definitive article to be rendered as "a god." For instance, in 1 Corinthians 8:5, Paul uses the plural *theoi* to refer to "gods" in contradistinction to the singular *theos/theō* mentioned immediately in the next verse to mean the God of the Bible.

19. Martin and Klann, *Jehovah of the Watchtower*, 29

20. Ibid., 48.

What MacArthur Overlooks

So then, why would the handling of John 1:1 and 1 Corinthians 14:2 by the Jehovah's Witnesses and MacArthur, respectively, be considered poor Greek?

First, what is overlooked, and which leads to a distortion of the text, is the fact that "the Greek had no indefinite article"[21]—meaning, we should be careful before placing an indefinite article, like "a," in our English translations. H. E. Dana and Julius R. Mantey, in their *A Manual Grammar of the Greek New Testament*, state, "It is important to bear in mind that we cannot determine the English translation by the presence or absence of the article in Greek."[22]

Second, typically, when no definite article is used with a noun, the noun functions like an adjective that "indicates the quality or characteristics of the noun."[23] Therefore, when *theos* (God) is used without the definite article, its implication is exactly the opposite of MacArthur's interpretation. Dana and Mantey write "that without the article *theos* signifies divine essence, while with the article divine personality is chiefly in view."[24] Quoting an earlier writer, they add, "*Theos* occurs without the article where the Deity is contrasted with what is human, or with the universe as distinct from its Creator . . . "[25] It appears, then, that is what Paul does in 1 Corinthians 14:2. By saying *theō* without the definitive article, he is contrasting God with what is human ("does not speak to men but to God"). But for MacArthur, *theō* without the article means a false god, which is exactly contrary to what the apostle John is saying when he writes *theos ēn ho logos*, which literally means, according to Ray Summers, author of *Essentials of New Testament Greek*, "the word was divine."[26]

21. Summers, *Essentials of New Testament Greek*, 129.

22. Dana and Mantey, *Manual Grammar of the Greek*, 150–51.

23. Summer, *Essentials of New Testament Greek*, 16.

24. Dana and Mantey, *Manual Grammar of the Greek*, 139–40.

25. Ibid., 140.

26. Summers, *Essentials of New Testament Greek*, 130.

Failing to Check His Work

Here, proper research would have forced one to check first whether *theō* used without the definitive article *tō* is found elsewhere in the New Testament, and if so, then see how it is typically translated. What is the purpose of this inquiry? To see whether it makes better sense to translate *theō* without the definite articles as "a god," a rendering preferred by MacArthur.

As for the first question, had MacArthur checked his work, he would have realized that while *theō* is normally used with *tō* (when functioning as an indirect object), there are several exceptions where the definitive article is not used with *theō*. I found eight such cases; there may be more: Romans 2:17; 1 Corinthians 10:20; 2 Corinthians 5:11; Galatians 2:19; 1 Thessalonians 1:9 and 2:15; Hebrews 12:23; and 1 Peter 2:5. Pointing this out is not simply to criticize MacArthur's less than thorough research, but also to underscore that the Radical Middle demands rigor and fairness to determine whether the approach of both/and is warranted, particularly over contentious matters.

Now, consider the following two Scriptures in which the definitive article *tō* is not placed before *theō* (used as an indirect object). In 1 Peter 2:5 ("You yourselves like living stones . . . to offer up spiritual sacrifices acceptable to God through Jesus Christ"), the phrase "acceptable to God" has no definite article *tō* in front of *theō* (in God), just as in 1 Corinthians 14:2. However, no Bible translates this as "acceptable to a god" (*euprosdektous theō*). The same translation exists in 1 Corinthians 10:20a which reads, "No, I imply that what pagans sacrifice they offer to demons and not to God." Concerning this phrase "and not to God" (*kai ŏu theō*), the definite article *tō* is not placed in front of *theō* ("to God"), just as in 1 Corinthians 14:2. It would be ludicrous to translate this verse as, "they sacrifice to demons and not to a pagan deity," since under this silly interpretation, Paul is supporting demons over pagan deities.

So what does this all mean? With all due respect to Pastor MacArthur, I find his research rather weak and his usage of Greek quite poor. Unfortunately, it does not stop here.

Cessationist Argument Based on *Glōssa* in 1 Corinthians 14

What makes the reading of 1 Corinthians 14 even more confusing is MacArthur's insistence in *The Charismatics* that *glōssa* (tongue) "used in the singular in 1 Corinthians 14:2, 4, 13, 14, and 19 . . . refer[s] to the counterfeit pagan gibberish (unintelligible speech) that was being used by many [*some* in his later publication] of the Corinthian believers,"[27] while its plural usage *glōssai* (tongues) refers to the true gift of languages. This implies that roughly half of the Corinthians spoke in real tongues (i.e., languages) while the other half spoke in pagan babbles. To distinguish one group from the other is why MacArthur needs to say that "tongue" used in the singular means pagan gibberish, and "tongues" in the plural means known languages.

A Groundless Assertion

It must be clearly stated that this assertion lacks any significant degree of support in Greek grammar regarding singular and plural nouns. And since MacArthur does not cite any source, I am led to believe that this is his own conjecture. I believe this is a groundless assertation that was the furthest thing from the apostle Paul's mind.

Reading 1 Corinthians 14 According to MacArthur's Logic

When 1 Corinthians 14 is read in accordance with his logic, the result is, again, quite preposterous. For instance, 1 Corinthians 14:13–14 would read: "Therefore, one who speaks in 'counterfeit pagan gibberish' should pray that he may interpret. For if I pray in 'counterfeit pagan gibberish,' my spirit prays but my mind is unfruitful." If this is indeed what Paul was saying, one wonders why Paul did not simply tell the Corinthians to stop speaking gibberish instead of encouraging them to interpret it.

In chapter 4, under "Making Light of the Bible," I wrote that the effort to maintain one's systematic theology at all costs often produces an unintended effect of making a travesty of the Bible. I gave the example of Reformed theologian R. C. Sproul, who insists that *holou tou cosmou* in 1 John 2:2 "does not refer to all people in the entire world,"[28] even though it means exactly that: the whole world and everyone in it. What Pastor MacArthur does is hardly any different: he makes a caricature of God's word in his efforts to justify his airtight version of hard cessationism. This is the hermeneutics of logocentrism of either/or, which is fueled by

27. MacArthur, *Charismatics*, 159.
28. Sproul, *What is Reformed Theology?*, 177.

"suppressing . . . one truth in the supposed interests of others . . . for the sake of a tidier theology."[29]

Cessationist Argument Based on False Gods in 1 Corinthians 13:1

The problem with MacArthur's research continues. As noted earlier, he asserts that the tongues of the Corinthians may have been the same as tongues spoken by the followers of "two false gods called Cybele and Dionysius"[30] (a.k.a., Bacchus). Against the backdrop of 1 Corinthians 13:1 in which Paul says, "If I speak in the tongues of men and of angels, but have not love, I am a noisy gong or a clanging cymbal," MacArthur writes:

> And used in the worship of both of these gods was speaking in tongues (ecstatic babble) accompanied by *clanging symbols, smashing gongs, and blaring trumpets.* There is no way to be sure Paul had these mystery religions in mind when he wrote 1 Corinthians 13, but it is fairly certain that he definitely had the corruption of the gift of tongues in mind.[31] (italics his)

MacArthur, then, cites William Barclay, a well-known British commentator, as his source to justify his claim. While that is not objectionable, MacArthur's usage of Barclay's comment is problematic.

Loose Citation (Inaccuracy)

Why is that a problem? It is because Barclay says something quite different in his commentary on *1 Corinthians* than what MacArthur asserts, ostensibly based on Barclay's work. Barclay writes:

> Paul begins by declaring that a man may possess any spiritual gift, but if it is unaccompanied by love it is useless. (i) He may have the gift of *tongues*. A characteristic of heathen worship, especially the worship of Dionysus and Cybele, was the clanging of cymbals and the braying of trumpets. Even the coveted gift

---

29. Packer, *Evangelism and the Sovereignty of God*, 25.

30. MacArthur, *Charismatics*, 163.

31. Ibid., 163. Notice how MacArthur begins with "no way to be sure," which then becomes "fairly certain," and ends with feeling "definite." That seems like building an argument on sand.

of tongues was no better than the uproar of heathen worship if love was absent.[32]

Evidently, "the uproar of heathen worship" here refers not to speaking in ecstatic babble but noisy instruments—meaning, Barclay says nothing about the Corinthians imitating pagan babble. On the contrary, he acknowledges that the gift of tongues is what the Corinthians had. The problem was their lack of love, which made their worship no better than noisy paganism. MacArthur's reference to Barclay's commentary to argue that the Corinthians spoke in pagan gibberish is a loose and inaccurate citation, and therefore quite misleading.

A Better Source for MacArthur

Ironically, according to Richard and Catherine Clark Kroeger, "speaking in tongues . . . was known in the ancient ecstatic religions; and Aristophanes in *Frogs* mentions 'the tongue of Bacchos' [in which] . . . a heathen might babble without consciousness of what he was saying." But this source would not have helped MacArthur's argument because the same authors concluded that "in 1 Corinthians it is clear that the gift of ecstatic language is a gift of the Holy Spirit (1 Cor 12:10)."[33]

EXAMINING THE VIEW THAT TONGUES HAVE TO BE KNOWN LANGUAGES

So then, if the gift of tongues spoken in the Corinthian church was not counterfeit pagan gibberish, then was it a known language? That does not appear to be the case since the apostle Paul states that "no one understands" the tongues spoken in the Corinthian church (1 Cor 14:2), which is contrary to what occurred in Jerusalem at Pentecost when believers miraculously began speaking in known human languages. On that day, "God-fearing Jews from every nation" (Acts 2:5b NIV) who had come to Jerusalem to celebrate the feast of Pentecost, heard the one hundred and twenty disciples praying in tongues, and said, "Are not all these who are speaking Galileans? And how is it that we hear, each of us in his own native language" (Acts 2:7b–8). Obviously, since the crowd understood

---

32. Barclay, *Letters to the Corinthians*, 117.
33. Kroeger and Kroeger, "Pandemonium and Silence at Corinth," para. 16.

what was being said *without* any interpretation, the tongues spoken in Jerusalem were known languages. Therefore, MacArthur insists, tongues must be known languages.

Couldn't Someone in Corinth Have Understood Tongues Without Translation?

Recall now what MacArthur believes happened in Corinth: "Since the gift of tongues consisted of authentic foreign languages on the day of Pentecost, then the same was true for the believers in Corinth."[34] Was this a sizable group in Corinth who allegedly spoke real languages when they spoke in tongues? Since MacArthur reduced the number of those Corinthians who spoke counterfeit pagan babble from "many" in his 1978 book to "some" in his 2013 book, perhaps the group that spoke real languages was larger than he previously thought. So what?

Let's say that some or all of these languages spoken in Jerusalem were also spoken whenever the Corinthian congregants spoke in tongues, a sizable group, during their Sunday worship services. Now imagine that there was at least one foreign visitor attending most, if not all, of their services. This is not an unlikely scenario since "Corinth was a rich and populous city with one of the greatest commercial trades in the ancient world . . . [that drew] the traders and the sailors from the ends of the earth."[35] So, if some of them were in attendance whenever the Corinthians were speaking in tongues in known languages, could these visitors have understood what was being said without interpretation, soon or later, just like what happened at Pentecost? MacArthur answers no, saying, "But in the Corinthian church, where those languages [i.e., known languages spoken at Pentecost] were not known, a translator was required; otherwise, the congregation would not understand the message and, therefore, would not be edified."[36]

Note that this statement assumes two things: first, none of the Corinthian congregants had come from fifteen nations and regions mentioned in Acts 2:9–11, including Mesopotamia, Asia, and Rome; and second, none from these multiple nations ever visited the church in Corinth. That's not plausible. Of course, some from these nations, however few,

---

34. MacArthur, *Strange Fire*, 141.

35. Barclay, *Letters to the Corinthians*, 2–3.

36. MacArthur, *Strange Fire*, 142.

were part of the Corinthian congregation; of course, some members knew at least one language spoken on the day of Pentecost; of course, some from these nations visited the church in Corinth at some point in time. So what does that all mean?

The Implication of Paul's Insistence that No One Understands

If and when known languages spoken at Pentecost were spoken in the Corinthian church, then, contrary to what MacArthur says, someone in that church could have understood them without the help of a translator, soon or later. Nevertheless, the apostle Paul is adamant that no one is able to understand the tongues spoken in the Corinthian church, including the visitors who, contrary to the onlookers in Jerusalem who responded to tongues with wonders, would respond critically. Paul states, "If, therefore, the whole church comes together and all speak in tongues, and outsiders or unbelievers enter, will they not say that you are out of your minds" (1 Cor 14:23)? Again, it bears repeating that even without translation, some foreign visitors from multiple nations mentioned in Acts 2:9–11 could have understood the tongues spoken on any given Sunday if the Corinthians happened to be speaking their languages. The apostle Paul, however, did not foresee such recognition happening, ever! Why? It is because the tongues spoken in Corinth were not known languages, and without interpretation, they are, in effect, gibberish to outsiders and unbelievers.

Two Types of Tongues in the Radical Middle

So, are there, as the apostle Paul asserts in 1 Corinthians 12:28, "various kinds of tongues?" Apparently so: On the one hand, it can be a known language, which is the case in Acts 2, as "each one heard them speaking in his own language" (Acts 2:6b NIV). On the other hand, a biblical tongue can be nonlinguistic, which is the case in 1 Corinthians 14, for Paul confidently asserts, "For anyone who speaks in a tongue . . . no one understands him" (1 Cor 14:2). What this seems to indicate is that the New Testament presents two kinds of tongues in an antithetic relationship: linguistic tongues versus nonlinguistic tongues. It is also an antinomy because they are both "logical, reasonable or necessary" according to *The Shorter Oxford Dictionary.*

Reasonableness of the Linguistic Tongue

The fact that the first occurrence of the word "tongue" was linguistic is reasonable and necessary, if one takes the following view with respect to what happened at Pentecost. Recall that in Genesis 11, what was once one nation (*ethnos*), prior to humans' attempt to build the tower of Babel in defiance of God (Gen 11:4), became many nations when "the LORD confused the language of all the earth. And from there the LORD dispersed them [the nations] over the face of all earth" (Gen 11:9b). When their confusion from an inability to "understand one another's speech" (Gen 11:7b) is contrasted with the reaction of amazement (Acts 2:7) by people from the nations gathered at Pentecost upon hearing "in [their] own tongues the mighty works of God" (Acts 2:11b), it signaled the launching of the Great Commission to redeem, by the power of the Holy Spirit (Acts 1:8), the nations still bearing the mark of God's punishment (Matt 24:7). A nonlinguistic tongue could not have served this purpose.

Reasonableness of the Nonlinguistic Tongue

On the other hand, it stands to reason to believe that the nonlinguistic tongue is a private prayer language for personal edification, for the apostle Paul tells the Corinthians, "The one who speaks in a tongue builds up himself" (1 Cor 14:4a). Evidently that was said in the context of Paul's rebuke of the Corinthians for speaking in tongues publicly without interpretation, which does not edify the church. Therefore, Paul's point seems to be that praying in tongues for personal edification is not as important as using that gift to edify the church; but that, in no way, precludes speaking in tongues as *one* of the spiritual means to edify oneself before serving others. Robert Saucy, who does not see a clear biblical warrant for the edifying of self, nonetheless, writes:

> In recognition of the personal edification that comes through speaking in tongues, the apostle may simply be acknowledging the truth that to experience the manifestation of the Spirit in the operation of a gift does bring some personal blessing, just as a teacher receives blessing in his teaching. It is no doubt true that the proper ministry of any gift helps the minister of that gift to grow personally, but this is never taught as the primary function of "spiritual gifts."[37]

37. Saucy, "Open but Cautious View," 134.

Saucy is of course right, since "each has received a gift . . . to serve one another" (1 Pet 4:10). Thus, it is imperative that continuationists are mindful of serving others after edifying themselves through prayer, including praying in tongues, and develop a ministry that includes the interpretation of tongues for the edification of the church (chapter 7).

In this manner, in the pneumatology of the Radical Middle, both the linguistic and nonlinguistic tongues are equally embraced as biblical, with the understanding that most of the tongues spoken today are of the latter type.

EXAMINING THE VIEW THAT SPEAKING IN TONGUES CEASED IN THE FIRST CENTURY

The second issue with respect to the gift of tongues is whether it came with an expiration date. As noted in chapter 1, 1 Corinthians 13:8–12 is the text upon which cessationism has built its case that the gift of tongues disappeared in the first century:

> Love never ends. As for prophecies, they will pass away; as for tongues, they will cease; as for knowledge, it will pass away. For we know in part and we prophesy in part, but when the perfect comes, the partial will pass away. When I was a child, I spoke like a child, I thought like a child, I reasoned like a child. When I became a man, I gave up childish ways. For now we see in a mirror dimly, but then face to face. Now I know in part; then I shall know fully, even as I have been fully known.

MacArthur, speaking for all cessationists, says that "the New Testament gift [of tongues] ceased after the apostolic age ended and never returned."[38]

MacArthur's Understanding of 1 Corinthians 13:8–10 Based on Greek

As for the reason concerning its cessation, he breaks with most cessationists who attribute its disappearance to the completion of the canon.[39] To

38. MacArthur, *Strange Fire*, 148.

39. Some see in *to teleion* (the perfect thing) the mature church. That has as much merit as seeing the completed canon in that phrase since the Greek word for church, *ekklesia*, is nowhere to be found in 1 Corinthian 13.

the latter, that is what "when the perfect comes" and "then see face to face" mean, but not to MacArthur, who says, "It seems that 'the perfect thing' has to be the eternal state—the new heaven and new earth . . . 'Face to face' in 1 Corinthians 13:12 can only be explained as being with God in the new creation."[40] To the Reformed, the eternal state begins when Christ returns; to the dispensationalists, after the thousand-year reign of Christ on earth. In light of the entire context of Scripture, MacArthur's view is more reasonable since the phrase "face to face," used several times throughout Scripture, always refers to a personal encounter between God and man[41] or between two individuals.[42] Insisting that "face to face" refers to the completion of Scripture is to shun the consistent meaning associated with this expression throughout the Bible (meeting God) in favor of injecting a foreign meaning into 1 Corinthians 13:8.

Cessationist Argument Based on *Pauō* in the Middle Voice (1 Cor 13:8)

So then, what is MacArthur's rationale for insisting that the gift of tongues ceased after the apostolic age ended in the first century? It has to do with the middle voice in biblical Greek, which does not exist in English but only has the active and passive voice.

What follows is a discussion about the middle voice relating to the Greek verb *pauō*,[43] meaning "to stop" or "cease," which is used in 1 Corinthians 13:8 to say that tongues will cease: "As for prophecies, they will pass away; as for tongues, they will cease [*pauō*]; as for knowledge, it will pass away." Note that although a contributor to *Strangers to Fire* (2013) ably deals with this issue, the author is not aware of MacArthur's particular argument, and therefore, does not deal with it, probably because

---

40. MacArthur, *Charismatics*, 165–66. The same idea is maintained in *Strange Fire* (147–48): "The believer's entrance into the Lord's presence best fits Paul's use of 'perfect.'"

41. Gen 32:30 (NIV): "So Jacob [said] . . . 'I saw God face to face, and yet my life was spared'"; Exod 33:11 (NIV): "The LORD would speak to Moses face to face, as a man speaks with his friend"; Judg 6:22b (NIV): "[Gideon] exclaimed, 'Ah, Sovereign LORD! I have seen the angel of the LORD face to face!'"

42. The apostle John says to Gaius the elder, "I hope to see you soon, and we will talk face to face" (3 John 14).

43. *Pausontai*, the future middle voice of *pauō*, is used here.

this article was first presented in 1977, two years before *The Charismatics* came out.[44] I will try to do that here from a similar yet distinctive angle.

Does Pauō Mean Ceasing by Itself?

In *The Charismatics*, MacArthur argues that the middle voice used with *pauō* signifies that "the gift of tongues will have ceased by itself *before* the perfect thing"[45] (italics his). He then explains basic grammatical concepts of the middle voice in Greek to justify his position, which is repeated in *Charismatic Chaos* to reach the same conclusion: "The gift of tongues will 'stop itself.' When is not stipulated, but they won't be around when the perfect thing arrives."[46] Actually, that is not quite true. By saying that tongues will cease on their own before the perfect comes, MacArthur does stipulate the when: at whatever time the tongues may cease, it will have to be before the perfect thing (i.e., the ushering of eternity prompted by Christ's second coming, or at the end of the one-thousand reign of Christ). So while MacArthur takes a different route than other cessationists, he arrives at the same destination: The gift of tongues ceased after the apostolic age ended. But, if it is shown that the ceasing of tongues is contingent upon the coming of the perfect (1 Cor 13:10), understood even by MacArthur as the arrival of eternity, then there is no scriptural basis to justify the removal of tongues until that moment arrives. Of course, MacArthur would not agree with that since, to him, *pauō* in the middle voice mean that tongues must disappear from the church before, not at the time of, the coming of the perfect.

Does Pauō Mean to Cease Permanently?

In *Strange Fire*, MacArthur adds a new twist, stating that the Greek verb *pauō*) "means 'to cease permanently,' indicating that the gift of tongues would come to an end once and for all."[47] So what's the twist? In *The Charismatics* (1978) MacArthur says that "*pauō* . . . simply means 'to

44. See Elbert, "Face to Face," 493–520. Keener points out that Elbert's paper was first presented in 1977.

45. MacArthur, *Charismatics*, 165. In this way, MacArthur translates the middle voice as reflexive.

46. MacArthur, *Charismatic Chaos*, 389.

47. MacArthur, *Strange Fire*, 148

stop,"[48] but in *Strange Fire* (2013) he presents *pauō* as if a sense of finality ("once and for all") is part of its inherent meaning. Actually, this change is already introduced in *Charismatic Chaos*, but unlike *Strange Fire*, MacArthur provides an explanatory footnote having to do with the middle voice in the Greek.[49] Much fuller explanation, however, is given in *The Charismatics*, which is examined in the following section in light of two questions. First, does the middle voice in Greek really mean what MacArthur says? Second, can a sense of finality be inferred from the word *pauō* itself as MacArthur insists?

The Truth about the Middle Voice in Greek

First, it must be said that anyone who attempts to build a whole doctrine (in this case, the doctrine that tongues disappeared in the first century) on account of the middle voice in Greek should show some restraint. A. T. Robertson, an eminent Greek scholar of the past generation warned, "We must not fall into the error of explaining the force of the middle by English translation."[50] It is because "no single principle can be found to cover all the cases,"[51] for, according to another Greek expert, James Moulton, "the sphere of the middle was . . . not at all sharply delimited."[52] With that caveat in mind, let's delve into the middle voice in Greek.

How the Middle Voice Differs from the Passive Voice

MacArthur's thesis is that the middle voice "always gives an emphasis to the subject doing the acting."[53] Meaning what? First, consider this simple sentence in the passive voice: "Tom is hit by a ball." Here, Tom is the subject and the ball, an agent. Obviously, the passive voice always requires an agent. So, if "as for tongues, they will cease" in 1 Corinthians 13:8 is given in the passive voice, it would mean that tongues will cease as the direct result of the coming of the perfect (eternity/the second coming). And, since the perfect has not come yet, it stands to reason that tongues

48. MacArthur, *Charismatics*, 165.

49. This footnote appears in MacArthur, *Charismatic Chaos*, 389.

50. Dana and Mantey, *Manual Grammar of the Greek*, 157.

51. Ibid., 157.

52. Ibid., 157.

53. MacArthur, *Charismatics*, 166.

still exist. But the ceasing of tongues in 1 Corinthians 13:8 is given in the middle voice, which, to MacArthur, means the subject is doing the acting by itself. What does that look like? Whereas in the passive voice, we would say "Tom is hit by a ball," in the middle voice, according to MacArthur, we would say "Tom hits himself." In his mind, an agent, whether it be a ball or the coming of the perfect, is not needed in the middle voice. So, regarding 1 Corinthians 13:8–10, MacArthur believes that *pauō* in the middle voice means that "the gift of tongues will have ceased by itself *before* the perfect thing"[54] (italics his). That is to say, the ceasing of tongues has nothing whatsoever to do with the arrival of the eternal state, prompted by the second coming of Christ.[55]

A Different Understanding of the Middle Voice

But, several works on Greek grammar indicate that, whereas MacArthur sees no need for an agent in the middle voice, the aforementioned Greek experts H. E. Dana and Julius Mantey believe otherwise, saying, "while the active voice emphasizes the action, the middle stresses the agent . . . [and] describes the subject as *participating in the results of the actions*"[56] (italics theirs). Consider the following example Dana and Mantey give: The Greek verb *bouleuō* in the active voice means "I counsel," but in the middle voice (*bouleuomai*) it "means *I take counsel*: the subject acting with a view to participation in the outcome"[57] (italics theirs). In this example, the subject is the counselee, the agent is the counsel given by the counselor, the action is taking the counsel, and the outcome is getting well. However, according to MacArthur's grasp of the middle voice that requires no agent (the perfect thing), *bouleuomai* would mean, "I counsel by myself" (a ludicrous claim). And that is how he translates *pauō* (cease) in the middle voice in 1 Corinthians 13:8: The tongues will cease by themselves. In contrast, "the dominant opinion among New Testament scholars today . . . is that . . . [1 Corinthians 13:8] makes no

54. Ibid., 165.

55. In 1 Corinthians 13:8, where prophecy and knowledge are also mentioned, the Greek verb for both is *katargeō*, meaning "to make to cease," which is used in the future passive voice (*katargēthontai*). This would mean that they will eventually pass away as the direct result of the coming of perfect (agent).

56. Dana and Mantey, *Manual Grammar of the Greek*, 157.

57. Ibid., 157.

comments about tongues ceasing on their own, apart from the interven-tion of 'the perfect.'"[58]

However, there is one Greek scholar who appears to give credence to MacArthur's position on *pauō*. Dallas Theological Seminary professor Daniel Wallace, under the rubric of what is called "indirect middle," states the implication of *pauō* in the middle voice "*may* be that tongues were to have 'died out' of their own *before* the perfect comes" (italics his).[59] Notice that this is what MacArthur claims. Wallace, then, uses the example of Luke 8:24 in which *pauō* in the middle voice is also used. It reads: "And they went and woke him, saying, "Master, Master, we are perishing!" And he awoke and rebuked the wind and the raging waves, and they ceased [*epausanto* from *pauō*], and there was a calm." Now, imagine that *pauō* is used in the passive voice, in which case it would mean that the wind is stopped by Jesus' rebuke. In this scenario, the wind does nothing to stop by itself; it is completely acted upon by the agency of Jesus' rebuke. So what changes in the middle voice? As seen earlier, while the agent is still needed in the middle voice, the focus is on the manner of the subject's response. Wallace explains it this way: "The elements are personified in Luke 8 and their ceasing from turbulence is therefore presented as voli-tional obedience to Jesus"[60]—meaning, the wind did not stop by itself, but did so willingly in response to Jesus' command. The difference between the passive and middle voice here is this: in the passive voice, the wind is forced to stop; in the middle voice, the wind willingly stops—either way it requires Jesus' rebuke (an agent).

This view corresponds to what W. E. Vine notes about the general usage of *pauō* in Scripture, that it "is used chiefly in the middle voice in the New Testament, signifying 'to come to an end, . . . a willing cessation' (in contrast to the passive voice which denotes a forced cessation)."[61] This means that *pauō* in the middle voice stresses the *manner* of the subject's ceasing in response to what the agent does: volitionally rather than forced, indirectly rather than directly. Obviously, this does not preclude an agent.

---

58. Wallace, *Greek Grammar*, 422.

59. Ibid., 422.

60. Ibid., 422.

61. Vine et al, *Expository Dictionary of Biblical words*, 93.

Does Pauō Tell Time?

Lastly, MacArthur's assertion that the word *pauō* itself carries time dimension in general, and finality in particular ("to cease permanently"), is groundless. Thus, Wallace, breaking from MacArthur's assertion that the gift of tongues, having long stopped itself, "won't be around when the perfect thing arrives,"[62] adds, "This is not to say that the middle voice in 1 Corinthians 13:8 *proves* that tongues already ceased! This verse does not specifically address *when* tongues would cease . . ."[63] (italics his). But, it actually does—at whatever time the perfect comes, the gift of tongues will cease volitionally. Why? I like the way my AMI colleague (a serious student of biblical Greek) with whom I was corresponding commented: "The perfect is an indirect catalyst, but the tongues cease on their own volition from the beauty of the perfect, like a person loses her voice in the presence of something magnificent."[64] That is so true: Why would anyone want to speak to God in tongues in heaven when you are face-to-face with him? I would gladly and willingly cease speaking to God in tongues.

The Gift of Tongues has Not Expired

So, in view of all that has been discussed regarding the gift of tongues, it is scripturally unwarranted to assert that the gift of tongues ceased in the first century when the canon of the New Testament was completed or when the apostolic age ended. Instead, tongues will disappear when the perfect comes to usher us into the presence of God. Meanwhile, it is still in operation today as both linguistic tongues (however rare) and nonlinguistic tongues.

This concludes the hermeneutical response to several arguments of hard cessationism with respect to the gift of tongues. The next chapter will address flawed versions of continuationism regarding the same gift.

62. MacArthur, *Charismatic Chaos*, 389.

63. Wallace, *Greek Grammar*, 423.

64. Doug Tritton, email to author, January 26, 2017.

QUESTIONS FOR REFLECTION & DISCUSSION

1. In your opinion, how has a Western-centric worldview both strengthened and weakened our understanding of Scripture?

2. The apostle Paul, under inspiration, told the Corinthians, "Now concerning spiritual gifts, brothers, I do not want you to be uninformed" (1 Cor 12:1). So why do we need to know about spiritual gifts? What are we missing out on? (1 Cor 12:4–31).

3. What would you say to cessationists about the validity of the gift of tongues for today?

4. Have you ever asked the Lord to give you this gift? What led you to ask for it? If you did not receive this gift, are you okay with it? Why or why not? Read Titus 3:5–6.

5. This chapter contains more discussions based on biblical Greek than any other chapters. What does that mean to you? Before you answer, consider this joke I once heard from a famous pastor. After reading a passage, he asked, "Do you know what this means in Greek?" After pausing, he deadpanned, "Same as in English." Now answer the question.

7

The Gift of Tongues in the Radical Middle: A Hermeneutical Response to Flawed Versions of Continuationism

THE FACT THAT ONLY cessationism has been highlighted thus far for its imbalanced (i.e., logocentric) approach to Scriptural passages referring to tongues, does not mean that Pentecostals and charismatics are above reproach. There are at least five things that some continuationists believe about the gift of tongues and its practice that rightfully concern cessationists.

MY PERSONAL HISTORY

I know these matters well personally, having cut my theological teeth with a charismatic congregation—a Pentecostal Holiness church— among the several hundred Korean congregations that were to be found in Los Angeles in the early 1980s. I remained a disciple of the pastor for three years, which included numerous weekly services, daily 5:30 AM prayer meetings, and 3-hour Bible studies, all of which left an indelible spiritual mark on me. I left the church a long time ago, but not without having acquired a daily habit of spending a protracted amount of time in prayer (including in tongues), along with reading and studying the Bible. At the same time, my ensuing studies at a cessationist seminary gave me an opportunity to think about what to believe and not believe about the sign gifts, and how to practice and not practice them.

From my perspective, it is reasonable that Pentecostals and charismatics, especially in their earlier days, have been called out for being doctrinally shaky and, at times, unsound. I would hope, for instance, that they no longer teach what I found in a Pentecostal/charismatic Sunday School curriculum (published in 1962), which I once used to teach my youth group in the early 1980s, because some parts are truly biblically deficient. According to the text, "salvation always precede[s] receiving the Holy Spirit [because] salvation is a gift to the sinner . . . The Holy Spirit cannot come into an unclean vessel."[1] The author seems unaware of the doctrine of regeneration by which "[God] saved us, not because of works done by us in righteousness, but according to his own mercy, by the washing of regeneration and renewal of the Holy Spirit, whom he poured out on us richly through Jesus Christ our Savior" (Titus 3:5–6). But that teaching pales in comparison to, as cited in chapter 1, the doctrine of "Unitarian Pentecostals . . . who say one must speak with tongues to be saved."[2] In terms of doctrinal importance, I do not believe the five problems that I am about to present are as essential as these two just mentioned (i.e., salvation preceding the receiving of the Holy Spirit; speaking in tongues as a prerequisite to salvation) that affect our view of salvation. Having said that, Pentecostals and charismatics must think differently on some of their beliefs and practices, and let cessationists know that the pursuit of word matters to them as much as Spirit.

Let me frame the concerns of cessationists in the form of a few questions. First, is it biblically warranted to believe that baptism in the Holy Spirit is a subsequent event to salvation? Second, is it biblical to believe that speaking in tongues is the initial evidence that a person has received the baptism in the Holy Spirit? Third, biblically speaking, should Pentecostals speak in tongues in public worship services attended by outsiders and unbelievers? Fourth, how exactly should tongue-speaking be interpreted in public gatherings? (This reflects my concern more so than that of cessationists.) And finally (already expressed through Robert Saucy), is the private usage of the gift of tongues biblical?

1. Clayton, *My Faith*, 50.
2. Synan, *Spirit Said "Grow,"* 8.

A ONE-STAGE OR TWO-STAGE SALVATION

Before discussing the matter of whether speaking in tongues is the initial evidence of baptism in/with the Holy Spirit, we must recognize an even more fundamental (read, antithetic) difference between cessationists and continuationists. Ironically, a clear recognition of this antithesis can actually bring both to the center where they can coexist in tension, as long as each side concedes one of their doctrines that is essential to them, but not to the matter of salvation.

A Fundamental Difference

This fundamental difference between continuationists and cessationists pertains to the number of stages involved in salvation.

Pentecostals and Charismatics: Two-Stage Way of Salvation

On the one hand, Pentecostals and charismatics hold to what amounts to a two-stage way of salvation, which is largely the result of privileging the book of Acts over the Epistles. Now, unlike the abovementioned Pentecostal author who claimed that "salvation always precedes receiving the Holy Spirit," most Pentecostals and charismatics do believe that the Holy Spirit is involved at the moment of salvation, but they do not refer to that as receiving the Holy Spirit. Prominent charismatic Kenneth Hagin writes, "There is a work of the Holy Spirit in the new birth, but that is not called receiving the Holy Ghost—that is called being born-again, receiving eternal Life. There is an experience following salvation called receiving, or being filled with the Holy Ghost."[3] This two-stage path of salvation stems from the record that those who already believed were "filled with the Holy Spirit" at Pentecost (Acts 2:4a). According to Acts 8:15–16, the Samaritans, after believing without receiving the Holy Spirit, received him later.[4] In Ephesus, "the Holy Spirit came on" (Acts 19:6) to a group

---

3. Hagin, *Why Tongues?* §47–48.

4. This is one highly unusual case since believing without the Spirit seems to go against Paul's teaching in 1 Corinthians 12:3b: "No one can say 'Jesus is Lord' except in the Holy Spirit." One view is that God allowed this one-off event to ensure that the Jews and Samaritans, who were archenemies, do not develop two separate churches. By having Peter and John come down to impart the Holy Spirit to the Samaritans, the latter naturally came under the ecclesiastic leadership of the Jerusalem church.

of twelve disciples (i.e., believers) who "ha[d] not even heard that there is a Holy Spirit" (Acts 19:2b). So, on the strength of the book of Acts, Pentecostals and charismatics advocate a two-stage way of salvation.

Cessationists: A One-Stage Way of Salvation

On the other hand, cessationists, prioritizing the Epistles over the book of Acts, believe that salvation and baptism in the Spirit occur simultaneously. The privileging of the Epistles by cessationists, on the sequence of salvation and baptism in the Spirit, stems from their belief that the book of Acts is a historical narrative, while the Epistles are doctrinal instructions.[5] MacArthur states that "the only teachings in the book of Acts that can be called normative (absolute) for the church are those that are doctrinally confirmed elsewhere in Scripture."[6] So if Acts and the Epistles seemingly contradict each other (cf. Acts 8:14–17 with 1 Corinthians 12:3 or Titus 3:5–7), the latter are given the precedent. This, of course, makes certain theological sense since early church doctrine and practice were not yet settled during this transitional period that Luke covers in Acts. And Paul's testimony from the Epistles works in concert with the one-stage path of salvation (i.e., salvation and baptism in the Spirit occurring simultaneously); one clear verse to this effect is 1 Corinthians 12:13, "For in one Spirit we were all baptized into one body." Here, both belief and baptism in the Spirit occur simultaneously, which is how one is incorporated into Christ's body.

Bridging the Gap between Cessationists and Continuationists

In any case, neither side will budge from their respective theological views, and like many hardliners of other beliefs, no amount of evidence will sway their minds. I attempted to justify the one-stage salvation view to Pentecostal pastors in Mexico, but to no avail: the two-stage way of salvation remains a key doctrinal view for Pentecostals. The same can be said about the conviction held by cessationists regarding their one-stage salvation view. Nevertheless, despite this theological gap, when this matter is hermeneutically processed through the Radical Middle, the

---

5. I slightly altered Grudem's statement, that "Acts 2 is historical narrative while 1 Corinthians is doctrinal instruction." Grudem, *Systematic Theology*, 1072.

6. MacArthur, *Charismatics*, 85.

outcome is an understanding that may allow both pneumatologies to coexist in tension.

The Baptism and Filling of the Spirit: Same or Different?

A possible alleviation of this tension begins with the question of whether it is biblical to treat "baptized with the Holy Spirit" and "filled with the Holy Spirit" as interchangeable phrases. I think so, since Luke uses two different Greek verbs—*baptizō* (Acts 1:5), meaning "to baptize," and *plēroō* (Acts 2:4), meaning "to fill" (the actual word is *plēthō*; *plēroō* is its derivative), to refer to what happened at Pentecost. In Acts 1:5, Luke says, "John baptized with water, but you will be *baptized* with the Holy Spirit not many days from now"; and in Acts 2:4, he describes its fulfilment as, "And they were all filled with the Holy Spirit and began to speak in other tongues as the Spirit gave them utterance." So there is little doubt that being baptized with the Holy Spirit and being filled with the Holy Spirit are synonymous.

However, also note that it is to the believers that the apostle Paul says, "Be filled (*plēroō*) with the Spirit" (Eph 5:18b). What does this imply? It seems reasonable to tell those who believe that salvation and baptism in the Holy Spirit occur simultaneously that they ought to be filled with the Spirit again after the rebirth. Does that constitute a second definite work of the Spirit for believers? At the very least, one can posit that while baptism and being filled with the Spirit may share much in common, they are not one and the same, since baptism in the Spirit is a one-off event ("baptized into Christ"—Gal 3:27), and the filling of the Spirit is a more routine event.[7] John Stott writes in his book *Baptism & Fullness*: "As an initiatory event the baptism is not repeatable and cannot be lost, but the filling can be repeated and in any case needs to be maintained. If it is not maintained, it is lost. If it is lost, it can be recovered."[8]

Recognizing this difference between baptism and filling of the Spirit is the key that can enable cessationists and continuationists to coexist in tension, since being filled with the Spirit as a post-salvation experience seems reasonable and necessary to their respective theologies. But, for

7. This understanding is supported by the fact that *plēroō* is used in the present imperative active (*plēousthe*). "In the active, it may indicate a command to do something in the future which involves continuous or repeated action." Zodhiates, *Complete word Study*, 869.

8. Stott, *Baptism & Fullness*, 48.

this conciliatory approach to work, each must concede, as hinted earlier, one of their doctrines that is essential to them, but not to the matter of salvation. We'll discuss this issue next while addressing whether speaking in tongues is the initial evidence of baptism in the Spirit.

SPEAKING IN TONGUES AS THE INITIAL EVIDENCE OF BAPTISM IN THE HOLY SPIRIT

So what doctrine do continuationists and cessationists need to concede in order to coexist in relative peace, without having to extensively alter their views on one-stage or two-stage way salvation?

What Continuationists Need to Concede

As for Pentecostals and charismatics, one doctrine they must concede is the belief that speaking in tongues is the initial evidence of baptism in the Spirit. This position, drawn entirely from Acts, is the result of the hermeneutics of logocentrism. Remember that these hermeneutics take form when people cherry-pick their desired interpretation while dismissing its opposite, appealing to selective Scriptures that justify the preferred view and ignoring other verses that point in a different direction. This is often what ardent advocates of their respective systematic theologies accomplish, while claiming to remain faithful to Scripture. What I labor to point out in this book is that hand-selected knowledge is not always equivalent to biblical knowledge based on the entire Scripture. And selective reading is what Pentecostals and charismatics do when they rely on the book of Acts, their most privileged book, to justify their pneumatology: if we receive the same Holy Spirit that people at Pentecost received, "[we] would have the same initial sign they had—the Bible evidence—speaking with tongues."[9] But, when considering the entire book of Acts, we clearly see that while speaking in tongues can be evidence, it is not the *only* evidence indicative of being baptized with the Spirit.

---

9. Hagin, *Why Tongues?* §29–30.

Some Spoke in Tongues, Some Did Not

First, note that there are at least six situations throughout Acts in which, while their situations are not alike, they roughly follow the pattern of believing first and then (or simultaneously) experiencing baptism or filling in the Spirit. While tongues are spoken in three situations, in the other three instances the text is silent as to whether those filled with the Spirit spoke in tongues. Yet Pentecostals and charismatics typically ignore the latter, much like the author of the abovementioned Sunday School curriculum. Christal Clayton, after raising the question, "What is the initial outward evidence that a person has received the baptism in the Holy Spirit?"[10] lists only Acts 2:4, 10:44–46, and 19:6 as scriptural proof. Since the believers in these passages (the one hundred twenty believers gathered in the upper room, Cornelius and his guests, and the believers whom Paul met in Ephesus) all spoke in tongues after being filled with the Spirit, Pentecostals can make a case for speaking in tongues as the initial evidence for baptism in the Spirit.

But, the hermeneutics of the Radical Middle does not play favorites—meaning, it recognizes all relevant Scriptures addressing a particular matter. So it notices that none of the following people appearing in the book of Acts are said to have received the gift of tongues, even though they were baptized or filled with the Spirit: first, the three thousand who became believers and received the gift of the Holy Spirit (Acts 2:38–41) shortly after the one hundred twenty received tongues; second, the several thousand who became believers (Acts 4:4) and were "filled with the Holy Spirit" (Acts 4:31); and third, the Samaritan believers who received the Holy Spirit through Peter and John (Acts 8:17). Now whatever Simon the magician saw when Peter and John laid hands to bestow the Spirit upon new believers was probably an outward manifestation (Acts 8:18), but Luke remains silent on what that was—to assume tongues is an educated guess at best, but not a sure bet. And along with these passages in Acts, other relevant passages in the Epistles (e.g., Gal 3:27; Rom 6:3) do not say that speaking in tongues specifically accompanies baptism in the Holy Spirit.

10. Clayton, *My Faith*, 56.

Other Signs for Being Filled with Spirit

So, then, what are some other signs that would indicate that we are filled with the Spirit? It is telling that Paul's command for the believers "to be filled with the Spirit" (Eph 5:18b) is immediately followed by "addressing one another in psalms and hymns and spiritual songs, singing and making melody to the Lord with your heart, giving thanks always and for everything to God the Father in the name of our Lord Jesus Christ" (Eph 5:19–20). This is pointing not to speaking in tongues but to a different, changed dialogue of praise between believers, which corroborates what Paul says earlier in the letter: "Let no corrupting talk come out of your mouths, but only such as is good for building up" (Eph 4:29a). The apostle then ends this section of Ephesians 5 with the command to "submit to one another out of reverence for Christ" (Eph 5:21). That speaks of a changed life. What does this imply? The passage indicates a general renewal of spirit after conversion that is marked by changes in one's speech and conduct. The conclusion: the pneumatology of the Radical Middle embraces speaking in tongues as valid evidence of baptism in the Holy Spirit; but it also acknowledges a changed tongue and life as evidence of the same.

What Each Side Needs to Concede: Cessationists

As for cessationists who prioritize the Epistles, which provide normative beliefs and practices for all churches to the present day, they must remain consistent with their hermeneutical rule of priority with respect to whether tongues must be real languages. The book of Acts says yes (Acts 2:7–8), but, as previously pointed out, chapter 14 of the first Epistle to the Corinthians says not necessarily so (1 Cor 13:1, 14:2). Therefore, cessationists should reconsider their approach of relying solely on the book of Acts to insist that tongues must be real languages.

Making it Work for the Sake of Unity

It is always "difficult for people of differing positions to fellowship together,"[11] whether between Calvinists and Arminians, or Reformists and dispensationalists. In the case of cessationist and continuationist

11. Saucy, "Open but Cautious View," 144.

conflicts, the degree of difficulty is even higher (more so in the aftermath of *Strange Fire*) because, as Saucy notes, "many of [their] issues directly affect behavior within the corporate church."[12] Unless both groups privilege and value the unity of the body of Christ over stubbornly maintaining their own dogma, nothing will change. They need to make it work, recognizing that the clarity of Scripture is not as strong as other doctrinal truths regarding these matters—"for now we see in a mirror dimly" (1 Cor 13:12a). Without humility and love, there is no unity. (How these inner qualities relate to one another is discussed in the last chapter.) Therefore, on the one hand, cessationists must relent from their position that the gift of tongues has ceased; on the other hand, continuationists need to relent from their position that speaking in tongues is the initial evidence of being baptized with the Spirit. And those who relent for the sake of practicing the right hermeneutics and desiring unity demonstrate how much they are spiritually growing and maturing in both word and Spirit.

SHOULD TONGUES BE SPOKEN IN PUBLIC WORSHIP SERVICES?

Now to a matter I feel many tongue-speakers simply ignore: whether tongues should be spoken in worship services open to everyone, including unbelievers. Perhaps some people have grown so accustomed to doing so in public, that the warnings which Paul very clearly writes about concerning the practice fall on deaf ears.

The Real Reason the Corinthians were Rebuked

The undeniable truth is that Paul calls out the Corinthians, not for speaking in counterfeit pagan gibberish, but for the abusive practice of the gift of tongues and prophecy. Consider Paul's admonitions to them: "I thank God that I speak in tongues more than all of you. Nevertheless, in church I would rather speak five words with my mind to instruct others, than ten thousand words in a tongue" (1 Cor 14:18–19).

Evidently, Paul does not mind speaking in tongues, but the church is not his preferred place to do it. Why? Paul explains it this way: "If, therefore, the whole church comes together and all speak in tongues, and outsiders or unbelievers enter, will they not say that you are out of your

12. Ibid., 144.

minds" (1 Cor 14:23)? The reason for the visitors' reaction is obvious: When the whole church speaks in nonlinguistic tongues all at once (and I have been in such situations many times), it can feel jarring to observers. "They will think you are crazy" (1 Cor 14:23b NLT). So what does Paul suggest? "If any speak in a tongue, let there be only two or at most three, and each in turn, and let someone interpret. But if there is no one to interpret, let each of them keep silent in church and speak to himself and to God" (1 Cor 14:27–28).

Through all his commands, Paul says three things: first, in public worship services, the whole church should not speak in tongues in such a way that it will alarm outsiders (e.g., people unfamiliar with tongues); second, establish a structure or program in a service where individuals can speak in tongues in an orderly fashion followed by interpretation; third, if there is no interpretation, then those who speak in tongues should do so silently during the service so that outsiders or unbelievers are not ostracized.

Speaking in Tongues in its Proper Perspective

This is really a question of what value we attach to speaking in tongues. In 2008, I spoke before a large group of Assemblies of God pastors in the city of Monterrey, Mexico, who had gathered for their annual district convention under the theme of spiritual gifts. During my lecture I shared what is outlined in the Corinthians' Epistle concerning tongues. That evening, while some lead pastors and I were waiting at a restaurant, one of them asked me somewhat curtly, "Brother Ryun, if there is no visitor attending our Sunday service, can we all speak tongues?" Sensing that he was somewhat offended by my teaching, I replied with a slight smile, "Do you really want a service where there are no unbelievers to hear the good news? Is that the purpose of our gathering: To speak in tongues?"

I spoke to this pastor out of personal experience because I had been saved in a church where everyone, including me, prayed out loud in tongues, and I have preached in countless Pentecostal churches in Mexico where people pray out loud (and loudly). However, since my perception of this matter has long changed (while accepting that pastors can think differently on this matter), whenever I pray in tongues during worship services, I do it quietly so as not to disturb the worship experience of others. But I think praying in tongues audibly with like-minded believers in prayer meetings should be permissible.

How Can Continuationists and Cessationists Worship and Pray Together?

As in any conflicts, unless some compromises are made by all sides, it is hard to imagine cessationists and continuationists genuinely worshiping together. Yet, it can happen. In 2010, I was invited to preach at a special prayer service sponsored by the Evangelical Ministerial Confraternity of Chihuahua (CMECH), during a time when the city was suffering from high levels of violence inflicted by drug cartels fighting among themselves. Although this association was interdenominational, most pastors who attended its monthly gathering were Pentecostals and charismatics, and its leadership reflected as much. One lone non-Pentecostal leader at the meeting was my good friend Pastor Javier, the senior pastor of the largest Baptist congregation in the city, who was not particularly fond of Pentecostals when we first met in 2003. But, as his perception of them changed, he decided to join the leadership when it was extended to him by the then-president of CMECH, Pastor Heriberto, an Assemblies of God minister and also a friend (more on him at the end of the book).

Now this prayer meeting was scheduled to be held at Javier's church. The Sunday before, during the announcement, Javier stressed that many Pentecostals would be attending this prayer meeting. So when I asked him why he made such an emphasis, Javier said: "Since they have been fairly warned, either they decide not to come or come with the right expectation." That encouraged me to make the following comment while preaching at this meeting before the time of prayer began: "My Pentecostal and charismatic brothers (a good number of them knew me personally), this is a Baptist church and the house rule is no speaking in tongues. So, if you want to speak in tongues loudly, go outside and do it. I am sure when the Baptists go to a prayer service held at your church, they will return the favor."[13] While I did not know what to expect, I was surprised by the degree to which the subsequent prayer meeting was conducted in a Baptist style—meaning, there was no one praying out loud at the

---

13. I do concede that when Pentecostals gather to pray among themselves (not a worship service open to anyone), they should pray as they are led, including praying in tongues.

same time. First, Pastor Heriberto, as if he were a Baptist, offered a calm public prayer that must have lasted over thirty minutes. Then we broke into groups and each person offered sentence prayers. Later, when we started praying individually, the atmosphere was quiet. I did not notice anyone leaving but I found out I was wrong when, a couple of weeks later, I ran into Pastor Carlos, another Assemblies of God minister, who at that time was the president-elect of CMECH for the coming year. Whether he was joking or serious, Carlos, without much facial expression, told me he went outside the church to pray in tongues. I thanked him.

HOW TONGUES OUGHT TO BE INTERPRETED IN PUBLIC GATHERINGS

The fourth issue is a matter of how to interpret tongues, a subject that is rarely discussed, much less practiced, among continuationists. However, I saw an incidence of this during the aforementioned Convergence Conference held in Oklahoma City in October 2017. In an afternoon session in which Francis Chan was the speaker, a person sitting in front began speaking in tongues during a pause; everyone heard it since his voice was the only one echoing in the large auditorium. Shortly after its conclusion, someone offered its interpretation that began with "Thus says the Lord . . ."

Common Problems with the Interpretation of Tongues

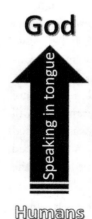

There are two problems with how the tongues were interpreted at the said conference. First, since speaking in tongues is a prayer from man to God, its interpretation should not be God speaking, which is the interpretation that was offered at the conference. Allow me to offer an analogy. I am fluent in Spanish, so imagine that I am offering a public prayer in Spanish and someone is interpreting it in English. So, if I prayed, "*Querido Dios, te digo que somos una gente orgullosa e infiel; por eso, necesitamos arrepentirnos,*" its interpretation should be, "Dear God, I say to you that we are an arrogant and unfaithful people; therefore, we need to repent." Notice that the interpretation is what I said to God and not the other way around.

Now, imagine that I do not know any Spanish, but these same Spanish words came out of my mouth through the exercise of the gift of (linguistic) tongues—a miracle to be sure, and one which the Spirit is evidently trying to speak through my words (Rom 8:26–27). But, should its interpretation be any different than the scenario in which I know the language? I do not think so. The interpretation of tongues should not begin with what God said to us, but what we said to God in tongues through the Holy Spirit who resides in us.

The second problem is this: "Thus says the Lord" implies that the ensuing words are a direct revelation from God. This matter is elaborated upon in the next chapter addressing the gift of prophecy; suffice it to say for now, the canon is closed, which means there is no more, "Thus says the Lord."

How to Tell Whether the Right Interpretation of Tongues is Given

How, then, can we tell whether the right interpretation has been given? Discerning this is to be accomplished in the same way that the church is to weigh whether prophetic words given in a gathering are from the Lord. The apostle Paul, right after concluding his instruction on proper practice of tongues in the church (that tongue-speakers should keep quiet if there is no interpreter) says, "Let the prophets speak two or three, and let the other judge" (1 Cor. 14:29 KJV). The Greek word translated here as "judge" is *diakrinō*, which means to "to make distinction . . . to determine."[14] So on what basis can the hearers determine or distinguish whether the interpretation just heard is from the Lord? In the same way the Bereans tried to determine whether Paul's teaching was from the Lord. Luke writes: "Now the Berean Jews were of more noble character than those in Thessalonica, for they received the message with great eagerness and examined the Scriptures every day to see if what Paul said was true" (Acts 17:11). This suggests that one prerequisite for developing a public ministry involving the sign gifts, particularly the interpretation of tongues and prophecy, is a congregation knowledgeable about Scripture, which is God's general will for all believers.

A brief comment is needed here. There are many things in life that we never have to pray about. For instance, we need not ask God, "Lord, since my spouse is uncaring towards me, should I run away with my

14. Zodhiates, *Complete word Study,* 902.

assistant?" or "God, give me wisdom to successfully rob that bank next to my office." If God were to respond audibly, he would simply tell them, "Don't waste my time; read the book that tells my general will." Therefore, if the interpretation falls within the parameters of God's general will, then we should not fight too hard against accepting it.

Let me share an experience I had while serving in Mexico, a year after the great tsunami in 2004 that claimed an untold number of lives in southeast Asia and which has to do with the interpretation of tongues. One day, a charismatic Methodist who was visiting my home shared how God revealed to her that earthquakes were about to happen in China and Tanzania. Taking her words at face value and because of the heightened awareness of what the tsunami had done, I encouraged her to warn the Chinese and Tanzanian consulates about what she believed was going to happen. Perhaps suspecting a hint of skepticism on my part, she suddenly did something that startled my wife and me: she fell into some sort of trance in which she spoke in tongues for a few minutes. She followed her trance with her own interpretation: "*Ryun, tenga más fe, así dice Dios*"—meaning, "Thus says the Lord, 'Ryun, have more faith.'"

How did I take this? Since the need to have more faith falls within the biblical parameters, I accepted that. Nonetheless, I shared with this

well-educated woman two things. First, one's consciousness is not lost while praying in tongues; tongue-speakers maintain their mental faculties—meaning, they can start and stop tongues at any time. Recall what Paul says if there is no interpreter: "The speaker should keep quiet in the church" (1 Cor 14:28b NIV). If someone is in a trance like what allegedly happened to her, then it would be impossible to comply with this command. Second, the interpretation of tongues should not begin with, "Thus says the Lord" (or anything equivalent), since the tongue speaker is praying (that is, saying something) to the Lord, not God saying something to the speaker (that would be a type of prophecy).

THE USE OF TONGUES FOR PERSONAL EDIFICATION

In chapter 6, I agreed with Saucy's view that "the proper ministry of any gift [including speaking in tongues] helps the minister of that gift to grow personally, but this is never taught as the primary function of 'spiritual gifts.'"[15] Having noted this, I would like to share how personal edification from speaking in tongues (a secondary function) has helped me to serve more diligently (the primary result).

My Personal Practice of Speaking in Tongues

I have prayed in tongues as part of my daily prayer for close to thirty-five years; in short, praying in tongues has been *part* of my daily spiritual routine that "strengthen[s me] with power through his Spirit in [my] inner being" (Eph 3:16) so that I may be more fruitful in my family (e.g., being more forgiving and less temperamental), ministry (e.g., teaching more with my heart), and personal walk with God (e.g., being more holy and loving).

One practical benefit has to do with intercessory prayer that I took to heart a long time ago. Therefore, there are some nonfamily members for whom I have been praying regularly for over twenty-five years. Sometimes, however, I am not sure what to pray for those whom I have not seen for a while, and this is where I find praying in tongues useful. As I pray in tongues while I think about them and their general needs, I believe that some aspects of what the apostle Paul talks about in Romans 8:26–27 are taking place:

> Likewise the Spirit helps us in our weakness. For we do not know what to pray for as we ought, but the Spirit himself intercedes for us with groanings too deep for words. And he who searches hearts knows what is the mind of the Spirit, because the Spirit intercedes for the saints according to the will of God.

In a manner of speaking, if groaning can pass for prayer, then so should nonlinguistic tongues. Now, while I pray in tongues, I also pray with my mind, which Paul additionally instructs us to do while praying in tongues. "For if I pray in a tongue, my spirit prays but my mind is unfruitful. What am I to do? I will pray with my spirit, but I will pray with my mind also" (1 Cor 14:14–15).

15. Ibid., 134.

What about Those Who Do Not Speak in Tongues?

However, an irrefutable fact remains that, as hinted earlier, not all believers are to receive this gift, which is what the apostle Paul rhetorically asks the Corinthians who coveted this gift, "Do all speak with tongues?" (1 Cor 12:30b). The answer, of course, is no. But don't those believers who cannot speak in tongues have the disadvantage of not getting the "extra help" to grow spiritually? The answer again is no, because "it is the Spirit who gives life" (John 6:63a), not speaking in tongues. "The words that [Jesus] ha[s] spoken to [us] are spirit and life" (John 6:63b). So I trust that "the Holy Spirit, whom [God] poured out on us richly" (Titus 3:5b–6a), and the intake of God's word are sufficient to promote spiritual growth, so that we "may have life and have it abundantly" (John 10:10b), whether one speaks in tongues or not.

Desiring the Gift of Tongues

Having said that, we must also heed what the apostle Paul additionally writes: "I thank God that I speak in tongues more than all of you" (1 Cor 14:18), "I want you all to speak in tongues" (1 Cor 14:5a), and "earnestly desire the spiritual gifts" (1 Cor 14:1b). So we should encourage people to seek whatever gifts God has for us, including the gift of tongues, or to discover the gifts that were given at our rebirth but have not yet manifested.

Several years ago, a church asked me to teach about the gift of tongues in a meeting organized for that purpose. So, after completing the teaching portion on the matter, I prayed for the attendees to receive the gift of tongues. First, I called for a general time of prayer in which people were told to pray as they normally would and indicate with their hands if they wished to receive the gift of tongues. As I visited each person whose hand was raised, I told the individual, "While you pray, if you sense some unintended words coming out of your mouth, just let them out." I did not know whether anyone had received tongues until, after the meeting, when three people came up to tell me that they did in fact receive the gift of tongues. Having said this, we must be very cautious in promoting spiritual gifts in general and tongues in particular, lest we lose something even more valuable in the process, which is discussed next.

The Downside of Seeking Too Many Spiritual Gifts

In wrapping up this section about desiring the gift of tongues, let me share two stories that tellingly point to a dark side of desiring this gift without moderation or a clear scriptural understanding. In chapter 3, recall the story I told of many youths who were speaking in tongues fervently without the assurance of salvation. What happened there? These youths desired the gift of tongues so much that they lost the sight of its Giver—Jesus Christ—and his redemptive work on the cross. The second story takes place in Acapulco, Mexico, in 2004. I was there to offer a week-long intensive theological course to thirty Mexican pastors belonging to a non-Pentecostal denomination that was nonetheless open to the gifts of the Spirit. During our break, a pastor in his forties asked, "Is it really true what you said, that we can be filled with the Holy Spirit without speaking in tongues?" After hearing my further explanation, this pastor, feeling relieved said, "No one knows that I do not speak in tongues, but I am often asked to pray for people to receive tongues. Your teaching freed me from fear, guilt, and shame."

In light of these two stories, let me reiterate: speaking in tongues, when understood correctly, can be a sign that one believes and is filled with the Spirit; but it is not the only sign; a renewal of spirit, demonstrated through a lifestyle change in words and actions, may be a better indicator (Eph 5:19–21). This matter, too, must be viewed in the Radical Middle of both/and.

CONCLUDING REMARKS ABOUT THE GIFT OF TONGUES

It is sad that those who love the Lord and value his words are engaged in this ongoing conflict over spiritual gifts of all things, at the expense of fracturing the body of Christ and discrediting the church before the world. What I have attempted to do in chapters 6 and 7—amending incorrect biblical understandings held by both cessationists and continuationists regarding the sign gifts in general and tongues in particular—may not be sufficient to restore the fractured church; nevertheless, it is necessary to implicate both sides, as there is enough blame to go around. Therefore, I say to my cessationist brothers to accept tongues both as a linguistic and nonlinguistic spiritual gift from the Lord and to rein in their naturalism under God's word. To my continuationist brothers, I implore them to accept speaking in tongues as well as "addressing one another in psalms" (Eph 5:19a). as evidence of the baptism in the Holy Spirit. And I ask them to please rein in their postmodernist take of the spiritual gifts, in which anything goes on account of the Holy Spirit—including abusive practices—under God's word.

QUESTIONS FOR REFLECTION & DISCUSSION

1. What do you think about the debate over one-stage or two-stage salvation? Feel free to wax theological or philosophical about it.

2. How can we be filled with the Holy Spirit? Do we need to do something? Do we need to stop doing something? Or is it a combination of both?

3. What would you say to those who speak in tongues publicly? (1 Cor 14:33)

4. What spiritual gifts do you believe the Lord has given you? Have you cultivated them?

5. Are you helping the body of Christ with the gifts that you have been given?

8

The Gift of Prophecy
in the Radical Middle

IN THE PREVIOUS CHAPTER, after addressing the deficiencies of several cessationist arguments, including Western-centric and naturalistic missteps that reject the viability of the sign gifts for today, we began a detailed examination of each sign gift, beginning with the gift of tongues. The key finding is that the Bible presents two types of tongues in antithesis: the linguistic tongues featured in Acts 2 and the nonlinguistic tongues spoken by the Corinthians. In the Radical Middle paradigm, both types of tongues are embraced as biblically valid. In this chapter we will examine the gift of prophecy.

TWO KINDS OF PROPHETS?

"Two kinds of prophets?" That's the question MacArthur raises in *Strange Fire*, no doubt because he feels how that question is answered indicates whether one is true to Scripture. MacArthur, clearly disagreeing with Pentecostals and charismatics who believe that there are, in fact, two kinds of prophets, unequivocally declares that such belief "is not biblical."[1] Believing that continuationists invented an additional kind of prophet to justify their unbiblical practices, he says,

---

1. MacArthur, *Strange Fire*, 119.

In an attempt to circumvent the clear-cut parameters of Scripture (and maintain some form of modern prophecy), charismatics are forced to propose there are actually two kinds of prophets described in Scripture—one that was infallible and authoritative, and a second kind that was not.[2]

Contra to this view, the first objective of this section is to help cessationists see that two kinds of prophets stare up at us from the pages of Scripture. The second objective is to tell continuationists to be more cautious, especially with their wording, and take themselves less seriously when they prophesy.

The First Kind of Prophet

So then, according to charismatics and Pentecostals, who is the first kind of prophet? The following is MacArthur's description of how continuationists define them:

> The first category includes Old Testament prophets, New Testament apostles, and the authors of Scriptures. Their prophecies consisted of the perfect transmission of God's words to God's people. As a result, their prophetic proclamations were both error-free and immediately binding on the lives of others.[3]

Would MacArthur disagree with this? Not likely, since the first category of prophet corresponds to those described by the apostle Peter as "men [who] spoke from God as they were carried along by the Holy Spirit" (2 Pet 1:21b), and the biblical writers whom the Holy Spirit inspired (2 Tim 3:16) to produce "prophecy of Scripture" (2 Pet 1:20b).[4] MacArthur calls the divine means through which these prophets and biblical writers received revelation from God as "the revelatory gift of prophecy."[5] The question, then, is whether there is still a need for the revelatory gift of prophecy today. Reformed cessationist Louis Hodges says:

2. Ibid., 118.

3. Ibid., 118–19.

4. On the one hand, some biblical writers whom the Spirit inspired to pen different books of the Bible and the prophets who spoke from God are one and the same person, such as Isaiah and Daniel. On the other hand, the same cannot be said about the writers of historical books, such as Kings in the Old Testament and Acts in the New Testament, since they were inspired to chronicle, for the most part, accounts of what others did and said.

5. Ibid., 126.

> Most Reformed theologians agree with Gaffin's assessment that
> prophecy is a revelatory gift in the New Testament; it involves
> the receipt of direct revelation which God intends to be given
> to his people. An important result of the completion of the New
> Testament canon and the former ways of God's revealing him-
> self having ceased, is the absolute sufficiency of Scripture which
> negates both the need and place for new or private revelation
> today.[6]

Reformed theologian Richard Gaffin maintains that since the prophetic gifts functioned as part of "the apostolic founding of the church"—
with the completion of the canon being the key to that process—once the
church was founded and the canon closed, there was no longer a need for
such gifts.[7] Of course, MacArthur would agree with this Reformed position, for he declares, "*God's revelation is complete for now. The canon of
Scripture is closed*"[8] (italics his). So for cessationists, the terms "inspired,"
"canon" (i.e., those books recognized as authoritative for having met the
divine standard), "revelatory," and "direct revelation" are reserved only
for the first category of prophets whose prophecies became Scripture.
This means that there should not be anymore inspired prophets running
around today, proclaiming more direct revelation from God. And this
is one main reason MacArthur recoils at Pentecostals and charismatics
because some of them "claim to have received a direct revelation from
God."[9] Is this a fair assessment? We will evaluate it later.

The Second Kind of Prophet

Who then is the second kind of prophet, according to charismatics
and Pentecostals? MacArthur states, "Charismatics contend there was
a second tier of prophets in the New Testament church: congregational
prophets who spoke a form of prophecy that was *fallible* and *nonauthori-
tative*, and that came into existence in the New Testament times"[10] (italics
his). Although MacArthur is not amused by this additional category of

---

6. Gaffin, *Perspective on Pentecost*, 59, 72, cited in Hodges, *Reformed Theology Today*, 112.

7. Gaffin, "Cessationist View," 61.

8. MacArthur, *Charismatic Chaos*, 71.

9. MacArthur, *Strange Fire*, 109.

10. Ibid., 119.

"second tier of prophets" and calls it unbiblical, proving their existence in both Testaments is not hard to do.

BIBLICAL CASE FOR THE SECOND KIND OF PROPHET

Let me begin the probe with this question: Is there any direct revelation given to humanity through the revelatory gift of prophecy that is not included in the canon of Scripture? That question was settled a long time ago when the early church canonized twenty-seven books as the New Testament to go along with thirty-nine books of the Old Testament. The church, then, still valued several Christian literatures that were excluded from Scripture, such as *Didache* and *The Shepherd of Hermas,* but none of them (in time, for some) were considered inspired or canonical.

The correct response, therefore, is a resounding no since all direct revelation that God has ever given to humanity through the first kind of prophet is in the canon of the Bible, otherwise known as prophecy of Scripture. So I will call this canonical prophecy.

Having said that, does Scripture present a category of noncanonical prophecy? Yes, for it is evident that both testaments present prophecies that are not part of direct revelation from God. How so? There are several individuals who appear in the Bible who prophesied, but we do not know what they said because none of their prophecies are recorded in Scripture. Craig Keener notes that "a survey of the prophets mentioned in the historical books of the Old Testament reveals that most of them, in fact, did not write Scripture."[11] I would add the Pentateuch to that list as well.

Meaning what? Their prophetic words were neither inspired nor canonical, otherwise they would have been included in books that the early church later recognized as inspired and canonical. At least the content of *Didache* and *The Shepherd of Hermas,* noncanonical books that supplemented Christian education in the early church, was known, but no one knows what was said when these noncanonical prophecies were uttered since their content is omitted from the Bible.

---

11. Keener, "Are Spiritual Gifts for Today?," 158. Saucy also recognizes this, saying, "Clearly both the Old and New Testaments indicate that there were many prophecies that were never included in the canonical Scriptures." Saucy, "Open but Cautious View," 68.

So Many to Choose from

Once we have the category of noncanonical prophecy that is not part of Scripture, recognizing the second type of prophet in the Bible is not hard to do. Consider the following three cases selected from many.

Saul (from Historical Books)

Let's begin with Saul in the Old Testament, who prophesied before becoming the king of Israel. First Samuel 10:11 (NIV) says, "When all those who had formerly known him saw him prophesying with the prophets, they asked each other, 'What is this that has happened to the son of Kish? Is Saul also among the prophets?'" Saul also prophesied as king: One day, "he stripped off his his robes and also prophesied in Samuel's presence. He lay that way all that day and night. That is why people say, 'Is Saul also among the prophets?'" (1 Sam 19:24 NIV). But none of the prophetic words Saul spoke were inspired or canonical, since they were not included in the prophecy of Scripture; neither was any new direct revelation given when Saul prophesied.

The Seventy Elders (from the Pentateuch)

The same holds true for the seventy elders under Moses, who writes this about them:

> Then the Lord came down in the cloud and spoke with [Moses], and he took some of the power of the Spirit that was on him and put it on the seventy elders. When the Spirit rested on them, they prophesied—but did not do so again. However, two men, whose names were Eldad and Medad, had remained in the camp. They were listed among the elders, but did not go out to the tent. Yet the Spirit also rested on them, and they prophesied in the camp. (Num 11:25–26)

With respect to what these elders prophesied, which is not included in Scripture, was it part of the revelatory gift of prophecy? Of course not.

Returning to the narrative, something interesting happens. Like cessationists getting upset at continuationists for prophesying today,

> Joshua son of Nun, who had been Moses' aide since youth, spoke up and said, "Moses, my lord, stop them!" But Moses replied,

"Are you jealous for my sake? I wish that all the Lord's people were prophets and that the Lord would put his Spirit on them!" (Num 11:27–28 NIV).

Does this sound like Moses expected thousands of the Lord's people—whom he wished would prophesy—to join the ranks of the first kind of prophet whose inspired writing became Scripture? Unless there is a second category of prophet, the answer has to be yes by default. But of course what Saul or the seventy elders prophesied was neither inspired nor canonical; nevertheless, what they said were prophecies—not of the first kind, but the second (defined later).

It is also interesting to note what Moses says here: "I wish that all the Lord's people were prophets," which resonates with what Paul would say 1,500 years later to the Corinthian believers: "Now I want you all to speak in tongues, but even more to prophesy" (1 Cor 14:5a).

Silas and Judas (from the New Testament)

The pattern of people uttering noncanonical prophecy continues into the New Testament. This kind of prophecy was no doubt helpful to the church, but none of it became part of Scripture. Consider what happens in Acts 15. "Some men came down from Judea to Antioch and were teaching the brothers: 'Unless you are circumcised, according to the custom taught by Moses, you cannot be saved'" (Acts 15:1 NIV). In response, "Paul and Barnabas were appointed . . . to go up to Jerusalem to see the apostles and elders about this question" (Acts 15:2b NIV). Later, after much discussion, Peter says, "We believe that we will be saved through the grace of the Lord Jesus, just as they will" (Acts 15:11). Then a letter is drafted by the apostles and elders that explains their decision. Since the entire letter is recorded in Acts 15:23–29 as part of the inspired Scripture, its content came by way of the revelatory gift of prophecy. The letter then is taken to Antioch by Judas and Silas "where they gathered the church together and delivered the letter" (Acts 15:30b NIV). After it is read, Judas and Silas have more to say to the Antioch believers. Luke writes, "And when they had read it, they rejoiced because of its encouragement. And Judas and Silas, who were themselves prophets, encouraged and strengthened the brothers with many words" (Acts 15:31–32).

So what prophetic words were said by the two? No one knows, since Luke was *not* "moved by the Holy Spirit" (2 Pet 1:21b NASB) to record them in Acts. Meaning what? The "many words" Judas and Silas said prophetically were neither canonical nor inspired by the Spirit; that is, no new or direct revelation from God was given to the church through them.

Biblicality of the Second Kind of Prophet

What does this all mean? The prophetic words uttered by Saul and the seventy elders in the Old Testament and by Judas and Silas in the New Testament, point to the existence of two kinds of prophecy and prophets in Scripture. Consider what Robert Saucy, a cessationist theologian at the time of writing (1972), says about the prophetic ministry of Judas and Silas. He writes:

> The primary function of the prophets was to bring God's message to the early church for the purpose of edification (1 Cor 14:3–4). This was done either through bringing new truth, or by giving insight into truth which was already known. Judas and Silas are seen as prophets exhorting "the brethren with many words" upon the occasion of bringing the decision of the Jerusalem council to Antioch. This action was probably characteristic of the prophets' function in the church. It does not appear that they were used as the apostles to bring permanent revelation but, rather, a message from God to meet the needs of the immediate situation of the church.[12]

Before proceeding, understand that new truth or permanent revelation imparted by God and attained through the revelatory gift of prophecy refers to all that is included in the canon of Scripture. That recognition will help to answer this question: How many types of prophets does Saucy see in the early church? He in effect identifies two. The first type of prophet was one who brought new and permanent truth; this refers to direct revelation from God that became Scripture. The second type Saucy identifies is one who "g[ave] insight into truth already known" which no doubt refers to Scripture.[13] The insight itself was neither canonical nor inspired by the Spirit since it never became part of the canon of the Bible.

12. Saucy, *Church in God's Program*, 138–39.

13. Admittedly, when Luke was writing Acts in the early 60s AD, not all revelations that would eventually be included in the New Testament had been given. Nevertheless, the early church, in addition to upholding the Old Testament as Scripture, was aware of, though they had not formerly declared, which extant writings were divinely authoritative (Col 4:16). What is said in the Muratorian Canon of Rome in the second

Two Types of Prophets and Prophecy

To introduce new terms as a matter of clarification, the following redundant question is raised: Do two kinds of prophecies in Scripture necessarily mean that there are two types of prophets in the New Testament? Yes. One type is those exercising the revelatory gift of prophecy, such as Paul and Peter, who received new and permanent revelation that became Scripture. I would classify them as "primary prophets" and their inspired writings as "primary prophecy." The other type is prophets like Judas and Silas who never received new and permanent revelation, but whose message was nonetheless from God "to meet the needs of," according to Saucy, "the immediate situation of the church." I would identify them as "secondary (i.e., congregational) prophets" and their noninspired prophetic words as "secondary (i.e., congregational) prophecy." From this point on the terms "primary and secondary prophet/prophecy" will replace "first and second kinds of prophets/prophecy."

Does Paul Mean Primary or Secondary Prophecy in 1 Corinthians 14?

One place where the apostle Paul talks extensively about prophecy is 1 Corinthians 14. Paul opens the chapter by telling the Corinthians to "earnestly desire the spiritual gifts, especially that [they] may prophesy" (1 Cor 14:1). He then adds, "I want you all . . . even more to prophesy" (1 Cor 14:5a), "you can all prophesy one by one" (1 Cor 14:31a), "earnestly desire to prophesy" (1 Cor 14:39a). What are we to make of Paul's expressed desire for the Corinthians? Are we to assume that he expected new, permanent, and direct revelation to be the outcome of what amounts to secondary or congregational prophecy in the Corinth church? Of course not! It was, nevertheless, prophecy; it is just that this type of prophecy, unlike primary prophecy, was neither inspired nor canonical.

---

century shows the high level of awareness and concerns that the early church had in regard to the canonicity of Scripture: "There are extant also a letter to the Laodiceans and another to Alexandrians, forged under Paul's name to further the heresy of Marcion. And there are many others which cannot be received into the Catholic Church. For it is not fitting for gall to be mixed with honey." Bettenson, *Documents of the Christian Church*, 29.

Two Types of Prophets and Prophecy in the Radical Middle

Speaking hermeneutically, I do not understand how MacArthur, a gifted Bible teacher, can say, "When all the passages regarding prophecy in the New Testament are considered, the charismatic position is immediately exposed as baseless and unbiblical," when 1 Corinthians 14, which contains words related to "prophecy" fourteen times (ESV), is ignored in chapter 6 of *Strange Fire*, which addresses prophecy.[14] At the least, he should have let us know his take on 1 Corinthians 14:29, which indicates that the kind of prophecy practiced in Corinth was not always correct (explained later). What does this omission imply? It indicates that when the Bible is *not* allowed to speak for itself, given that it is read through the rose-tinted spectacles of systematic theology (in this case, hard cessationism), we only see what we want to see through the hermeneutics of logocentrism of either/or. To cessationists, prophecy is either a revelatory gift through which direct revelation that became Scripture is received, or there is nothing else—that is, no other kind of prophecy. And any scriptural evidence to the contrary is simply ignored.

However, when Scripture is interpreted through the hermeneutics of the Radical Middle of both/and, one can readily see that the Bible presents two kinds of prophets, each imparting prophecies that are related (explained later) but not identical to each other. In fact, they are antithetic to each other in that while primary prophecy is inspired, canonical, and revelatory, secondary prophecy is just the opposite: not inspired, not canonical, and not revelatory—meaning, no new truth is given through it. But, the relationship between the two types of prophecy is an antimony. Recall what Packer says about antinomy: "It is not a real contradiction, though it looks like one. It is an *apparent* incompatibility between two apparent truths . . . seemingly irreconcilable, yet both undeniable"[15] (italics his). He reminds us not to "get rid of it, save by falsifying the very facts that led us to it."[16] I am afraid that is what hard cessationism has done by falsifying—that is, ignoring—Scriptures that clearly delineate secondary

---

14. MacArthur, *Strange Fire*, 126. He does refer to 1 Corinthians 14 once on page 121, but not in a substantial way. He merely adds part of 1 Corinthians 14:3 in a sentence to say that prophecy, as speaking forth God's truth, "*speaks edification and exhortation and comfort of men*" (the italicized words from 1 Corinthians 14:3).

15. Packer, *Evangelism and the Sovereignty of God*, 18.

16. Ibid., 21.

or congregational prophecy in addition to primary or the revelatory gift of prophecy.

On the contrary, in the pneumatology of the Radical Middle, both primary and secondary prophecy are fully embraced, meaning that they are believed and practiced (but not always well) accordingly. For that to happen we need to have a better understanding of secondary or congregational prophecy and how it relates to the revelatory gift of primary prophecy. Recall how Packer, with respect to handling antinomy, puts it:

> Think of the two principles as, not rival alternatives, but . . . complementary to each other . . . Note what connections exist between the two truths and their two frames of reference, and teach yourself to think of reality in a way that provides for their peaceful coexistence . . . This is how antinomies must be handled.[17]

Taking a cue from Packer, what follows is an attempt to provide a peaceful coexistence between the two categories of prophecy delineated in Scripture.

DIFFERENCES BETWEEN PRIMARY AND SECONDARY PROPHECY

Despite the case for two kinds of prophets that has been presented in a straightforward manner, many cessationists I am sure are still not convinced. So what concerns them about accepting the two types of prophets/prophecy and makes them ignore what seems evident in Scripture? Their concerns can best be addressed by way of showing differences between the two kinds of prophecy in terms of their origin, understanding of forthtelling/foretelling, purpose, and margin of error.

Differences in the Origin

As for the origin of prophecy, the essential difference between the two is whether the prophecy is given directly or indirectly from God. And this has big implications.

17. Ibid., 21.

Primary Prophecy: Directly from God

The first kind, the revelatory prophecy, that yielded new truth and permanent revelation which then became inspired Scripture, came *directly* from God. This implies that since the New Testament canon has long been completed, there is no more direct revelation from God and no more prophets who receive them today. But since Pentecostals and charismatics typically preface their prophetic words by saying, "Thus says the Lord," which in the Old Testament was always followed by direct revelation from God, their words, in effect, claim equality with Scripture. And as long as Pentecostals and charismatics do that, thereby taking themselves too seriously, they bear much responsibility for criticisms leveled by concerned cessationists.

Secondary Prophecy: Indirectly from God

On the other hand, with respect to those New Testament prophets who, according to Saucy, gave "insight into truth which was already known" but they themselves gave no new truth, what was said was *indirectly* given by God (thus making it secondary prophecy). What is helpful here is the concept of forthtelling, which simply means "to speak forth" and not foretelling (making predictions). But, speak forth from what? The answer to that is Scripture, the inspired writings of primary prophets who spoke directly from God. Since secondary prophets speak forth from Scripture, it seems reasonable to say that their prophecies came indirectly from God. This is not to say, however, that cessationists and continuationists think alike about forthtelling, which is discussed next.

I think this is a good place to present a definition of "secondary" or "congregational prophecy" (a.k.a., the gift of prophecy): it is Scripture, a thought, a word, or an image[18] in our minds that is spontaneously prompted by the Holy Spirit, giving us insight into a certain scriptural truth that would, as Saucy says, "meet the needs of the immediate situa-

18. For those who might balk at this, isn't it true that prophets like Jeremiah (1:11–12) and Ezekiel (1:4–28) saw vivid images from the Lord? To those who may say, "Those images were given as part of direct revelation that became Scripture," my reply is this: the fulfillment of the promise given to Joel on the day of Pentecost includes young men seeing visions and old men dreaming dreams (Acts 2:17b). Suffice it to say, these are not canonical or inspired visions and dreams since none of them have been and will be added to Scripture. It stands to reason that these experiences are normative, more or less, for all believers in whom resides the Holy Spirit.

tion of the church." By church, it could mean an entire congregation or individual believers in whom the Holy Spirit resides (more on this later).

Theologically, I would reason that the Holy Spirit, having been deposited in our hearts (2 Cor 1:22), "knows the thoughts of God" (1 Cor 2:11 NIV) and then "bears witness with our spirit" (Rom 8:16) to give us "what to say" (Matt 10:19b NIV); and we say this in accordance with diverse manners through which individuals express themselves. These are human words describing the thoughts originating from the Holy Sprit from within. Thus, I would not agree with those continuationists who see secondary or congregational prophecy as the "Spirit taking over and speaking directly from Christ through you, in words that you had never intended to use at all."[19] This definition comes dangerously close to being the revelatory gift of primary prophecy that produced Scripture.

Differences in Forthtelling Between Cessationists and Continuationists

Cessationists might find it odd that a continuationist would stress the importance of forthtelling when talking about prophecy, since they are alarmed by the perception that continuationists claim to receive new revelation from God ("Thus says the Lord") and advocate foretelling.

The truth is that what cessationists mean by forthtelling is not the same as what continuationists mean by the same term.

Forthtelling According to Cessationists

For cessationists, the forthtelling aspect of prophecy is, according to MacArthur, "any authoritative proclamation of God's Word."[20] In all fairness, this view is not entirely without merit, since the reason the Bible is called "prophecy of Scripture" (2 Pet 1:20b) is because it is the outcome of the revelatory gift of prophecy; therefore, it can be reasoned that when pastors speak forth from the Bible (i.e., forthtelling), they are being *prophetic*. And this is why Saucy says (and which MacArthur agrees) that "the ministry of the prophets . . . was taken by the regular local ministry

---

19. Green, *I Believe in the Holy Spirit*, 171
20. MacArthur, *Strange Fire*, 121.

of pastor-teachers."[21] So, to cessationists, there are no more prophets to-day because they have been replaced by pastors and Bible teachers.

Forthtelling According to Continuationists

But, there is one major difference between the cessationist version of forthtelling and that of continuationists: the role of the Spirit. Recall that, according to Saucy, secondary prophets like Judas and Silas gave insight into truth already known "to meet the needs of the immediate situation of the church."[22] What does this imply? Unlike pastors who forthtell God's word with a *prepared* sermon based on Scripture, people operating in the gift of prophecy forthtell in a *spontaneous* manner, which is what meeting *immediate* needs implies.

Now, this does not necessarily mean that the Spirit is involved beyond how we typically attribute his role in our lives. For instance, imagine a situation in which someone with a dire need just told you about her circumstance, so you immediately informed the church to address it. Is the Spirit involved in this type of situation? Yes, of course: whether small or big things, it is "not by might, nor by power, but by my Spirit, says the Lord of hosts" (Zech 4:6b).

Nonetheless, is it also possible to sense the dire need of a brother or sister without being told, that is, you suddenly sense something—a Scripture, word, phrase, or image? If this is true, then can such spiritual sensitivity be attributed to the prompting of the Holy Spirit? Consider Matthew 10:19–20, where Jesus says,

> When they deliver you over, do not be anxious how you are to speak or what you are to say, for what you are to say will be given to you in that hour. For it is not you who speak, but the Spirit of your Father speaking through you.

This situation and my hypothetical situation are alike in the sense that what is said to a friend in need or persecutor is done in an impromptu manner; it is not something rehearsed beforehand. Keep in mind that this is not a situation in which the gift of revelatory prophecy is at work to produce a new and permanent revelation that will become part of Scripture. Instead, this is a case of spontaneous forthtelling, prompted

21. Saucy, *Church in God's Program*, 139. Saucy's entire quote is cited later when making a different point.

22. Ibid.,138–39

by the Spirit, not from a prepared sermon, but from God's word and its principles committed to one's memory or consciousness. Jesus puts it this way: "But the helper, the Holy Spirit, whom the Father will send in my name, he will teach you all things and bring to your remembrance all that I have said to you" (John 14:26). But, unlike sermons, these are unrehearsed words spontaneously shared with those who have an urgent need to hear such things. And if this sort of prophecy is spurred by a genuine prompting of the Spirit, then what is said will give insight into truth that is already known—the Scriptures.

I can just imagine many cessationists feeling uncomfortable because they assume that forthtelling prompted by the Spirit is tantamount to hearing the literal voice of God. For instance, consider the viewpoint of radio Christian host Greg Koukl, whose "Stand to Reason" ministry (based in California) has ably defended the Christian faith for many years. In criticizing *Experiencing God*, a popular course designed to help people know and do the will of God on the premise that he still speaks to individual believers, Koukl says:

> Does the Holy Spirit speak to our hearts? That depends entirely on what one means by the word "speak" . . . The Bible doesn't teach we must "hear" God before we can make decisions. It's just not there. When the text says, "Listen to the voice of the Lord," the word "listen" is synonymous with "heed." It's much like a mother saying, "Listen to me when I tell you to do something." It's an appeal for obedience . . . We should seek God's "voice" in the place Scripture tells us to: the word. Spiritual maturity is not the ability to hear God's voice. It's the ability to know, understand, and apply Scripture in every circumstance . . . Must I hear the voice of God and receive personalized direction—special assignments for my life? . . . I'm not dictating what God can or can't do. He can intervene in any way he chooses. However, we must base our teaching and conduct on the Scriptures, not on what might be possible for a sovereign God.[23]

As I was reading this, I was reminded of an argument with my wife over some spiritual matters which turned personal and made me feel self-righteous. On the third day of still feeling this way, while I was praying, these words—"Be not overly righteous"—suddenly entered into my consciousness. That short phrase, which I read many times, is from Ecclesiastes 7:16a. To put it scripturally, the Holy Spirit testified with my

---

23. Koukl, "Experiencing God," 7.

spirit (Rom 8:16) and reminded me (John 14:26) that I was being an arrogant fool; furthermore, the Spirit gave me "what to say" (Matt 10:19b NIV). So I stopped praying and immediately apologized to my wife with *my* words that expressed what the Spirit revealed to me that day through Ecclesiastes 7:16a. What happened? Word and Spirit worked side by side to produce repentance and obedience in me. In other words, I heeded the voice of God, and as a result grew spiritually in humility and love which led to a restoration of marital unity. And since the said critic of *Experiencing God* also writes, "I'm not claiming there's no subjective element in knowing God . . . my principal concern is where we get our information about God,"[24] he should not have any problem with my encounter since what I obtained from the Spirit was a Scripture.

What Forthtelling Prompted by the Spirit Looks Like in Real Life

Here is another true story that shows how forthtelling prompted by the Spirit works; ironically, this involved someone who does not believe in secondary or congregational prophecy.

You already met Pastor Javier, the senior pastor of Jerusalem Baptist Church that my family and I attended for eight years in Chihuahua, Mexico. He made such a moving statement at the close of one Sunday service that it led to examining whether I was truly depending on God in my ministry. Javier, seeking to encourage his congregants to come and pray on Wednesday nights, said, "Those who come to mid-week prayer services are not the most spiritual but the most needy." Because this remark very much moved me, and because I was teaching on prophecy at that time, I later asked Javier whether he had prepared to say that. "No," he said, "it was a thought that came to me at the spur of the moment." Being

24. Ibid., 7.

somewhat coy, I asked my friend, "Would you say the thought came from you or the Holy Spirit?" After a pause (perhaps sensing where I was going with this), he said, "The Spirit." Then I said to Javier: "You do not need to call what you said prophetic since that makes you feel uncomfortable. However, it seems to me that the Spirit prompted you to share insight into truth already known, like 'My house shall be called a house of prayer' (Matt 21:13a), or 'Out of the depths I cry to you, O Lord!' (Ps 130:1a), with spontaneous words to meet the urgent needs of your church." This Baptist pastor did not disagree. After all, isn't that what Jesus promised to the persecuted who have an urgent need for apt words to defend their faith before the persecutors? "For what you are to say will be given to you in that hour. For it is not you who speak, but the Spirit of your Father speaking through you" (Matt 10:19b–20). I truly hope no one says that this promise applies only to the persecuted.

While Javier's spontaneous words were addressing the collective needs of the church to pray corporately (as many members were facing challenging issues at the time), my personal needs were also being met. The truth was that I saw myself more as a missionary who was sent to meet the needs of pastors, than as one with *real* spiritual needs. So when I felt overwhelmed with preparations for my daily classes, I would skip Wednesday prayer meetings (something personally important) to prepare, often feeling justified since it was God's work, and since I would always spend a prolonged period of time in prayer every morning. But Javier's spontaneous words gave insight into truth which I already knew but needed to be reminded of. That is, I was reminded of Martha—one who was "distracted with much serving" and complaining about her sister who sat at the Lord's feet listening to him—to whom Jesus said, "But one thing is necessary. Mary has chosen the good portion, which will not be taken away from her" (Luke 10:38–42). Martha needed to be with Jesus just as much as Mary, but her commitment to serve slowly ebbed away Martha's need for Christ. That was me (and still is). Having been given insight into truth already known through the Spirit's prompting of Pastor Javier, my urgent spiritual need was exposed and met. So I came to church that Wednesday evening to pray, despite having much to do that evening, as an expression of my need to depend on Christ. And I grew spiritually, having been reminded of the need to depend on the Lord, as a result—in word and Spirit.

Differences in Foretelling Between Cessationists and Continuationists

As for foretelling, that is, predicting the future, the gap between continuationists and cessationists is even greater, since the latter simply do not believe in it. Their case is further emboldened by many predictions that have not come true. The effects of missed predictions are not quite what Paul told the Israelites in Rome, who said one thing and did another—"The name of God is blasphemed among the gentiles because of you" (Rom 2:24)—but it certainly provides fodder for skeptics and critics of Christianity. On this matter, continuationists, heeding what is a legitimate concern of cessationists, ought to be very cautious with their predictions. In the following section, some general guidelines for foretelling are extracted from two cases of foretelling, one that was fulfilled and one that was not.

A Failed Foretelling

In the previous chapter, I mentioned what a female visitor to my house told my wife and me: "I received words from the Lord that earthquakes are about to happen in China and Tanzania." In all honesty I felt skeptical, but there was no *biblical* reason for me to doubt her words because, although most secondary or congregational prophecies consist of forthtelling, some can be foretelling (e.g., Agabus in Acts 11:28). But I do not think I was in the wrong to tell this woman to warn the Chinese and Tanzanian consulates about what she believed was going to happen. Is that not one reason why prophetic words are given: To serve as a warning? (Ezek 33). Nevertheless, the fact that she had no desire to do so and fell into a trance through which she had God tell me to have more faith, had the effect of making her prophecy less credible (though not entirely illegitimate). Eventually when the said earthquakes never materialized, I figured my visitor had it wrong. Yes, people can be wrong—that is the premise of 1 Corinthians 14:29: "Let two or three prophets speak, and let the others weigh what is said."

A Successful Foretelling

Having said that, foretelling does happen, as is evident in the following story involving a Mexican missionary to India. He first shared this with me in 2009 and I recently confirmed it in 2018.

In 2004, Agustin Jimenez, a first-term Assemblies of God missionary based in Chihuahua, was busy visiting churches to raise support before leaving for India in 2005. While visiting a church in the nearby city of Delicias, the host pastor told Jimenez, out of the blue, "In India a Samaritan will show you the way." Agustin, who was once my student, told me he had no idea what that meant.

Fast forward four years, to 2008. By now Jimenez and his family had been in India for four years, mostly to learn the language and to prepare for a second missionary term by trying to discern what his next phase should consist of. So, after learning about the Tharu people and praying about working with them, he went to northeastern India, bordering Nepal, to speak to a long-time German missionary operating an orphanage there to inquire about the prospect of working with the Tharu people. While the German missionary was telling Agustin that he should speak to a Tharu pastor named Lok Bahadur who comes to the orphanage every six months, Bahadur suddenly appeared. (I guess it had been six months since his last visit.) When they sat down to talk, the first thing Pastor Bahadur said to Jimenez about his people was, "We are like the Samaritan people; we are poor and oppressed!" At that point, Agustin remembered what was said to him four years earlier: "In India, a Samaritan will show you the way." What happened? The prophetic words uttered in 2004 confirmed the ministry that the Lord had prepared for missionary Agustin Jimenez.

Therefore, he used his furlough spent in Mexico to prepare himself to train and disciple the Tharu pastors in his second term through using my courses. I was happy to be a small part of what God was doing through this Mexican missionary whose future work had been prophetically foreshadowed four years earlier. So Agustin returned to India in 2009 for his second term during which time he worked with the Tharu pastors until 2013. After returning home on his second furlough, he and his family could not return to India because of visa problems. But, according to Agustin, numerous Tharu pastors whom he trained are doing quite well in ministry.[25]

Remember, no new or permanent revelation was proclaimed. There are two key concepts in this story that are based on truth already known: first, the pastor in Delicias did not invent Samaritans, an oppressed group disliked by the Israelites that fit well with the Tharu people; second, discipleship, as Agustin was planning to do, is always God's will.

General Guidelines for Foretelling

In light of both stories told here about the failed prophet and Agustin, I would advise would-be foretellers to be measured in their words and not speak with absolute certainty (e.g., no "Thus says the Lord"). And if they truly believe in their predictions, they should follow through by their actions. So if one is predicting an earthquake in such and such areas, then that person should warn those who live there. If they are unwilling to do this and are consistently wrong in their predictions, they should stop attempting to predict the future and focus more on "speak[ing] five words with [their] mind in order to instruct others" (1 Cor 14:19), rather than dismay people with incorrect foretelling. This is to say, I would rather that would-be prophets do less foretelling and do more Spirit-prompted forthtelling—that is, spontaneously giving insight into scriptural truth in such a manner that the immediate needs of the church and people are met.

---

25. Agustin confirmed the entire story told here in a telephone called made on April 22, 2018. He also graciously allowed me to use these photos for this publication. He is currently working with Tarahumara Indians in Chihuahua.

Differences in the Purpose of the Two Types of Prophecy

Addressing differences in the purpose and margin of error between the two types of prophecy is necessary to adequately respond to the cessationist charge that so-called prophetic words spoken today constitute new and permanent revelation. In the next two sections, let me explain why this accusation is simply biblically untrue.

To Encourage

The purpose of primary prophets has been articulated numerous times: to receive new and permanent revelations from God that would become "prophecy of Scripture" (2 Pet 1:20b). I need not add anything more than what has already been said on this matter.

As for secondary or congregational prophets, the purpose for their ministry is clearly spelled out in Scripture. The apostle Paul tells the Corinthian congregation, "The one who prophesies speaks to people for their upbuilding and encouragement and consolation" (1 Cor 14:3). This is exactly how "Judas and Silas, who were themselves prophets" also affected the Antiochian congregation with their prophetic words: They "encouraged and strengthened the brothers with many words" (Acts 15:32).

What Being Encouraged by Prophetic Words Looks Like in Real Life

I know what it feels like to be encouraged as a result of receiving prophetic words because I received a terse prophetic message a year after I had come to Chihuahua to serve as a missionary.

One morning in 2002, feeling frustrated over not having many ministry opportunities at the outset of serving in Mexico, I prayed, "Lord, when do I leave here?" A few hours later, an elderly woman, whom I did not know, called me and said, "I want to share a word from the Lord. He said that you ought to stay here in Chihuahua."[26] Yes, I was shocked at hearing what this anonymous woman said to me. Later, I shared her words with my wife to, in effect, weigh what was said, even though believ-

---

26. Georgina Pérez V., email sent to author, June 3, 2006. I discovered her identity in 2005, about three years after her call in 2002. Then, in her email sent to me in 2006, Mrs. Pérez made a reference to that call, saying, "*Hace bastante tiempo yo hablé por teléfono para darle una palabra del Señor que decía que usted permaneciera aquí en Chihuahua.*" (Its translation is in the text.)

ing that the thought expressed through this woman's words came from the Spirit was easy, especially considering what I had prayed earlier that day. And I was so encouraged because her words gave me fresh insight into Galatians 6:9: "And let us not grow weary of doing good, for in due season we will reap, if we do not give up." And that's how Agustin felt when he heard from the Tharu pastor, "We are like the Samaritan people; we are poor and oppressed." In both cases, these prophetic words based on truth already known confirmed our call to missions.

Notice that while no new or permanent revelation was given to me, what the Spirit prompted this woman to say was based on prophecy of Scripture. Recall what a Macedonian man told a wavering Paul in a dream, "Come over to Macedonia and help us" (Acts 16:9b). Based on that permanent revelation, would it be wrong to say that the Lord met my urgent needs that day by way of providing directions? So, whereas Paul went to Macedonia (westward) instead of Bithynia (eastward), I ended up staying put in Chihuahua for another nine years. Although nothing changed for me that day with regards to increased ministry, I felt much more hopeful about my future. It was as if God were saying, "You are there because it is my will; be patient because you are going to be really busy for me." And that's how my missionary journey would unfold in Mexico as the Lord used me to train hundreds of pastors, missionaries, and church leaders all over Mexico, while producing various theological materials for them to use in their churches and schools. In looking back, there is little doubt in my mind that that prophetic phone call from an unknown Christian woman was the turning point in my ministry.

Differences in the Margin of Error

Another means to show the difference between primary and secondary prophecy is addressing the margin of error. What does this mean? While primary prophecy that led to canonical Scripture had no margin of error, the apostle Paul assumed that secondary prophecy could be erroneous, and this is what bothers MacArthur.

What MacArthur is Unwilling to Recognize

MacArthur is troubled by the teaching that presents the first kind of prophet (the primary) as "infallible and authoritative and a second kind that was not."[27] Thus, what cessationists get hung up on is that "charismatics may claim that New Testament prophets were not held to the same standard as their Old Testament counterparts."[28] MacArthur, finding "such an assertion [to be] entirely without warrant,"[29] says, "The true prophetic office demanded 100 percent accuracy. Insofar as they declared a new revelation from God to the church, New Testament prophets were held to that standard."[30] Of course, I agree completely with this, as long as we are talking about primary prophecy that became "prophecy of Scripture" (2 Pet 1:20b).

Now, since cessationists do not acknowledge the existence of secondary prophets, it is difficult to appeal to them with the following point because it is about secondary prophecy. But if the premise of two types of prophecy is accepted, then one can readily see that the margin of error allowed in secondary or congregational prophecy, addressed in 1 Corinthians 14, is higher than the one imposed on primary prophecy that became Scripture; in fact, absolutely no margin of error was tolerated for the latter. To that end Moses states:

> But the prophet who presumes to speak a word in my name that
> I have not commanded him to speak, or who speaks in the name
> of other gods, that same prophet shall die. And if you say in your
> heart, "How may we know the word that the Lord has not spo-
> ken?"—when a prophet speaks in the name of the Lord, if the
> word does not come to pass or come true, that is a word that the

27. MacArthur, *Strange Fire,* 118.
28. Ibid., 119.
29. Ibid., 119.
30. Ibid., 129.

Lord has not spoken; the prophet has spoken it presumptuously. You need not be afraid of him. (Deut. 18:20–22)

Evidently, with respect to primary prophecy, 100 percent accuracy was demanded. And the punishment in the Old Testament for false prophecy was severe enough to serve as a strong deterrent for potential false prophets. But this simply is not the case with respect to secondary prophecy presented in 1 Corinthians 14. So what does Paul say?

What Paul Says about the Accuracy of Secondary Prophecy

One way to address the margin of error regarding secondary or congregational prophecy and the need to discern an accurate one from an inaccurate one is to consider another criticism leveled at continuationists—this one by someone who actually recognizes the gift of prophecy but does not like its widespread practice. Dealing with this criticism allows us to see Paul's assumption that the margin of error is part and parcel of secondary prophecy, which therefore would require quality control.

Greg Koukl, the previously mentioned critic of *Experiencing God*, says:

> Historically, first-person private revelation has been reserved to a very select group of people: prophets, Jesus Christ, the apostles, or those with unique gifts in the body of Christ. In each case, first-private revelation is given to a properly qualified select few who then pass it on to the rest of the church to study it in a third-personal public way. The main thesis of *Experiencing God* is that this kind of special revelation isn't unique, but meant to be an ordinary part of every Christian's life . . . I'm not questioning the possibility of God working through gifted people, like prophets. Yes, I believe such things are possible, biblically. That some are given the gift of prophecy or knowledge is not a debate for me. But should everybody be a prophet, receiving God's word directly? No.[31]

Notice two things here: First, Koukl sees that prophecy, at the outset, is first-person private revelation, after which it is to be shared with others (third-person public). I agree since the apostle Paul stipulates that

---

31. Koukl, "What's Wrong with 'Experiencing God?,'" 1–2, 5. This article, which I accessed from the Stand to Reason website on September 20, 1998, appears to have been removed since the link is dead. The citation here is based on a downloaded copy of this blog.

"the one who prophesies builds up the church" (1 Cor 14:4b). This cannot be done unless what is received privately is shared publicly. That is why Paul, while prescribing what a typical worship service should include, writes, "When you come together . . . let two or three prophets speak" (1 Cor 14:26a, 29a). This depicts ordinary believers sharing in "a third-person public way" what was initially a first-person private revelation. How many people are needed to constitute this third-person public way? It may be a roomful of people or just one other person (e.g., like your Christian spouse), since Jesus says, "For where two or three are gathered in my name, there am I among them" (Matt 18:20).

Second, Koukl believes that while God still speaks today through the gift of prophecy, it is not for every believer. I agree with the first half of this statement but not with the second, in light of chapter 14 of 1 Corinthians, which is Paul's instruction for "all those who in every place call upon the name of our Lord Jesus Christ" (1 Cor 1:2b). Accordingly, who ought to prophesy? We already saw that Paul, under inspiration, wants "all those who . . . call upon the name of . . . Jesus" to "speak in tongues, but even more to prophesy" (1 Cor 14:5a), "prophesy one by one" (1 Cor 14:31a), and "earnestly desire to prophesy" (1 Cor 14:39a). These words of Paul indicate that the receiving of private revelation—words or images prompted by the Spirit—should be normative for all believers. Afterwards, any messages received privately ought to be shared in third-person public.

So why is it so important to publicly share a first-person private revelation? It is not just to encourage people, but to make sure that it is obtained from the Spirit, not from one's wild imagination. How else would one understand Paul's instruction on how to carry on prophetic ministry in the church: "Let the prophets speak two or three, and let the other judge" (1 Cor 14:29 KJV). As has already been mentioned in chapter 7, the Greek word translated here as "judge" is *diakrinō*, which means to "to make distinction . . . to determine."[32] Why is this necessary? Recall how secondary prophecy (a.k.a., the gift of prophecy) is defined earlier: a Scripture, thought, word, or image that the Holy Spirit spontaneously impresses upon the mind in such a manner that the person senses that it may be from God. This individual then would share this impression in his or her own (human) words, which are neither inspired nor infallible. As is readily seen, this definition leaves room for the possibility of mod-

---

32. Zodhiates, *Complete word Study*, 902.

ern prophecies being incomplete or flat out wrong because, as the saying goes, "to err is human," especially with words since "we all . . . stumble in what [we say]" (Jas 3:2). What God gives as prophecy to a person is accurate, but the way people express or even interpret it may be wrong.

Here is my all-time blunder of misspeaking in everyday life. Once, on my way back from a very tiring church retreat, I stopped by a flower shop to buy a bouquet of flowers and card for my wife to commemorate our wedding anniversary. My wife was happy at first that I remembered the special day, but upon reading what was written in the card, was not amused. When I looked at the card to see why, I was shocked that instead of writing, "I am so happy to be married to you," I wrote, "I am so sorry to be married to you." It was a sincere human error, but an error nonetheless.

In a similar manner, there is always a possibility of such human error in some degree when prophetic words are shared. The more grievous kinds, of course, are those that go outside biblical parameters. Since this is so, the way a prophetic word is prefaced should indicate that it is not an "inspired utterance" (the kind that led to Scripture), while signaling the possibility of it being incomplete or erroneous. Therefore, as said before, "Thus says the Lord" is not appropriate, but something like, "I feel led by the Lord to say . . ." or "I could be wrong, but I sense the Spirit saying to me . . ." is prudent.

Criteria of Judgment

So by what criteria can hearers determine or distinguish whether the prophetic words are from the Lord? This can be accomplished in the same way that the Bereans tried to determine whether Paul's teaching was from the Lord (Acts 17:11).[33] What 1 Corinthians 14:29 assumes is this: What is said under the rubric of congregational (secondary) prophecy could be fallible and certainly not authoritative as "prophecy of Scripture" (2 Pet 1:20b). What Paul commands is that all secondary or congregational prophecies are to be tested (1 Thess 5:21–22)[34] by God's general will found in Scripture. If some fall outside of biblical parameters, then they should be discarded.

---

33. "Now these Jews were more noble than those in Thessalonica; they received the word with all eagerness, examining the Scriptures daily to see if these things were so."

34. "Do not despise prophecies, but test everything."

Let me now share some practical ways to discern whether alleged prophetic words are really from God. Pastor Jack Hibbs, the senior pastor of Calvary Chapel Chino Hills in California supported me and my family when we went to serve in Mexico. According to him, one day, a woman whom Pastor Jack did not know approached him after the service, telling him that she had a word from God. Being preoccupied, he repeatedly told this person to wait. She got increasingly impatient and angry, beginning to cuss at him. As a result, the question of whether this woman had really received a prophetic message from the Lord was easily answered. Pastor Jack said regarding this, "That one was easy to discern. Her reaction told me that her words were not from the Lord."[35]

Well, since not every case is that easy, let me present two situations that were not as easy to make a judgment call.

The first one involves the aforementioned Mexican sister, whom God used to encourage me with prophetic words in 2002. In 2006, she shared another message allegedly from the Lord. She wrote me in an email (making her first-person private revelation into third-person public): "A few days ago, I was praying, and the Lord put this thought in me to encourage you and to tell you to write a book called the *The Lies of the Da Vinci Code*. Think about it and do it. I think it is the will of the Lord and the time."[36] This idea did not come out of thin air, since I had conducted multiple conferences in the city to address many inconsistencies and inaccuracies contained in in the novel *The Da Vinci Code* that affected the faith of many. However, after carefully weighing in prayer what she said and seeking advice from a fellow believer (my wife, that is) about it, I reached a different conclusion. For one, I had been researching for several months to write a curriculum called *Comparative Systematic Theologies,* to unify feuding Baptist and Assemblies of God pastors (among others). In the end, Christ's call for "all of them" to "be one" (John 17:21a NIV) weighed more heavily on me than exposing the inaccuracies of Dan Brown's novel based on revisionist history, particularly since numerous books against it were already inundating the market. Subsequently, I came to firmly believe that the Lord wanted me to work on the comparative systematic theology curriculum, which I finished a year later. So, while I thanked this godly woman for caring about my ministry, I told her that what she told me may not have been from the Lord.

35. Robin Knapp, email sent to author, March 20, 2018. Pastor Jack confirmed the story through his assistant, Robin.

36. Georgina Pèrez V., email sent to author, June 3, 2006.

On another occasion, a pastor in Chihuahua asked me to get involved with a situation involving Miguel, a leader at his church and also my former student at a nearby Bible institute.[37] Miguel firmly believed that God told him to go to China as a missionary without his young family. So I said to him, "Brother, God may have told you to '[leave] houses or brothers or sisters or father or mother or children or lands, for [his] name's sake' (Matt 19:29), but you should first abide by 1 Timothy 5:8 before leaving: 'But if anyone does not provide for his relatives, and especially for members of his household, he has denied the faith and is worse than an unbeliever.'" Notice two things that happened here: First, this conversation took place in the presence of three pastors (one more joined in). In this way, what was initially a first-person private revelation to Miguel was converted into a third-person public matter. Second, Scripture (primary prophecy) was used to weigh what Miguel claimed were prophetic words (i.e., secondary prophecy). As a result of this meeting Miguel decided to wait.

Thus, I believe that for a church to develop a healthy prophetic ministry, any would-be prophets must first acknowledge that the validity of their alleged prophetic words is not finalized until it is reviewed in a third-person public way. And those who have the task of weighing the biblical validity of secondary prophecy must first demonstrate an adequate knowledge of Scripture—that's a must.

Have Secondary Prophets/Prophecy Disappeared from the Church?

The final discussion is to examine Saucy's claim that the ministry of prophets has been replaced "by the regular local ministry of pastor-teachers."[38]

First, all continuationists should acknowledge that primary prophets—those foundational prophets (and apostles) who completed the task of building the church (Eph 2:20) and producing the canon of Scripture with permanent truth given to them—died out in the first century. But, what about secondary prophets who did not bring new truth but gave "insight into truth which was already known" in Scripture through the prompting of the Spirit?[39] Are they still around? Or, did they also die

37. Not his real name.
38. Saucy, *Church in God's Program*, 139.
39. Ibid., 138.

out after Scripture was completed? For an answer, consider what Saucy wrote when he was a cautious cessationist in 1972, and later as a non-cessationist in 1996.

What Saucy Claimed in 1972

So what did Saucy say on the matter in his 1972 book, *The Church in God's Program?*
Then he said,

> The ministry of the prophets as speaking inspired utterances from God gradually died out after the end of the apostolic age and the completion of the canon [of Scripture]. Their place of exhortation was taken by the regular local ministry of pastor-teachers.[40]

Before proceeding, it is important to note what Saucy means by "inspired utterances from God." Since he ties in its dying out with the completion of the canon, it seems reasonable to posit that "inspired utterances from God" refers to direct revelation that became Scripture. Therefore, it is accurate to say that the role of the inspired prophets was taken by pastor-teachers, since they preach and teach out of Scripture generated by direct revelation given to these primary prophets.

What Saucy Did Not Address in 1972

The key thing to note here is that the phrase, "the prophets as speaking inspired utterances from God," does not include prophets like Judas and Silas because, as noted earlier, they never spoke inspired utterances— meaning they never received direct revelation from God since Scripture includes none of their prophetic words. Therefore, Saucy's statement that primary prophets who received "inspired utterances from God" died out in the first century, does not answer the question of whether second-ary prophets, who never received "inspired utterances from God," also died out. There is little doubt that Saucy assumed in 1972 that second-ary or congregational prophets were also replaced by pastor-teachers; but that to me is a system-induced (i.e., cessationism) theology, since no New Testament verse says this. That is to say, prophets (the kind who

40. Ibid., 139.

spontaneously give insight into God's word through the Spirit's prompting) and teachers (those who prepare their Bible lessons beforehand) are always distinguished throughout Paul's writing. 1 Corinthians 12:28 says, "And God has appointed in the church first apostles, second prophets, third teachers . . . ." Ephesians 4:11–12a (NIV) reads, "It was he who gave some to be apostles, some to be prophets, some to be evangelists, and some to be pastors and teachers, to prepare God's people for works of service." When these passages are read without the bias of cessationism, one can readily see that prophets and pastor-teachers are differentiated.

What Saucy Said in 1996

And it appears that my former professor no longer held (not entirely anyway) the view that the ministry of prophets was taken by pastor-teachers. If I was still unsure about his stance while reading "An Open but Cautious View," the appendix removed any doubts. Saucy writes: "One of the key evidences for seeing a form of prophecy that is less than fully inspired and authoritative is Paul's call for the 'weigh[ing] carefully [*diakrinō*] what is said' in the church (1 Cor. 14:29)."[41] This is to say, among many spiritual gifts still in operation to "sustain [the church] to the end" (1 Cor 1:8a), one is "a form of prophecy that is less than fully inspired and authoritative," but still good enough for the "upbuilding and encouragement and consolation" of people (1 Cor 14:3b).

CONCLUSIVE REMARKS ABOUT THE GIFT OF PROPHECY

I will admit that I get annoyed when those who engage in prophetic ministry seem to put more importance on their ministry than those who proclaim the exposition of "prophecy of Scripture" (2 Pet 1:20b), which is more important than any secondary or congregational prophecy. And I strongly disagree with the practice of prefacing any prophetic words with, "Thus says the Lord." But I am just as perturbed by cessationists who say they honor God's word, which they do for the most part, but not when it comes to spiritual gifts.

I would ask both cessationists and continuationists to embody the pneumatology of the Radical Middle of both/and, and be "open but

41. Saucy, "Open but Cautious View," 146.

cautious." Acknowledge that there are two kinds of prophets outlined in Scripture. The primary kind that imparted new and permanent revelation is no more, but through their inspired writings, we have "prophecy of Scripture" (2 Pet 1:20b). It is more important than any modern prophecy. The secondary kind that spontaneously gives insight into Scripture (i.e., truth already given) through the prompting of the Spirit "to meet the needs of the immediate situation of the church"[42] is still with us; in fact, we are told to eagerly desire the gift of prophecy (1 Cor 14:1). Therefore, handle with care this prophetic responsibility so that we may all be mutually encouraged and strengthened. We should prophesy and receive prophecy in the Radical Middle while sustaining tension created between reasonable faith and reasonable doubt, since we are told to "not despise prophecies" (1 Thess 5:20) and also to "test everything; hold fast to what is good" (1 Thess 5:21).

QUESTIONS FOR REFLECTION & DISCUSSION

1. Are there two types of prophecy or just one presented in Scripture? What is the biblical argument in favor of two? (1 Cor 14:29–31; Num 11:24–30; 2 Pet 1:20–21)

2. What is the main reason cessationists insist that there is only one type of prophecy presented in the Bible and that it has long since ceased? (Rev 22:18–19)

3. What do continuationists need to watch out for when they prophesy? (1 Cor 14:29–33)

4. How should the gift of prophecy be used? (Acts 15:32; 1 Cor 14:3)

5. Do you think when Paul says, "I want you all to speak in tongues, but even more to prophesy" (1 Cor 14:5a), he expected everyone to get the gift of prophecy? (1 Cor 12:29). Can you prophesy without having the gift of prophecy? If you are hesitating to answer, try this question: Can we evangelize without having the gift of evangelism?

42. Saucy, *Church in God's Program*, 138–39.

9

The Gift of Apostleship in the Radical Middle

PERSONALLY, THE WORD "APOSTLE" or "apostolic" carried a negative con-notation to me while serving in Mexico during the 2000s for two reasons. On the one hand, what is called *El movimiento apostolic*—which has a robust presence in the state of Guajajara and Jalisco—is unitarian, mean-ing they have broken with the historic Trinitarian creed of the church. On the other hand, those claiming to be apostles among *los evangélicos* (i.e., Bible-believing Protestants) had a reputation of being very authori-tative and given to prosperity theology. For instance, some in this group charged money for their prayer and counseling services, and allowed no one to touch them lest their anointing be compromised.[1] Therefore, rejecting the validity of the gift of apostleship for today may appear pru-dent so as to avoid problems associated with this gift; nonetheless, such overly precautionary measures are based on experience, not Scripture. And this is where MacArthur's argument comes up short, because while his citing of the excesses of modern-day apostles can bring shivers down one's spine (for instance, he cites Peter Wagner's claim that God acted to end mad cow disease in Europe through his apostolic decree),[2] he once again *completely* ignores Scriptures that are inconvenient to his preferred position.

1. Hugo Martinez, email sent to author, January 29, 2018.

2. MacArthur, *Strange Fire*, 87. MacArthur rightfully points out that "the disease still exists in Europe."

TWO KINDS OF APOSTLES?

As was the case with the gift of tongues and prophecy, it is quite evident that Scripture presents two kinds of apostles. In fact, Robert Saucy, whose work (1996) MacArthur cites approvingly in *Strange Fire* (123), says precisely that in his 1972 work, *The Church in God's Program*: "It would appear that there were two categories of apostles, those sent specifically by the church (2 Cor 8:23; Phil 2:25; Acts 14:4, 14), and those who had been directly commissioned by the risen Lord."[3] MacArthur also recognizes the latter group as apostles, namely the original Twelve disciples and Paul. As a matter of distinction, I would refer to them as primary apostles, and those who are called apostles in the New Testament but are not included in the primary group, the ones Saucy identifies as "apostles . . . sent specifically by the church," or secondary apostles. But inexplicably, MacArthur mentions none of the secondary apostles in *Strange Fire* when discussing "the Biblical Criteria for Apostleship." And that has unfortunate implications.[4]

Primary Apostles

Of course, there is nothing wrong with what MacArthur presents as three biblical qualifications for apostleship in and of themselves, since these are extracted from the Twelve disciples and Paul, whom the Bible unequivocally calls apostles. MacArthur writes:

> The New Testament articulates at least three necessary criteria: (1) an apostle had to be a physical eyewitness of the resurrected Christ (Acts 1:22; 10:39–41; 1 Cor 9:1; 15:7–8); (2) an apostle had to be personally appointed by the Lord Jesus Christ (Mark 3:14; Luke 6:13; Acts 1:2, 24; 10:41; Gal 1:1); and (3) an apostle had to be able to authenticate his apostolic appointment with miraculous signs (Matt 10:1–2; Acts 1:5–8; 2:43; 4:33; 5:12; 8:14; 2 Cor 12:12; Heb 2:3–4)"[5]

Obviously, these criteria are well attested, scripturally. For instance, Paul, in defending his apostleship to those who questioned it, said, no

---

3. Saucy, *Church in God's Program*, 138.

4. MacArthur, *Strange Fire*, 91.

5. Ibid., 92. Matthias, who replaced Judas, would not pass the second criterion since he was not appointed by Christ but rather was chosen by lot (Acts 1:23–26).

doubt referring to himself, "The signs of a true apostle were performed among you with utmost patience, with signs and wonders and mighty works" (2 Cor 12:11–12). Therefore, Christopher Wright (first introduced in chapter 3), after noting the apostleship of the Twelve in *The Mission of God's People*, says,

> Undoubtedly the original Twelve had a unique status and role within the early church. They were the source of authoritative witness to the life, death, and resurrection of Jesus, and so it was vital that their voice, and later the writings of some of them, should be heard and should be decisive.[6]

Thus, these writings were included in the New Testament canon. As for the apostles, they became part of "a holy temple in the Lord" (Eph 2:20–21), meaning "in this church-house the apostles and prophets are the foundation, along with Christ as the 'cornerstone.'"[7] Thus, the biblical evidence seems to warrant categorizing the Twelve disciples and Paul as primary apostles. As noted in chapter 8, once the church was founded and the canon closed, there was no longer any need for this type of apostle and prophet, so they ceased existing after the apostle John died at the end of the first century. Thus, MacArthur confidently asserts that "the biblical criteria for apostleship make it impossible for any credible claim to be made that there are still apostles in the church."[8] That is true but only under one condition: as long as the New Testament does not call anyone apostle who fails to meet MacArthur's apostolic criteria; however, the Bible plainly does call people apostles who do not fit under his criteria.

Secondary Apostles

An undeniable scriptural truth is that, as Christopher Wright notes, "we hear about quite a number of other people who are also described as 'apostles' in the more general sense."[9] So who are these people not mentioned in *Strange Fire*?

First, Luke refers to Barnabas as an apostle in Acts 14:14: "But when the apostles Barnabas and Paul heard of it, they tore their robes and rushed out into the crowd" (NASB).

6. Wright, *Mission of God's People*, 215.

7. Gaffin, "Cessationist View," 43.

8. MacArthur, *Strange Fire*, 91.

9. Wright, *Mission of God's People*, 216.

Then the apostle Paul refers to several people, three by name, as apostles in his Epistles. One of them is Epaphroditus, whom the church in Philippi sent to help Paul when he was under house arrest in Rome. While speaking of Epaphroditus, Paul uses the Greek word *apostolos*, a compound of *apo*, meaning "from," and *stellō*, meaning "to send"; from this, the word "apostle" is derived. But in Philippians 2:25, where this word is used,[10] popular versions such as the NASB, ESV, and NIV translate it as "messenger," although NASB's marginal note does say, "Lit. *apostle*." The same translation, "messenger," is rendered in reference to people whom Paul describes as *apostoloi ekklēsiōn*, literally meaning "apostles of churches,"[11] who were sent to Corinth, along with Titus, to ensure the reception of "the gift" the Corinthian congregation had "promised" (2 Cor 8:23, 9:5).

In addition, Paul calls his relatives, Andronicus and Junias, apostles in his Epistle to the Romans. He writes, "Greet Andronicus and Junias, my kinsmen and my fellow prisoners, who are outstanding among [*en* in the Greek] the apostles, who also were in Christ before me" (Rom 16:7 NASB). Inexplicably, however, ESV translates the Greek preposition *en* as "to," thereby rendering the affected phrase as "they are well known to the apostles." Grammatically, this change would mean that Andronicus and Junias were not apostles. This is puzzling because major translations, including the NIV, RSV, and NKJV, all agree with the NASB in rendering *en* as "among." In fact, neither Bruce M. Metzger's *Lexical Aids for Students of New Testament Greek* nor Sakae Kubo's *A Reader's Greek-English Lexicon of the New Testament* lists "to" as an English equivalent of *en*. Instead, Metzger translates it "in" or "by," and Kubo simply as "in." The previously mentioned Greek scholars Dana and Mantey offer a few more equivalents, such as "on, at, within, among" but "to" is not one of them.[12]

In addition, Christopher Wright notes that, in 1 Corinthians 15:7, "Paul says that Jesus appeared to 'all the apostles' after his resurrection. But he has just listed Peter and the Twelve in verse 5, so this would seem to refer to a wider group of people with some kind of apostolic ministry."[13]

---

10. "But I thought it necessary to send to you Epaphroditus, my brother and fellow worker and fellow soldier, who is also your messenger and minister to my need" (NASB).

11. Marshall, R. S. V. *Interlinear Greek-English New Testament*, 727.

12. Dana and Mantey, *Manual Grammar of the Greek*, 105.

13. Wright, *Mission of God's People*, 216.

So then, do these individuals whom the New Testament refers to as apostles meet MacArthur's three criteria for apostleship? While some of them may have met one or two criteria, none of them met all three—particularly being personally appointed by Christ. What then is the implication that apostles other than the Twelve and Paul are found in the New Testament?

Are there Still Apostles Today?

This implication naturally leads to the question of whether there are still apostles today. MacArthur would say no since, to him, "when the apostle John went to heaven, the apostolate came to an end . . . after the first century."[14] Yet, this conclusion is solely based on selective Scriptures that guarantee *that* conclusion. The textbook used for my hermeneutical class at Talbot says, as cited in chapter 2, "All of the relevant material on a given subject [is] to be collected together so that the pattern of divine revelation concerning that subject would be apparent."[15] Perhaps not liking the emerging pattern, MacArthur has not heeded Packer's warning which has already been mentioned several times in this book: "We are tempted to get rid of antinomies from our minds by illegitimate means: to suppress, or jettison, one truth in the supposed interests of the other, and for the sake of a tidier theology."[16] But, when the entire New Testament is considered, we would agree with Saucy who says, "It would appear that there were two categories of apostles, those sent by the church . . . . and those who had been directly commissioned by the risen Lord."[17] While the latter category of apostles surely ceased, what about the former category? Has that ended too? The key question is this: What qualifies Barnabas, Andronicus, Junias, and Epaphroditus to be apostles? We will now consider that.

The Gift of Apostleship

So then, how did they become apostles? That is like asking what makes Billy Graham an evangelist or Charles Spurgeon a pastor. At bottom, it

14. MacArthur, *Strange Fire*, 102.
15. Ramm, *Protestant Biblical Interpretation*, 56.
16. Packer, *Evangelism and the Sovereignty of God*, 25.
17. Saucy, *Church in God's Program*, 138.

is because these renowned men of faith were given the gift of evange-lism and the gift of pastoring, respectively, "for the common good" (1 Cor 12:7b). An exception should not be made for apostles on account that they must satisfy the apostolic criteria extracted from the original Twelve, since it is Scripture that calls Barnabas and others as "apostles," despite not meeting some or any of the criteria for primary apostleship. Evidently, they became apostles because they were "given through the Spirit" (1 Cor 12:8a) the gift of apostleship.

If indeed apostleship is reserved only for the original Twelve and Paul, then 1 Corinthians 12:29–30 really does not make much sense. He tells the Corinthian believers who coveted after more ostentatious gifts, such as apostleship, "Are all apostles? Are all prophets? Are all teachers? Do all work miracles? Do all possess gifts of healing? Do all speak with tongues? Do all interpret?" Here, Paul's concern stems not from Corin-thians seeking after coveted gifts that were no longer possible to attain, like apostleship, but seeking them for all the wrong reasons. It is likely that Paul was asking a rhetorical question to chastise the Corinthians who were disrespecting each other over spiritual gifts (1 Cor 12:14–26), as if to say, "You guys only want spiritual gifts that appear more ostenta-tious to upstage each other." Therefore, the apostle reminds them that no single individual can have all the gifts; but that reasoning does not nullify the validity of spiritual gifts such as the gift of apostleship. This is to say, the attainment of all these gifts was possible then as it is today. To believe otherwise is to say that 1 Corinthians is written only for the Corinthians in the first century. No, the Epistles are doctrinal instructions for every generation of believers.

The Apostles of Today

As to whether there are still secondary apostles today, nothing in the Bible suggests that they vanished as well, since their apostleship is predicated upon receiving the gift of apostleship and since the perpetuity of spiritual gifts stands. When the apostle Paul writes, "It was he [Christ] who gave some to be apostles" (Eph 4:11a NIV), he is not limiting its scope only to his time, since his belief is that Christ "will keep [the church] strong to the end" through spiritual gifts (1 Cor 1:8a). Since the end has not yet come, it stands to reason that the Spirit continues to "give [spiritual gifts] to each one, just has he determines," (1 Cor 12:14b NIV), including the gift of apostleship, "for the common good" (1 Cor 12:7b).

The Apostleship in the Radical Middle

In view of all that has been discussed, it should be said that when the matter of apostleship in the New Testament is addressed, the hermeneutics of the Radical Middle of both/and is once again needed because Scripture presents two types of apostles: the primary apostles who were directly appointed by Christ, and the secondary apostles who were appointed not by the Lord, but by the church in recognition of those who have the gift of apostleship. There is nothing inherently antithetic between these two types of apostles, but they have become, in effect, binary opposites because hard cessationism privileges, under the rubric of the hermeneutics of logocentrism, those Scriptures that support primary apostles, while ignoring other Scriptures that point to the existence of secondary apostles. The Radical Middle fully embraces both categories as biblical.

THE ROLE OF APOSTLES TODAY

So, then, what do apostles do today? Christopher Wright, noting the "sending" aspect of the word *apostolos*, simply says that other apostles not included among the original Twelve "were sent to do various tasks."[18] Whereas the mission of Epaphroditus, sent out by the church in Philippi, was to minister to Paul's need in Rome, and that of those sent out by Paul to the church in Corinth was to ensure the reception of the offering promised by that congregation, the mission of Barnabas, sent out first by the Jerusalem church and later by the Antioch church, looks a lot different.

The Apostolic Ministry of Barnabas

Based on what the apostle Barnabas did, it can be stated that secondary apostles, sent by the church and operating out of the gift of apostleship, are: first, prompted by a vision; second, driven by a pioneering spirit; and third, sustained through caring leadership.

18. Wright, *Mission of God's People*, 216.

A Visionary

So what prompts apostles to leave the comforts of home to go elsewhere, whether for a time or permanently, to carry out a new mission from God? One factor that prompts apostles is having a vision that others do not see clearly or miss out on entirely. It could be a vision to join in God's great work or to bring out the best in others with God-given potential.

First, consider who physically responded when the report of a great number of people in Antioch turning to the Lord "came to the ears of the church in Jerusalem" (Acts 11:22b). It was not the Twelve disciples, those appointed to an apostleship by Christ. They continued to hunker down in Jerusalem (Acts 8:1), still ministering mostly to the Jews (Gal 2:9) and in seeming obliviousness to the Great Commission (Matt 28:18–20). Instead, it was Barnabas, who was willing to be sent to the Greek city of Antioch, to organize the incipient Christian movement initiated by those who had been "scattered because of the persecution that arose over Stephen" (Acts 11:19–20). Later, the fact that Barnabas would leave his pastorate in Antioch to proclaim the gospel mostly to the Greeks in Asia Minor (Acts 13:1–13), suggests that uprooting himself from Jerusalem was prompted by envisioning this move as the first step toward proclaiming Christ "to all nations" (Luke 24:47).

As he began to pastor the church in Antioch, his visionary acumen resurfaced as the congregation grew under his pastoral care, and along with it, the needs of the church as well (Acts 11:24). By this time, Paul was likely forgotten by the Jerusalem church, as he had long since returned to his home in Tarsus to avoid persecution (Acts 9:30). But the thought (a vision, if you will) of Paul must have suddenly appeared in Barnabas's mind, even though Barnabas had only known Paul for a brief time (Acts 9:26–29; Gal 1:18–19) and had not seen for six to seven years.[19] Barnabas must have remembered Paul's call to ministry and remarkable testimony, and how he had leveraged his good reputation to ensure that the skeptical apostles accept Paul (Acts 9:27). Thus, when Barnabas began to look for help, instead of going to Jerusalem—a logical choice since there must have been several candidates to choose from—he went to "Tarsus to look for Saul, and when he found him, he brought him to Antioch. For a whole

---

19. Since it is believed that Paul was converted in 35 AD and left for his first missionary trip in 46 AD, while in between spending three years in Arabia/Damascus (Gal 1:17–18) and at least one year co-pastoring the church at Antioch with Barnabas (Acts 11:26), that leaves about 6–7 years spent in Tarsus.

year they met with the church and taught a great many people" (Acts 11:25–26a). What a pleasant surprise for a driven man like Paul (Gal 1:13–14; Phil 3:4–6), who likely felt restless as his stay in Tarsus became unexpectedly long. And it was the apostle Barnabas's visionary leadership that brought Paul back from obscurity in Tarsus (Acts 11:25–26) so that he could serve with Barnabas in shepherding the growing Antioch congregation. This then is how Paul's ministry to "carry [God's] name before the Gentiles and kings and the children of Israel" (Acts 9:15b) all began.

Later, Barnabas would do the same for Mark when Paul, before beginning his second missionary trip with Barnabas, rejected Mark for returning home in the middle of their first missionary trip (Acts 13:13). Separating from Paul, Barnabas took Mark under his wing and no doubt contributed greatly toward his eventual restoration, including becoming the first gospel writer as well as earning Paul's change of opinion of him, for shortly before the apostle's martyrdom he said, "[Mark] is very useful to me for ministry" (2 Tim 4:11b).

Suffice it to say, the apostle Barnabas had a vision of Paul and Mark's great potential for God, something no one else saw, and served diligently in order to bring it out. And those modern-day apostles suffering from egomania should realize that the apostle Barnabas gladly let Paul, a man he pulled out of obscurity, take the lead at some point during their partnership. Note that Luke introduces Barnabas first and then Paul, prior to and at the beginning of their missionary trip. Describing the completion of a trip taken by them prior to their first missionary journey, Luke writes, "And Barnabas and Saul returned from Jerusalem when they had completed their service" (Acts 12:25a). Referring to a situation taking place at the outset of the first missionary trip, Luke writes, "A Jewish false prophet named Bar-Jesus . . . was with the proconsul, Sergius Paulus, a man of intelligence, who summoned Barnabas and Saul and sought to hear the word of God" (Acts 13:7). But, Luke reverses the order in the middle of the trip, writing in Acts 13:46, "And Paul and Barnabas spoke out boldly," as if to mark the rising prominence of Paul over Barnabas.

A Pioneer

A key component to the apostolic tasks, based on what Barnabas accomplished with Paul in their missionary journey together from the years

AD 46–48, seems to be pioneering and planting new churches. Luke reports that after Paul and Barnabas "had preached the gospel to that city [Derbe] and had made many disciples, they returned to Lystra and to Iconium and to Antioch, strengthening the souls of the disciples, encouraging them to continue in the faith" (Acts 14:21–22a). The two apostles, then, organized the churches they planted and oversaw those who pastored them. Acts 14:23 (NIV) reads, "Paul and Barnabas appointed elders for them in every church, and with prayer and fasting, committed them to the Lord, in whom they had put their trust."

The sphere of their apostolic leadership also extended to the churches planted by someone other than the apostles themselves. Paul wrote an Epistle to the church in Colossae that was founded by Epaphras, who likely became a believer "during Paul's three-year ministry in Ephesus . . . and had carried the gospel to Colossae (cf. Col 1:7–8; Acts 19:10)."[20] The apostle Paul's influence did not stop there as he instructed the Colossians to share his letter with two other churches in Laodicea and Hierapolis, which Epaphras or his disciple(s) likely planted, but not Paul or Barnabas (Col 4:13–16).

An Overseer

What ensued in the apostolic ministry of Barnabas and Paul was their continuous overseeing of the churches they had planted. The sudden breakup of the ministry partnership of Barnabas and Paul just prior to their planned second missionary journey often overshadows what they were planning to do: "Return and visit the brothers in every city where we proclaimed the word of the Lord, and see how they are doing" [pôs ĕchosin] (Acts 15:36). This was not a case of lording over those placed in local leadership, since structurally (in terms of the vast distance separating the apostles from the churches they planted, along with the absence of modern means of communication and transportation) that was not quite possible. Instead, there was a lot of trusting on the part of the apostles; first in the Lord, and then in those who were given ministry responsibilities (Acts 14:23). A few times, they could actually talk face to face, as Paul and Barnabas were about to do before their mishap, yet the focus was not on checking out what "they are *doing*," but, as NASB renders the Greek

20. Barker, *NIV Study Bible*, 1813.

clause *pôs ĕchosin* more literally, to "see how they *are*." In other words, the apostles were more concerned with "being" rather than "doing."

Improving Your Apostleship

I began this section with my apprehension over using the word "apostle" or "apostolic" because of the way many apostles in Mexico (whether real or imagined) carry themselves publicly, with a sense of entitlement and reveling in how those around them treat them like kings. So I felt somewhat jolted when, as I was preparing to leave Mexico in 2011, Keith Park, the head of Acts Ministries International (AMI), offered me the position of Teaching Pastor for this fellowship of churches. The reason for my hesitancy is that the governance of this organization was apostolic, meaning AMI claimed to be led by three apostles. Since then, the AMI's governance and ministry structure has transitioned to the fivefold offices prescribed in Ephesians 4:11–12, meaning there is now one apostle, along with one prophet, evangelist, pastor, and teacher in the leadership.

So how does this function? Is the leadership dominated by the apostle and everyone else just follows him? No, because the new bylaw says, first, "The fivefold members serve together to prepare the AMI body of Christ for the work of ministry"; second, "The fivefold members, as ruling elders of their respective churches (1 Tim 5:17), participate in the decision-making process of all pertinent macro-affairs of AMI, such as ordination, discipline, missions, etc."; and third, "The fivefold team is led and directed by the apostle in acknowledgement of his authoritative role." As a result, open dialogue takes place among the fivefold in view of the authoritative role of apostle; after all, "God has appointed in the church first apostles" (1 Cor 12:28). But it has been an easy apostolic leadership to follow because the person occupying the office lives modestly, leads with a vision, is mindful of planting new churches, and is concerned more about how the workers *are* than with what they do.

That leads me to wonder whether cessationists would still vehemently deny that apostles exist today if modern-day apostles lived and ministered the way the apostles Barnabas and Paul did. Instead of enriching themselves with perks that typically come with being a leader, these two gave up all or most of what they had to serve as apostles. While Barnabas "sold a field that belonged to him" and gave all the proceeds to the church (Acts 4:37), Paul told the Corinthians who acted as if they "have become kings" (1 Cor 4:8b), not unlike many apostles of today, "We," referring specifically to apostles (1 Cor 4:9), "are homeless" (1 Cor 4:11b NIV). My hope is that cessationists are willing to tone down their rhetoric against continuationists when they see the apostles of today: first, living modestly; second, planting churches that preach "repentance and . . . faith in Jesus Christ" (Acts 20:21); and third, not lording over those who are under their leadership, but being concerned about "how they are" (Acts 15:36b NASB).

QUESTIONS FOR REFLECTION & DISCUSSION

1. Does Scripture present one or two types of apostles?

2. Again, why do the cessationists insist that all apostles died out in the first century? I made an argument that this is a matter of hermeneutics: What are the implications of that?

3. In view of how the original apostles lived and died, what's missing among many of the apostles today?

4. I said we need more apostles like Barnabas in the church today. What aspects of his life and ministry do you admire the most?

5. What does it mean to be an apostle in the mode of Epaphroditus whom the church of Philippi sent to take care of Paul's needs (Phil 2:25–30, 4:18), and the brothers whom Paul sent to Corinth to ensure the reception of the promised offering (2 Cor 8:23, 2 Cor 9:5)?

10

Divine Healing in the Radical Middle

SOME YEARS BACK, OUR organization (AMI) planted a church in an Eastern European country, led by an expatriate named Stefan, who was trained in one of our churches in the States.[1] In a country dominated by the Orthodox Church, the old guard known for its liturgical tradition, planting a church open to the Spirit was challenging to say the least. So Stefan, with a background in Brethren Church, wanted to incorporate what he referred to as the fullness of the gospel into the church's ministry in order to manifest the presence of God. For him, this meant physical healing.

Later, during my visit to this new church, a meeting was held to hash out differences in vision among the team members, because some felt uncomfortable with Stefan's overture toward what they deemed as an aggressive healing ministry, most of which he learned from the internet. When asked for his reasoning behind his framework for spiritual gifts, Stefan said,

> We are used to the ways of the Brethren Church: hoping for people to change through sharing the Bible, good character, and being nice. We have to impact the people, but these efforts will not accomplish that. Now, I want to add the manifestation of the Holy Spirit, like healing. That is how we can distinguish ourselves from the Brethren Church.

1. Not his real name.

For his proof text, he cited Isaiah 53:5: "But he was pierced for our transgressions; he was crushed for our iniquities; upon him was the chastisement that brought us peace, and with his wounds we are healed." This is the central Scripture upon which the classical Pentecostal doctrine on healing is established, as one Pentecostal writer puts it: "Divine healing was purchased—paid for at Calvary—included in the atonement."[2] The phrase, "by his wounds you have been healed," which the apostle Peter, looking back to the crucifixion, repeats in 1 Peter 2:24b, is understood by many charismatics and Pentecostals to mean that the thirty-nine stripes Jesus received "represent healing for *all* our diseases."[3] Evidently, Stefan agreed.

Out of my concern that he not go off the deep end with respect to a healing ministry, I asked Stefan what he thought of numerous arguments advocated by those who, in my opinion, were on the extreme side. His initial hesitation following my explanation suggested that he had not really thought about these matters. Although he finally indicated his disagreement with certain extreme views associated with healing ministry, I was not quite sure whether he understood their full implications. So what are those teachings on healing that "go beyond what is written" (1 Cor 4:6b)?

TEACHINGS ON HEALING THAT GO BEYOND WHAT IS WRITTEN

As a recent convert to the Pentecostal faith in the early 1980s, I used to transcribe word by word the sermons I heard on cassette tapes of Frederick K. C. Price, the founder and senior pastor of Crenshaw Christian Center, a charismatic megachurch in Los Angeles.[4] In terms of dynamism and clarity, he was as good as they come. While I gravitated toward his teaching at first, I began to see that something was off with respect to his thoughts on healing.

2. Clayton, *My Faith*, 61.

3. Bennett and Bennett, *Holy Spirit and You*, 116.

4. Price, now known as an apostle, has retired as the senior pastor of the church after serving there for thirty-five years.

Is Healing for All?

One of Price's books that clearly delineates his thoughts on sickness and healing is *Is Healing for All?*, which was first published in 1976 and rereleased in 2015. This work leaves no doubt about where Price stands on healing: "Praise God! Healing is for all!"[5]; "it *is* God's will for you to be healed"[6] (italics his). In fact, for Price, praying, "'Lord if it be thy will, heal them,' . . . is not a prayer of faith, but a prayer of doubt."[7] So Price would say to an individual who did not get healing, "If you say you've done what God said and you didn't get your healing, you're mistaken, because he said you'd get it."[8] Typical reasons given for not getting healed are because of the sick person's lack of faith or some unconfessed sin.

Furthermore, he espouses the view that if a Christian faithfully walks with the Lord, then that person will not get sick. Price says, "If I walk rightly, and if I walk in line with the word of God, I'm thoroughly convinced I can be free from sickness and disease."[9] Conversely, this is tantamount to saying, "I'm thoroughly convinced that if I am sick and in pain, that is because I did not walk rightly and according to the word of God."

The Worldview of Price

So what is behind his belief? It stems from Price's worldview that "sickness does not originate with or come from God. Sickness is of the devil."[10] To him, therefore, to be sick and not healed, despite the scriptural assertation that "by his wounds you have been healed" (1 Pet 2:24b), is to still be bound and deceived by Satan. For Price, this cannot possibly be part of God's will for us.

---

5. Price, *Is Healing for All?* §267.
6. Ibid., §716.
7. Ibid., §338.
8. Ibid., §302.
9. Ibid., §77.
10. Ibid., §445.

HOW DOES GOD HEAL?

How would the Radical Middle paradigm respond to this type of either/or teaching that stipulates the following: either healing is *always* God's will or if you are not healed, then something is wrong; either faithful Christians never get sick or if you are sick, then that means you are not faithful. Foremost, as a matter of proper hermeneutical procedure, instead of imposing our predisposed theology on the biblical text, Scripture should speak for itself. When we allow that, the scriptural reality that emerges is the outlook of both/and, not either/or. What does that mean? First, it purports that God does heal but not always; second, while righteous living can lead to better health, it does not make us invulnerable to sickness (amplified later). And when God does grant healing, he does it principally through two modes.

Prayer for Healing

First, God heals in response to prayers offered in faith. James 5:14–16 (NASB) says:

> Is anyone among you sick? *Then* he must call for the elders of the church and they are to pray over him, anointing him with oil in the name of the Lord; and the prayer offered in faith will restore the one who is sick, and the Lord will raise him up, and if he has committed sins, they will be forgiven him. Therefore, confess your sins to one another, and pray for one another so that you may be healed. The effective prayer of a righteous man can accomplish much.

The thought expressed here seems straightforward: pray in faith for healing. That is why I pray for healing—because of this passage. Not too long ago, I was encouraged when shortly after I had prayed for a young girl who was feeling ill all day, her father indicated to me that she was feeling all better. I felt glad to have prayed for her while visiting this family. I also have met numerous people who have been divinely healed from various ailments.[11] I, too, have experienced such healing myself, although fortunately none of the ailments I suffered from were too serious.

---

11. For instance, Erika Soto, a missionary sent by the Assemblies of God of Mexico to Mozambique, shared with me how the Lord healed her from cancer.

A Questionable Understanding of James 5:14–16

Be that as it may, in the hermeneutical hand of MacArthur, understanding James 5:14–16 as I do is problematic. That is, not wanting this passage to mean physical healing, he states,

> At first glance it appears to be teaching that sick believers can expect physical healing through the prayers of the elders. But such an interpretation is out of harmony with the context . . . The suffering James has in view is evil treatment, not physical illness.[12]

To justify this interpretation, MacArthur takes issue with the way the Greek word *asthenéō*, literally meaning "without strength,"[13] is translated in all major translations such NASB, ESV, NIV, and NKJV. While he admits that this Greek word is translated slightly more often as "sick" than "weak" (emotional or spiritual) in the New Testament, he believes that in James, the correct translation is "weak," not "sick." To buttress this point, MacArthur makes an additional argument based on Greek. First, he notes that the Greek word translated as "sick" in verse 15 ("the prayer of faith will save the one who is *sick*") derives from a different Greek word, *kámnō*. He then says the word "sick" is "misleading and not the best translation of *kámnō* which in its only other New Testament usage (Heb 12:3) clearly does not refer to physical illness."[14]

Again, what Pastor MacArthur does here is no different from what he does with 1 Corinthians 14:2 ("praying to a pagan deity"): this otherwise venerable pastor makes a claim that most, if not all, Bible translators do not make. For instance, Bible scholar Spiros Zodhiates notes that when *kámnō*, meaning, "to be weary from constant work, . . . [is] used in connection with *asthenéō*, to be sick, (as is the case here), it suggests the common accompaniment of sickness, weariness of mind which may hinder physical recovery."[15] Almost certainly, that is why all Bible translations I have seen on this passage (James 5:14–16) say "sick," not "weak." The fact that even cessationist Richard Gaffin says, "I do not deny that God heals (miraculously) today . . . in response to the individual and cor-

---

12. MacArthur, *MacArthur New Testament Commentary*, 276.

13. Zodhiates, *Complete word Study*, 894.

14. MacArthur, *MacArthur New Testament Commentary*, 278. Hebrews 12:3 reads, "Consider him who endured from sinners such hostility against himself, so that you may not grow weary [root: *kámnō*], or fainthearted."

15. Zodhiates, *Complete word Study*, 925. In Kubo's lexical aid, "to be ill" is listed first as the meaning of *kamnō*.

porate prayers . . . James 5:14–16, for instance, points us to that," shows how extreme hard cessationism has become.[16]

The Gift of Healing

Along with praying for healing, God also heals through the exercise of the gift of healing, for the apostle Paul unequivocally states that "to one is given through the Spirit . . . gifts of healing" (1 Cor 12:8a, 9b). Peter Wagner, in his *Your Spiritual Gifts Can Help Your Church Grow*, defines this gift as "the special ability that God gives to certain members of the body of Christ to serve as human intermediaries through whom it pleases God to cure illness and restore health apart from the use of natural means."[17] Of course, "the gift of healing does not give a person supernatural power over disease. He or she is simply a channel through whom God works when He desires to heal."[18] Many would agree that the two people in previous generations who exercised this gift with a great deal of anointing from the Lord were Kathryn Kuhlman and Oral Roberts, whose healing crusades drew thousands of the infirmed for a long time. Even if just a handful of countless testimonies is to be believed, many people were indeed healed at these crusades; but I am absolutely positive that not every single sick person returned home healed (explained later).

The Importance of the Matter of Healing

Since sickness is common to all of us at some point in life, healing always draws a great deal of people's interest, certainly more so when we are actually sick, thereby rendering us mentally vulnerable because infirm people desperate for a cure are likely to believe anything. Scripturally, there are certainly grounds for hope. But this hope must be qualified in light of what Scripture actually teaches about sickness, healing, and God's will. This must be clearly understood, because if the promised healing does not materialize and the blame is placed on the sick people themselves (i.e., blaming the victim), they will surely become disheartened.

---

16. Gaffin, "Cessationist View," 42.

17. Wagner, *Your Spirit Gifts Can Help*, 238.

18. Ibid., 239.

THE RESPONSE OF THE RADICAL MIDDLE TO TEACHING THAT GOES BEYOND WHAT IS WRITTEN

We just saw that God grants healing through the exercise of the gift of healing and praying in faith. Does this mean healing is guaranteed as long as the infirm have enough faith and confessed their sins, or someone with the gift of healing has prayed for them? Price would likely say yes, but what does Scripture say on this matter?

No from God

As the Teaching Pastor of AMI, I have my own blog on our organization's website. I began that blog in 2013 in response to what was said by the speaker at our tri-annual congregation conference. In one sermon he declared, "Don't take 'NO' for an answer from God." The speaker meant to underscore the importance of faith in prayer, but you need not flip through many pages of the Bible before finding God saying "no" to his people.

No from God in the Old Testament

The first significant no was when God said no to Moses who begged that he be allowed to enter the promised land (Deut 3:23–26). Specifically, with respect to healing, when King David pleaded with God for his child, birthed out of adultery with Bathsheba and stricken with sickness as a judgment against David, his desperate petition went unanswered: the child died (2 Sam 12:15–18). No amount of fasting or weeping was going to change God's decree, even after he had taken away David's sin: "The child who is born to you shall die" (2 Sam 12:14).

What if "I have all faith, so as to remove mountains?" (1 Cor 13:2b)—would that ensure God's healing? If that were the case, Elisha should not have died from illness, but he did. Second Kings 13:14a (NIV) reads, "Now Elisha was suffering from the illness from which he died." This renowned miracle worker, who once raised the dead (2 Kgs 4:34), likely would have prayed for his own healing, but obviously God did not grant that request.

No from God in the New Testament

And in the New Testament, the apostle Paul asked the Lord no less than three times to remove what he described as "a thorn in my flesh" from him. Second Corinthians 12:7 reads, "So to keep me from becoming conceited because of the surpassing greatness of the revelations, a thorn was given me in the flesh, a messenger of Satan to harass me, to keep me from becoming conceited." However, God said to the apostle, "My grace is sufficient for you" (2 Cor 12:9a)—meaning, Paul's request was denied.

So what does Paul mean by the Greek word *skolops* translated as "thorn?" Frederick Price, unwilling to entertain the possibility that a righteous person like Paul could get sick (thereby, ignoring the apostle's admission of having been sick while visiting the Galatians—Gal 4:14–16), insists that the "thorn" in the Bible refers not to "disease or sickness, but persons."[19] This view is not without reason since Moses does refer to the pestering presence of the Canaanites amid Israel as "thorns in your sides" (Num 33:55). Applying this to Paul's thorn in the flesh, Price concludes that this refers to "one of Satan's angels that was sent to harass and bug [Paul]"[20] and not sickness. What he fails to consider is that *skolops* (used only once in the New Testament) according to *Greek Dictionary of the New Testament*, figuratively means "a bodily annoyance or disability."[21] *An Expository Dictionary of Biblical Words* adds that Paul's "language indicates that it was physical, painful, humiliating."[22] Thus, I agree with C. Peter Wagner, a great advocate of charismatic causes, who commented that thorn in the flesh "in all probability was a physical problem of some kind, but God chose not to remove it."[23] Why? To "keep [Paul] from becoming conceited because of the surpassing greatness of the revelations" (2 Cor 12:7).

Therefore, in accordance with Scripture, first, it is not true that God *always* heals, and second, the reason for not getting healed is not always because of unconfessed sin or lack of faith (though it could be due to both, according to James 5:16 and Mark 6:5–6).[24] Instead, it may be God's

---

19. Price, *Is Healing for All?* §389.

20. Ibid., §149.

21. Strong, "Greek Dictionary of the New Testament," 65.

22. Vine, *Expository Dictionary of Biblical words*, 629–30.

23. Wagner, *Your Spirit Gifts Can Help*, 239.

24. "Therefore, confess your sins to one another, and pray for one another so that you may be healed. The effective prayer of a righteous man can accomplish much" (Jas

will that the sufferer is not healed or even dies from the illness, as was the case with Elisha. A case can be made that that's precisely what happened to Christ whose petition for the removal of his cup of suffering went unanswered and was finally withdrawn after his second plea in lieu of accepting God's will for his life. (Matt 26:37–39).

Real-life Ramifications

A key reason the matter of divine healing must be carefully considered is that the charismatic belief that "over every sickness there stands the will of God to heal" can have serious repercussions at all levels, including church and family.

Going back to my days of serving in Mexico, one Thursday, while taking a short break during my class with the Assemblies of God pastors, Pastor Edgar, a man in his late fifties who had just lost his wife to cancer, wanted to speak to me.[25] Usually a jovial man, on this day he was in a somber mood, even weeping, and it was not all because of his wife's passing. The leaders of the church just forced him to resign on account that his wife died, despite the whole church praying for her, in contrast to Edgar's teaching that it is always God's will to heal. While there had to be other conflicts that led to this ugly situation, the issue the church leaders hung their case against Edgar on was his inability to live up to his teaching. While consoling my friend, I gingerly told him this: "First, your wife did not die because you did not pray enough nor did not have enough faith; two, please reconsider your teaching."

Actually, this matter of healing hits close to home because I have lost two brothers-in-law and two sisters-in-law to cancer in the prime of their lives.[26] Many prayers were offered on their behalf by numerous concerned people, but the recipients of all these prayers eventually succumbed to the disease. It was devastating and even more so when my young daughter began to wonder why God did not answer. One of these deaths in particular stands out because my sister beautifully captured God's healing in the Radical Middle in her eulogy for her husband of seven years. For the first ten months of fighting this disease, she and her husband felt hopeful

---

5:16); "He could not do any miracles there, except lay his hands on a few sick people and healed them. And he was amazed at their lack of faith" (Mark 6:5–6).

25. Not his real name.

26. Two from my side (1996, 2005) and two from my wife's side (2007, 2014).

that God was going to heal—their hope being bolstered by the doctor's promising words of recovery. But suddenly (at least that is how it felt to them), the doctor said that my brother-in-law (Sun) had about two months to live. In the eulogy below, she shares how the Lord spoke to her while she was praying rather angrily at God, at first, after being told of her husband's dire prognosis:

> I begged God to cure my husband of this horrible disease and bring him home . . . Then God spoke to me that night telling me that all this time, I've been praying for my husband to get well according to *my* will (italics hers). God told me to change my will to *God's will* (italics hers). Whatever happens, trust God. This was a pivotal moment for me because I accepted God's will, regardless of whether his will was to cure Sun or to take him to heaven; it was God's will and his will is perfect, righteous, and good. When I took God's will over mine at that moment, he lifted up my unbearable heavy load and gave me a lighter load to carry. So the anger I thought I would have if God took my husband from me was no longer there because God filled my heart with this incredible peace that passes beyond any understanding; and I was so grateful to God for telling me this sooner than later because I had a chance to tell my husband how I felt now while he was still alive. Next day I shared this with Sun and told him, "If God wants you to stay here on earth, then you will, regardless of what doctors said, but if God calls you to go to heaven, go and do not worry about me and the kids and do not feel bad because either way, [God] will take care of us here on earth."[27]

I believe that my sister's faith in the face of her husband's rapidly deteriorating condition can be presented in the following paradigm of the Radical Middle:

Thesis: "God may heal my husband."

Antithesis: "God may take him home."

God's healing in the Radical Middle: "I accept both outcomes because God's will is perfect, righteous, and good."

---

27. Hedda Bong, the eulogy written for her husband and read at his funeral on March 7, 2005, at Fairfax Memorial Park, Fairfax, Virginia.

Faithful People Can Become Sick

The last item on Price's teaching on healing is most alarming because it can lead to falsely judging people, as well as living in denial: "If I walk rightly, and if I walk according to the word of God, I'm thoroughly convinced I can be free from sickness and disease."[28]

A Recipe for Judging and Pretending

It was said earlier that Price believes that "sickness does not originate with or come from God. Sickness is of the devil."[29] But elsewhere in the book he says that "all bad things are here in the world because of sin,"[30] which has a different ramification than the statement that sickness is of the devil.

First, the belief that the devil, not God, is the author of sickness assures Price that it is always the will of God, who opposes the adversary, to heal (John 10:10). But, can such assuredness be extended to his belief, that it is possible for believers to be free from sickness if their walk with God is faithful, in light of the admission that sin is what causes all bad things in the world, including sickness? This is actually a moot question because it is impossible not to sin as long as believers are in the world. First, it is hard not to sin in thought and action (Matt 5:27–28) when, according to the apostle Paul, "sin . . . dwells within [us]" (Rom 7:17b). Second, it is likely that for this reason the apostle John declares, "If we say we have no sin, we deceive ourselves, and the truth is not in us" (1 John 1:8). Echoing the same sentiment is the apostle James who says, "We all stumble in many ways. And if anyone does not stumble in what he says, he is a perfect man" (Jas 3:2a). This is not to say that believers have no spiritual wherewithal to avoid sinning; they certainly do, as John declares, "I am writing these things to you so that you may not sin" (1 John 2:1a). Nevertheless, because the apostle John understands that no believer will live perfectly, he quickly adds, "But if anyone does sin, we have an advocate with the Father, Jesus Christ the righteous" (1 John 2:1b).

In view of this, to say that imperfect humans living in a sin-tainted world can be absolutely free from sickness and pain as long as their walk

28. Price, Is Healing for All? §77.

29. Ibid., §445.

30. Ibid., §186.

with God is right is absolutely "go[ing] beyond what is written" (1 Cor 4:6b). And this belief will entice some people to assume the worst of the infirm or induce the sick to pretend to be well lest others may judge them.

I saw this firsthand during the time when my mother-in-law, who passed away in 1999, suffered mightily with a debilitating disease that paralyzed her completely. Some who prayed for her, upon seeing that she was not healed afterwards, laid the blame on her, saying, "Sister, you lack faith." But the most galling comment was telling her that she was sick and was not being healed because she lacked joy. My mother-in-law, a pastor's wife, was always gracious to those who came to pray for her, no matter what they said to her, but in private, she would lament to my wife as to why everyone was blaming her. So the approach of "your sickness indicates you are not right with the Lord" ended up adding great mental anguish on top of her physical pain.

Hermeneutics of Logocentrism to Uphold that Faithful People Do Not Get Sick

Recall that logocentrism is privileging the first term over the second in a binary opposition. When applied to the Bible, it takes the form of either distorting the meaning or entirely ignoring scriptural verses that do not back one's preferred theology. In chapter 4, this way of interpreting the Bible is referred to as "the hermeneutics of logocentrism," and this is the interpretive method through which Price promotes a teaching on healing that goes way beyond what is written in the Bible. In his *Is Healing for All?*, not even one person in the Bible who became sick, despite being righteous and faithful, is mentioned. Job (well known for having suffered immensely) is discussed, but not in the way you would think (I will elaborate on this later).

Look no further than the apostle Paul who, in his letter to the Galatians, reminded them of how sick he was when they first met him. He says, "You know it was because of a bodily ailment that I preached the gospel to you at first, . . . for I testify to you that, if possible, you would have gouged out your eyes and given them to me" (Gal 4:13, 15b). Then there is Timothy, pastor of the Ephesian church, of whom Paul gushed, "I have no one like him" (Phil 2:20a). Notwithstanding, Timothy experienced chronic abdominal pain, so much so that Paul told him to "stop drinking only water, and use a little wine because of your stomach and frequent illnesses" (1 Tim 5:23 NIV). The list does not stop here: Elisha fell ill and never recovered; Dorcas, "full of good works and acts of charity . . . became ill and died" as well (Acts 9:36b–37a); King Hezekiah, of whom it is said, "There was none like him among all the kings of Judah after him, nor among those who were before him" (2 Kgs 18:5b), suddenly "became sick and was at the point of death" (Isa 38:1a); even Daniel in whom "no error or fault was found" (Dan 6:4b) "lay sick for some days," (Dan 8:27a). Only by ignoring these biblical cases can Price make the claim that faithful believers are free from sickness.

As for Job, there does not seem to be any question that God allowed seemingly unbearable pain in his life, despite the fact that he was "blameless and upright, one who feared God and turned away from evil" (Job 1:1b). Incredulously, Price argues, based on his understanding of Job 1:12, that it was Job's fault that he suffered the calamity. Job 1:9–12 says:

> Then Satan answered the Lord and said, "Does Job fear God for no reason? Have you not put a hedge around him and his house and all that he has, on every side? You have blessed the work of his hands, and his possessions have increased in the land. But stretch out your hand and touch all that he has, and he will curse you to your face." And the Lord said to Satan, "Behold, all that he has is in your hand. Only against him do not stretch out your hand." So Satan went out from the presence of the Lord.

To Price, the phrase, "All he has is in your hand" means that "Satan didn't even know that . . . Job had [already] pulled the hedge [i.e., God's protection] down."[31] He adds, "As long as Job walked in *faith*, the wall—the hedge—was up. But when he started walking in unbelief and doubt the hedge was pulled down. Job pulled it down! . . . Job brought it upon himself."[32]

This is yet another example of privileging the theology we prefer by thoroughly distorting Scriptures that are inconvenient to uphold that theology, a.k.a., the hermeneutics of logocentrism. Does Price not realize that on the list of the three most righteous people in the Old Testament, compiled by God himself, is found Job, along with Noah and Daniel? (Ezek 14:20). Does he not know that the apostle James presents Job as a model of keeping one's "patience in the face of suffering" (Jas 5:10–11)?

---

31. Price, *Is Healing for All?* §103. King David speaks of God's protection in Psalms 5:11: "But let all who take refuge in you rejoice; let them ever sing for joy, and spread your protection over them, that those who love your name may exult in you."

32. Ibid., §119.

Only by ignoring these Scriptures and distorting the book of Job can Price insist that those who faithfully walk with God will never get sick.

Nothing to Celebrate About, but Why?

The fact that these exceptional people of faith experienced sickness despite their righteous walk is very telling about the power of sin itself, because without sin having entered the world, there would have been no sickness and pain, a point Price does not refute. But to stipulate that every sickness is a result of committing a specific sin or unfaithfully walking with the Lord is as cruel as what the Twelve disciples, upon seeing a man born blind, asked Jesus, "Who sinned, this man or his parents, that he was born blind?" (John 9:2b).

Perhaps we are all philosophers at heart, especially when bad things happen. When my sister-in-law was dying of cancer many years ago, one relative opined that it was because my family was not supportive of me in ministry (something I never felt). When a friend's wife was killed in an automobile accident, the father of the deceased opined that this tragedy occurred because my friend did not respond to God's call to enter full-time ministry. What philosophy did these people have in common? The same as that of the disciples: bad things happen because of the bad things we have done. What Jesus said to his men must have stunned them: "It was not that this man sinned, or his parents, but that the works of God might be displayed in him" (John 9:3). Christ then proceeded to heal him, and this redemptive story, having been included in the Gospel of John, has been retold to generations of people to remind them of God's great power and grace.

To be sure, nothing Jesus said on that day nullifies the view that specific sins can cause sickness. After all, Christ told an invalid person whom he had just healed, "Stop sinning or something worse may happen to you" (John 5:14 NIV). For instance, driving under the influence of alcohol (i.e., the sin of violating civic law or doing something that leads to dissipation) surely increases the likelihood of a car accident, while excessive drinking of alcohol (a.k.a., the sin of drunkenness) can damage the liver. But since finite humans cannot know why people get sick, we should not always try to figure it out. Instead, we should "weep with those who weep" (Rom 12:15b) and pray that "the sick person" will get "well" (Jas 5:15).

Healing in the Radical Middle

In view of all that has been discussed, what does divine healing in the Radical Middle look like? First, yes, God heals, and no, God does not heal regardless of the level of our faith or the sincerity of the confession of our sins. Second, divine healing in the Radical Middle accepts that, on the one hand, an unfaithful walk with the Lord (i.e., a life of sin) can lead to sickness, and on the other hand, a faithful walk with the Lord does not guarantee that the faithful will never fall ill.

THE IMPORTANCE OF A PROPER VIEW OF DEATH FOR HEALING IN THE RADICAL MIDDLE

I began this chapter with a tense meeting among young church planters in an Eastern European country, because a well-meaning young leader desperately wanted to incorporate a healing ministry into a new church. He sincerely believed that that was how the new church was going to distinguish itself from the tradition-bound Orthodox Church and Brethren Church.

What Really Impresses the Skeptics

Yet, had he asked the evolutionary biologist Richard Dawkins, arguably the world's most famous atheist, what would impress him the most about Christian believers, his answer would have surprised the young church planter enamored with divine healing. While I find much of the thoughts expressed in Dawkins' *The God Delusion* to be the atheist equivalent of preaching to the choir, I do agree with one thing he says. Dawkins, in the latter part of his book, tells a story of an abbot who told his dying colleague, "Congratulations! That's brilliant news. I wish I were coming with you."[33] He then writes:

> The abbot, it seems, really was a sincere believer. But it is precisely because it is so rare and unexpected that his story catches our attention, almost provokes our amusement . . . Why don't all Christians . . . say something like the abbot when they hear that a friend is dying? When a devout woman is told by the doctor that she has only months to live, why doesn't she beam with excited

33. Dawkins, *God Delusion*, 398.

anticipation, as if she has just won a holiday in the Seychelles? "I can't wait!" Why don't faithful visitors at her bedside shower her with messages for those who have gone before? "Do give my love to Uncle Robert when you see him . . ." Why don't religious people talk like that when in the presence of the dying? Could it be that they don't really believe all that stuff they pretend to believe?[34]

Unbeknownst to Dawkins, he is pointing to a proper perspective on death that is absolutely necessary for believers to embody in order to uphold God's healing in the Radical Middle.

Death Be Not Proud

It seems patently obvious that we who live in the affluent West, including believers, are very focused on living well here on earth, seemingly thinking that the longer we stay, the better. We have many books on how to live well but hardly any on how to die well.[35] For me, no one embodied an outlook on death more powerfully than my father, an immigrant from South Korea, who was told by his doctor, a Hindu, that he had only three months to live; a routine checkup led to discovery of terminal lung cancer that had long spread to his brain. How did he respond to this horrific prognosis that turned out to be very accurate? My sister, who translated for our father during that visit, said the following in her eulogy for him:

> On October 15, my dad was told he had cancer and that his life expectancy was about three months. I will never forget how my dad responded to his devastating news. As shocked as he was—since he never expected this kind of result—the first thing dad told the doctor was, "You say cancer, I say no problem. I like Jesus Christ. God blessed my life, I go when God calls." And then my dad pointed at the Hindu doctor and said, "You, Jesus Christ." I looked at the doctor, thinking maybe he was a bit offended by what my dad had just told him, but all he could say was he was happy to be here, to be in the moment with us

---

34. Ibid., 398–99.

35. *The Last Lecture* (2008) quickly comes to mind. Randy Pausch, a computer science professor and young father, wrote this book for his small children before his untimely death from cancer. He writes, "We cannot change the cards we are dealt, just how we play the hand." Pausch, *Last Lecture*, 17.

because people generally do not respond this way with this kind of devastating news.[36]

To the extent that this Hindu doctor was impressed by the Christian hope firmly expressed by my father, it was not a hope in the certainty of divine healing if he only had enough faith, but a hope in Christ and his promise: "Let not your hearts be troubled. Believe in God; believe also in me. In my Father's house are many rooms. If it were not so, would I have told you that I go to prepare a place for you? And if I go and prepare a place for you, I will come again and will take you to myself, that where I am you may be also" (John 14:1–3). Perhaps, those of us in the West are not looking forward to seeing the Father's house because we are quite content "to dwell in [our] "paneled," that is, luxurious, "houses" (Hag 1:4b).

My father never heard the phrase "Radical Middle"—he didn't have to; he simply embodied it. Choosing not to have any surgery, since it was useless at that point, he opted to pray for healing, that is, if that was God's will (1 John 5:14). "I cannot lose," I remember my dad telling me, "If God heals me, then I can continue to serve him here, but if he does not, then I am going to be with Jesus." That is the epitome of God's healing in the Radical Middle! And it makes praying for the sick, particularly those who are terminally ill, so much easier. So we pray for healing in faith and through the exercise of the gift of healing, knowing that "to live is Christ, and to die is gain" (Phil 1:21b). And when we approach healing and death in the Radical Middle, maybe it will give atheists like Dawkins, who have no hope for an afterlife, at least a moment to pause; it certainly appeared that the Hindu doctor was touched. In the meantime, until the day of our departure arrives, we serve God with all our hearts!

QUESTIONS FOR REFLECTION AND DISCUSSION

1. Let's share about our healing stories—you or maybe someone you know whom God healed miraculously. What did you learn from that experience?

---

36. Hedda Bong, the eulogy written for our father and read at his funeral on November 21, 2005, at Fairfax Memorial Park, Fairfax, Virginia.

2. Now, let's share about when the awaited healing didn't come and the person we loved passed away. What did you learn from that experience?

3. Why is the matter of divine healing so important? Can wrong teachings on this matter have grave consequences? What are some wrong teachings on this that we need to avoid?

4. We read about what impressed the atheist Richard Dawkins about Christian believers. Ultimately, what is the most powerful witness we can impart to the world? (2 Tim 4:6–8; Phil 1:21–23).

5. Are you hurt? Are you in pain? Take the time to pray for yourself. Sometimes we don't receive what we ask for because it isn't God's will (1 John 5:14), but other times, "you do not have, because you do not ask God" (Jas 5:3). Do you know anyone who is sick right now? Pray for that person.

11

Understanding the Western Mindset, Scripture, and the Disposition Necessary for the Radical Middle and Spiritual Growth

HAVING REACHED THE LAST chapter, recall what was said in chapter 1: one undeniable truth about the Christian movement has been its divisive nature, particularly among those who firmly believe in Scripture as God's eternal, unchanging word. And there is nothing quite like a fractured and feuding body of Christ that discredits the message of Christ to the world.

Why is it, then, that those who revere the Bible are more prone to divisiveness than those who have a low view of Scripture? (At least it seems that way.) Inasmuch as this has to do with attitude, a key contributing factor is a fundamental misunderstanding of the nature of the Bible. While most people who contend for Scripture are sincere, this mix-up has fostered an immature disposition that renders them unable or unwilling to "make every effort to keep the unity of the Spirit through the bond of peace" (Eph 4:3 NIV).

The objective of the final chapter is twofold. First, after succinctly presenting the nature of Scripture, I will argue how our misunderstanding of it has led to fracturing the body of Christ. Second, I will present a proper outlook that is necessary to maintain the unity of the Spirit amid conflicting situations as an outgrowth of spiritual growth and maturity.

A WESTERN MINDSET

In chapter 4, I mentioned Bart Ehrman, a leading critic of the Christian faith who, after having embraced the gospel in his youth, gave it up during his doctoral study at Princeton Theological Seminary.[1] He felt as if he was sold a faulty theological product at the Moody Bible Institute and Wheaton College, the two Christian institutions he attended. Among many problems he has with the New Testament is inerrancy, the belief that because Scripture is inspired by the Spirit (2 Tim 3:16–17), "everything that the Bible teaches or affirms, properly interpreted, is absolutely true. The Bible does not teach anything that is false or erroneous."[2] In response to this doctrine, Ehrman says, "How does it help us to say that the Bible is the inerrant word of God if in fact we don't have the words that God inerrantly inspired?"[3] By this he means that Scripture in its original autograph is full of factual errors. As a key example he notes that "the Mark 2:26 reference to Abiathar as high priest during the days of David" is incorrect since "according to 1 Samuel 21:2, Ahimelech was the high priest."[4] (See Appendix C for my response.) Having opened this can of worms but also needing to complete this book, I feel obligated to explain only briefly Ehrman's allegation and how it relates to the last chapter.

Scripture Seen through a Western Mindset

As I said elsewhere, one tendency with systematic theologians is a penchant for breaking the Bible down and then organizing the data into a tidy and airtight system built on precise terms and definitions. This appeals to their Western mindset that privileges a certain conception of reason and logic; therefore, for instance, numeric precision in historical narratives is expected. A problem, therefore, emerges whenever numeric imprecision is found in the Bible. Consider this example: How many times did Peter deny Jesus? Note that Mark in his gospel has Peter deny Jesus three times before the rooster crowed twice (Mark 14:72), while the rest of the

---

1. Ehrman, in a 2006 interview, said, "In short, my study of the Greek New Testament, and my investigation into the manuscripts that contain it, led to a radical rethinking of my understanding of what the Bible is. This was a seismic change for me." Burge, "Lapsed Evangelical Critic," 26.

2. Cowan and Wilder, *In Defense of the Bible*, 5–6.

3. Burge, "Lapsed Evangelical Critic," 26.

4. Ibid., 26.

gospel writers have the rooster crow only once before the denial. Is this a problem? Many years ago, Harold Lindsell, a serious theologian who taught at Fuller Seminary, thought so. "In his widely quoted *Battle for the Bible* . . . [he] found the differences between the gospels' accounts of Peter's denials so great that he postulated that Peter actually disavowed knowing Jesus *six* times!"[5]—three before the rooster crowed once and three more when the rooster crowed twice. Poor Peter!

The point, which Ehrman may not have heard during his formative years, is this: people tell their stories differently due to dissimilar personal and/or cultural orientations, and the Holy Spirit did not interfere with that while inspiring the biblical writers whose cultural context was Hebraic and Greco-Roman in antiquity, not Western in the twenty-first century. The central problem with skeptics like Ehrman, therefore, is their Western-centric orientation that demands precision, numeric or otherwise. Thus, they are unable to handle what are deemed to be discrepancies in the Bible that were not problematic to the original, non-Western audience.

Theologizing the Bible with a Western Mindset

Of course, cessationists would vehemently defend Scripture against the likes of Ehrman, but they do share one thing in common: a Western-centric orientation.

As pointed out in chapter 6, for cessationists, with respect to events occurring in the present that cannot be explained by science, their orientation is naturalism on the one hand, and rationalism on the other. But cessationists will not admit this; instead, they assert that their conclusion—the sign gifts have long ceased—is a result of sound hermeneutics. But the findings of chapters 6–10 show that their conclusion is quite imbalanced, because of its unsound hermeneutics of logocentrism, which privileges Scriptures that lend support to one's preferred theology, while ignoring or distorting inconvenient biblical texts. What is going on? It could be that cessationists are hiding their Western bias against the supernatural under the cloak of another Western bias that favors an airtight systematic theology that poses as advanced biblical knowledge. While no one may say that about continuationists, the penchant for prosperity teaching by a good number of them suggests that crass materialism—born

5. Blomberg, "You Asked," para. 1.

and bred in the West—is what drives their "faith." Apparently, cessation-ists and certain continuationists are joined at the "Western" hip.

THEOLOGICAL CONTENTIOUSNESS

Laying all the blame of theological contentiousness solely on how the West prefers to theologize is reductionistic, especially since both Jesus and the apostle Paul had to address this issue among the very committed: their own followers.

Contentiousness: A Problem from the Outset

At the very outset of this book, the following event involving John the apostle was mentioned. Once, he said to Jesus, "Master, we saw someone casting out demons in your name, and we tried to stop him, because he does not follow us." Jesus responded, "Do not stop him, for the one who is not against you is for you" (Luke 9:49–50). Here, John tried to stop another believer from doing a good thing, just because he was not one of the Twelve disciples. Instead of acting graciously toward others out of gratitude for being chosen by Christ, John took his position to mean admission to an exclusive club that gave him status and power to keep others out. This incident showed that John had room to grow in humility, love, and unity. (Thank God that John, in time, was transformed to be known as the apostle of love—that ought to give us hope.)

The early church was no different. Paul, describing the divisiveness at the church in Corinth, wrote: "For it has been reported to me by Chloe's people that there is quarreling among you, my brothers. What I mean is that each one of you says, 'I follow Paul,' or 'I follow Apollos,' or 'I follow Cephas,' or 'I follow Christ.' Is Christ divided?" (1 Cor 1:11–13a). The issues that separated these committed and yet divisive believers were not of fundamental doctrinal importance since these groups were united on those fundamentals, as evidenced by being taught by spiritual teachers who shared the same doctrines—but that made no difference. This shows that theological contentiousness is a problem which the more committed are prone to commit.

Contentiousness: Exacerbated by its Personal Nature

So why is it that among those who study the same book—the Bible— seriously, such as theologians and pastors, some are drawn to one theological direction while others pull toward another? That is to ask, why is it that ardent advocates of respective systematic theologies are so committed to defending their own positions as biblical while discrediting other viewpoints? While everyone would say, "Mine is biblically warranted," there is more than meets the eye. And we get to see this when these advocates lower their guard and share why their teaching is *personally* important to them.

The Making of a Strong Advocate of Positional Theology

For example, consider professor of theology Michael Horton at Westminster Seminary California. He is known for his Reformed-based positional theology that emphasizes what the believers already possess in Christ by virtue of having been imputed with the righteousness of Christ apart from works (2 Cor 5:21). Says Horton, "Every believer possesses everything of Christ's . . . Every believer is spirit-filled."[6]

But, he grew up in a church environment in which much emphasis was placed on what believers must do to attain what is called "the Higher Life" or "the Spirit-Filled Life."[7] What is in view is sanctification, that is, breaking free from the power of sin to live a holy life. Horton describes this approach as one driven "by imperatives: 'Do this.' 'Confess that.' 'Follow these steps,' and so on."[8] After agonizing over whether he was a carnal or spiritual Christian, this despite trying hard to be the latter, he moved on to the Reformed theology with its emphasis on the believer's position in Christ and resting in its permanence and security. Evidently, this transition was very personal, for he writes:

> I will have to explain why this issue is so important to me. I was raised in Bible churches pastored by those who had been taught by Zane Hodges, Charles Ryrie, and other proponents of the "carnal Christian" teaching . . . [and] "Higher Life" . . . As a teenager I had discovered the writings of the Reformers . . . The

6. Horton, *Christ the Lord*, 113.

7. Ibid., 112, 113.

8. Ibid., 114.

more deeply I delved into these works, the more cynical I became toward the schizophrenia I had experienced all along in trying to get from the bottom of the spiritual ladder to the point where I could finally be victorious . . . In most cases with which I have been familiar (including my own), those who have been nurtured in this environment . . . live in constant fear of whether they are "carnal Christians" . . . What they really need is Christ as the sufficiency for their faith, their justification, their sanctification and growth, their obedience and perseverance in faith to the end.[9]

There is no question that many Scriptures support Horton's positional theology that takes a dim view of having to "do this" and "confess that" to reach the Higher Life (Isa 28:10; Col 2:20–22).

But it is evident that he allows his past experience to so color his present hermeneutics that any Scripture that underscores human responsibility in sanctification is deprivileged, meaning reinterpreted or even ignored. So the apostle Paul's command to the Ephesian believers to "be filled with the Spirit" becomes "merely a figure of speech to him."[10] Paul's command to the carnal Corinthians (1 Cor 3:3), "Let us cleanse ourselves from every defilement of body and spirit, bringing holiness to completion in the fear of God" (2 Cor 7:1b), can hardly be mentioned from the pulpit. In so teaching, this earnest theologian privileges our permanent standing in Christ while deprivileging our actual state in which we are told to "work out your own salvation with fear and trembling, for it is God who works in you, both to will and to work for his good pleasure" (Phil 2:12b–13).

Sanctification in the Radical Middle, however, embraces both our permanent standing in Christ in which we are already "sanctified [and] . . . "justified" (1 Cor 6:11b), and our fluctuating state in which we are being set free from the power of sin (Rom 6:11–14) through the Holy Spirit. There is, of course, tension, which is essential for any growth, be it spiritual or muscular. But regardless of how we respond to God's command for us to "bring holiness to completion," we should always be reminded that nothing we ever do or fail to do makes us any more or less "holy and acceptable to God" (Rom 12:1b) in Christ.

9. Ibid., 30, 31, 32.

10. Ibid., 113. Recall what John Stott says on this matter: "The filling can be repeated and in any case needs to be maintained . . . The fullness of the Spirit is intended to be not a static but a developing experience." Stott, *Baptism & Fullness* 48, 61. Evidently, the command to be filled with the Spirit is more than a metaphor to him.

The Making of a Strong Advocate of Free Grace

Robert Wilkin, a strong advocate of free grace, is no different from his theological opposite, Horton, in that he too experienced a powerful release from a teaching that had long bound him. At the very outset of his work, *Confident in Christ*, under the heading of "Why I wrote this book," he writes:

> I was in [a small religious boy's club] from first through eighth grades . . . Over time I came to believe the club's teaching that salvation was only for those who were holy enough. I also accepted the teaching that if I ever did gain salvation; I would lose it forever if I committed even one sin. The club taught that sinless perfection was necessary to maintain my salvation, and that if I lost it, I could never get it back.[11]

One cannot help but feel great sympathy for a young Wilkin, getting crushed under the weight of such extreme legalism and agonizing over whether he was good enough for God's acceptance. It stands to reason that he found much comfort in a version of eternal security that guarantees salvation no matter what you do, including no longer believing. So how airtight does his soteriology get? Any mention of work in relation to salvation, including repentance, sets off alarm bells for a false gospel, leading to questioning the salvation of many. He says,

> Many pastors, Bible college professors, seminary professors, and missionaries believe in lordship salvation and hence need to hear the gospel of grace. Don't assume that they are saved just because they are pastors of churches that have words like Grace, Faith, Believer, or Bible in the name. The key is what they believe.[12]

How ironic that Wilkin is questioning others' salvation, the very thing that was done to him in his youth.

Evidently, as is the case with Horton, Wilkin's prior experience with rigid legalism affected his hermeneutics, for his conclusion is based solely on just one book of the Bible, the Gospel of John. He states: "The Fourth Gospel is the only book of all Scripture whose stated purpose is evangelistic, that is, to tell unbelievers what they must do to have eternal life (John 20:31)." Highlighting that John does not use the words "repent"

11. Wilkin, *Confident in Christ*, ix.
12. Ibid., 186.

or "repentance" in his gospel, Wilkin concludes that "this shows that repentance is *not* a synonym for faith in Christ and that it is *not* a necessary precursor to faith in Christ"[13] (italics his). His logic posits that since salvation does not correlate with turning from sin (i.e., repentance), then continuing to live in sin, even to the point of no longer believing, has no ramifications for salvation itself. Thus, in Wilkin's version of hermeneutics of logocentricism—where one book of the Bible is privileged while others are completely ignored—antithetic Scriptures such as 2 Corinthians 7:10a, "For godly grief produces a repentance that leads to salvation," or Luke 24:47, "Repentance for the forgiveness of sins should be proclaimed in his name to all nations," can therefore hardly be acknowledged.[14] In the Radical Middle, however, both faith and repentance are upheld equally: "Repent and believe in the gospel" (Mark 1:15b).

The Making of a Strong Advocate of the Radical Middle

This preceding section highlights one key reason why we turn theology into an airtight system and then defend it at all costs—a strong personal conviction emerging from a painful past. Of course, I am no exception. I must confess that a rather embarrassing incident in my past motivates me to advocate for the Radical Middle.

In 1985, just before turning 25, I was on the verge of losing my faith while attending a liberal seminary in Washington, D.C., because I did not know how to respond to the theological liberalism I had only read about in secondary sources; now, I was hearing it directly for the first time, and doubts kept creeping into my mind. It was a dark moment of despair captured by what I told my mother one day: "I don't know whether there is a God." In time, the Lord, in his wonderful grace and mercy, would rescue me from that massive confusion, which then left me with one deep conviction: I ought to spend the majority of my time and energy defending

---

13. Ibid., 201–2.

14. Actually, Wilkin did not invent this view. Some in Dispensationalism teach that unless a believer chooses to accept the lordship of Jesus, Christ is merely a savior to him. Though such believer will not experience a blessed earthly life, whether Jesus is his Lord is still up to him. Thus, the advocates of this view do not believe repentance (as in turning from sin) as a condition of salvation. Lewis Chafer, founder of Dallas Theological Seminary, who espoused this view, said: "The preacher has the obligation 'of preaching the Lordship of Christ to Christians exclusively, and the Saviorhood of Christ to those who are unsaved . . . The New Testament does not impose repentance upon the unsaved as a condition of salvation'" (Grudem, *Systematic Theology*, 715).

the gospel against the theological liberalism that corrodes it, rather than fight against fellow believers over issues that are far less important. It left an indelible mark in my life.

I am not saying that we should not try to correct those who err; in fact, the apostle Paul commands us to warn them, but not "as an enemy, but . . . as a brother" (2 Thess 3:15b). While the apostle's teaching is far more important than mine (after all, his words are inspired), that is what this book tries to do: "Not judge by appearances, but judge with right judgment" (John 7:24) to correct the errors of both hard cessationism and flawed aspects of continuationism through the paradigm of the Radical Middle. For what? To settle our petty differences so that together we can address more consequential matters such as theological liberalism, religious pluralism, social injustice, etc. (The danger of my view will be presented at the end.)

UNDERSTANDING THE NATURE OF SCRIPTURE TO PROPERLY THEOLOGIZE

Despite the problems of contentiousness and disunity prompted by uncivil dialogue among advocates of different airtight theologies, we in the West will continue to theologize because systematizing—whether it be a stamp collection or organizing a walk-in closet—is in our nature. But whether Calvinism or Arminianism, cessationism or continuationism, the true nature of Scripture must first be recognized before we theologize. If we fail to see it, then our adherence to any systematic theology, tidy and airtight, would only exacerbate the contentiousness that makes a mockery of Christ's prayer "that [we] may all be one" (John 17:21a).

Not a Theology Book

At the risk of raising the ire of some theology students, we need to understand first and foremost that the Bible itself is not a theology book— meaning, God did not write a systematic theology. Richard Gaffin, now a retired professor of biblical and systematic theologian at Westminster Seminary, agrees as well: "The Bible is . . . not a systematic-theological textbook or a manual of ethics (as it has long tended to be treated, at least in practice); it is 'not a dogmatic handbook but a historical book full of dramatic interest.'"[15] And this story is told through "different genres of inspired books from which we draw theology and doctrine."[16] The fact that Scripture consists of poetry (whose meaning is not always apparent), fictional narratives (parables), and many antithetic (i.e., two contradicting propositions) and antinomic (i.e., two opposites that are reasonable in themselves) revelations affirms the notion that Scripture does not immediately lend itself to be systematized.[17] Subsequently, the Bible should not be perceived primarily as a book of data to be organized into an airtight, logical, and tidy system under the rubric of one overarching or dominant theological outlook.

Scripture's Primary Intent

If Scripture is not a theology book, then what is its primary intent? Consider what Paul told the Philippians, some of whom must have disagreed with his teaching: "And if on some point you think differently, that too God will make clear to you" (Phil 3:15b NIV). It is safe to assume that Paul's disagreement with them was not over essential matters, or otherwise, he would have said to them what was told to the Galatians who insisted that circumcision, along with faith in Christ, was necessary for salvation (i.e., faith + works = salvation): "You have fallen away from grace" (Gal 5:4b NIV). But neither did Paul say, "Hey, let's agree to disagree"; instead, he said, "God will make clear to you," which, if said to us who live in a much more sensitive culture than Paul's (for better or worse), it would have made us feel slighted.

Now, pay attention to what Paul says next to the Philippians: "Only let us live up to what we have already attained" (Phil 3:16 NIV). While the apostle is certainly not discounting the need for further dialogue with those who disagree with his teaching, he seems to be far more concerned with them living a fruitful life based on God's already clear, revealed doctrine. John puts it: "Whoever claims to live in him must walk as Jesus did" (1 John 2:6 NIV). That is true spirituality—becoming more like Jesus. Suffice it to say, the main intent of God's word is to transform us, that is,

15. Gaffin, "Cessationist View," 54. The quote in the citation is from Vos, *Biblical Theology*, 26.

16. Park, "Introduction to AMI."

17. The Bible is not always chronological either. For instance, the order of Genesis 10 and 11 is reversed. After God "confused the language of all the earth" (Gen 11:9), then "the nations spread abroad on the earth" (Gen 10:32).

to grow to spiritual maturity, through the "renewal of [our] mind" (Rom 12:2b), not so that we do more theologizing, but as James says, "Not forgetting what they have heard, but doing it—they will be blessed in what they do" (Jas 1:25b NIV)—in other words, less theologizing, more doing the will of God.

Three Losses when Theologizing is Done Improperly

As indicated already, the ultimate outcome of theologizing in such a partial manner, fueled by a strong personal conviction that leads to a biased outlook, is contentiousness that leads to disunity, which diminishes the credible witness of the church. Along with this, there are at least three concomitant losses that further weaken the church's health and credibility.

The Loss of True Biblical Knowledge

First, recall what was said in chapter 3: Knowing well one's systematic theology does not necessarily mean that true biblical knowledge has been gained, because ignoring or distorting inconvenient Scriptures is obligatory to systemize the Bible rigidly from one dominant angle.

Mentioned in chapter 1 is what Thomas Ice, a dispensationalist theologian known for his teaching on the rapture, said about the Reformed theologian R. C. Sproul, who called the rapture a "silly idea": "Someone who thinks that the rapture is a silly concept doesn't know the Bible."[18] That was partially true. Sproul—a Reformed theologian (recently passed away), strong Five-Point Calvinist, and cessationist—certainly knew his Reformed theology and cessationism, perhaps better than the Bible itself (Matt 22:29).

This, then, is a common mistake that ardent advocates of different systematic theologies make, including cessationists and continuationists: while the advocates of each group believe that they are contending for the truth of God, they are actually contending for the rightness of their respective systematic theology (except when they focus on the essentials and allow the Bible to speak for itself).

---

18. Ice, "When Will the Rapture Come?"

The Loss of Grace

Second, it should be no surprise then that in an environment in which theologizing is done contentiously and with partiality, it engenders ungraciousness toward those with whom one disagrees. Once, Joshua Harris, the author of *I Kissed Dating Goodbye* and a well-known Calvinist pastor, quipped that those who spoke to him before he became a Calvinist about the doctrine of grace did so with very little of it. He says,

> I remember some of the first encounters I had with Calvinists. I'm sorry to say they represented the doctrine of grace with a total lack of grace. They were spiteful, cliquish, and arrogant. I didn't even stick around to understand what they were teaching.[19]

That's ironic, but it's all too true; the loss of grace is like losing our soul.[20]

The Loss of Doctrine

The third outcome when people witness ungracious battles fought among advocates of competing theological systems is not taking theology or doctrine seriously at all. When T. D. Jakes, a megachurch pastor in Dallas who hails from the United Pentecostal "Oneness" Church which has traditionally denied the Trinity, was asked about theology, he said, "I am too busy trying to preach the Gospel to split hairs. People in my generation are lost, in prison, wounded, and alone . . . Many of our generation are dying without knowing God—not dying for the lack of theology, but for lack of love."[21] (He has since changed his view on the Trinity.)[22] Of course, we do not want to throw the baby out with the bath water, meaning theology and doctrine are still very important, for Paul reminded Pastor Timothy, "Watch your life and doctrine closely. Persevere in them, because if you do, you will save both yourself and your hearers" (1 Tim

19. Reynolds, "Resurgence of Calvinism?" 33.

20. Yes, I do feel self-conscious over not being gracious enough toward those whose works I felt compelled to critique.

21. Pivec, "The 'D' word," 14.

22. Since making that statement, "Bishop T. D. Jakes says he has moved away from a 'Oneness' view of the Godhead to embrace an orthodox definition of the Trinity—and that some in the Oneness Pentecostal movement now consider him a heretic." Faust, "T. D. Jakes Embraces Doctrine," para. 1.

4:16 NIV). Since the Greek word *didachē*, translated here as "doctrine," is also rendered as "teaching" in the New Testament (2 John 1:9), it points to the importance of our teachings being established on sound doctrines.

Wisdom to Pick Our Doctrinal Battles

Although the Bible is not a theology book, we still need to draw theology and doctrine from it. Any deleterious doctrinal change will lead to erroneous beliefs with a fatal result, such as when people compromise the essentials of the historic Christian faith that have ramifications for salvation. Consider those who apparently used to worship and serve with the apostle John but left him to join the docetists who denied the humanity of Jesus (1 John 4:2–3; 2 John 1:7–9). That these docetists corrupted one of the essential doctrines of the Christian faith—the full humanity of Christ—cessationists and continuationists would agree. For those who take Scripture seriously, this is not too hard to recognize, since John, in reference to them, declared, "Every spirit that does not confess Jesus is not from God. This is the spirit of the antichrist" (1 John 4:3a).

And if the world judges cessationists and continuationists for agreeing with the apostle Peter, who declared that "there is salvation in no one else, for there is no other name under heaven given among men by which we must be saved" (Acts 4:12), because it goes against politically correct religious pluralism, then that is par for the course: "If the world hates you, know that it has hated me before it hated you," said Jesus (John 15:18). That is a God-honoring witness of the church to the world.

What Would the Apostle Peter Say to Cessationists?

So what would the apostle Peter, who later died for his belief in the exclusivity of Christ (John 21:19), say to cessationists and continuationists who fight over spiritual gifts? To answer that question, it helps to remember what really alarmed Peter upon realizing that "there are some things in [Paul's letters] that are hard to understand" (2 Pet 3:16a). He was startled that "the ignorant and unstable twist [them] to their own destruction, as they do the other Scriptures" (2 Pet 3:16b). Not only did their twisting hurt them but it no doubt affected the church at large, for "a little leaven leavens the whole lump" (1 Cor 5:6b).

Considering that, what would Peter say to cessationists who ignore and distort inconvenient Scriptures to protect their cessationism while telling continuationists, "I have no need of you" (1 Cor 12:21b), thereby fracturing the body of Christ? I imagine that he may say this:

> If you are not going to consider the entire Scripture to study the sign gifts, then leave that matter alone. Doing nothing is better than misrepresenting Scripture that speaks of two types of tongues, prophecies, and apostles. God still heals, but not always. Instead, I prefer that you accept the validity of the sign gifts for today, and then gently point out to continuationists, as brothers caught in some errors (2 Thess 3:15), how they can practice spiritual gifts more biblically and orderly (1 Cor 14:33).

And being familiar with the apostle Paul's writing, Peter might gently remind them that their fight is not with continuationists; rather, they ought to "fight the good fight of the faith. Take hold of the eternal life to which [they] were called" (1 Tim 6:12a).

What Would the Apostle Peter Say to the Continuationists?

Then the apostle Peter may remind continuationists to use their gifts for the "common good" (1 Cor 12:7), to edify the church (1 Cor 14:5), and to "serve others" (1 Peter 4:10). And to those who are enamored with prosperity teaching, "Gain all you can . . . Save all you can . . . Give all you can."[23] And finally, to those among Pentecostals and charismatics for whom the term "charismaniac" has been coined, he may gently remind them, "Love the giver of spiritual gift, not the gifts themselves."

And to both cessationists and continuationists, the apostle Peter may quote from a man whom he called "our beloved Paul" (2 Pet 3:15b): "I appeal to you, brothers, by the name of our Lord Jesus Christ, that all of you agree, and that there be no divisions among you, but that you be united in the same mind and the same judgment" (1 Cor 1:10). As Paul and Peter, whose relationship may have been strained after Paul's public rebuke of Peter over the latter's hypocritical act that compromised the gospel (Gal 2:11–14), eventually became dear brothers, here's hoping that one day cessationists and continuationists will call each other dear brothers as well. But this will not happen unless we all embody the character of Christ.

23. Wesley, "Use of Money," paras. 5, 13, 21.

KEY DISPOSITIONS FOR THE RADICAL MIDDLE

We saw earlier what may happen when a theological disagreement between two passionate believers reaches a boiling point: acting ungraciously toward each other and saying condescendingly, "You don't know your Bible" as if to mean, "If you really knew the Bible, then you would see the rightness of my theology." For sure, biblical knowledge is necessary to effectively theologize in the Radical Middle since, when facing a pair of antithetic revelations, the path of least resistance is *not* taken, that is, a genuine attempt is made to consider both claims regardless of their seeming contradiction. That can be a lot of work. But having much knowledge of the Bible, or more accurately, a particular understanding of it (a.k.a., systematic theology) can actually work against embracing the Radical Middle. While knowledge is necessary for the Radical Middle, that alone is insufficient; the possessor of knowledge must also embody a certain disposition or attitude (i.e., the character of Christ) without which there is no willingness to accept the Radical Middle. For that matter, neither will we grow spiritually.

Humility

The first disposition necessary for the Radical Middle is humility. According to James who writes, "God opposes the proud but gives grace to the humble" (James 4:6b), humility can be defined as the absence of arrogance and pride, which the Corinthians, feuding over who possessed more ostentatious spiritual gifts, had in abundance. So Paul told them, "For now we see in a mirror dimly, but then face to face. Now I know in part; then I shall know fully, even as I have been fully known" (1 Cor 13:12). Since "face to face" refers to that time when we will be with God in heaven, "see[ing] in a mirror dimly" and "know[ing] in part" speak of our experiences here and now. Suffice it to say, these descriptions point to a lack of complete clarity with respect to what we know in this life about God and his plans, as opposed to in heaven when complete lucidity will replace this unclarity. I believe a humble disposition stems from recognizing two related but distinctive limitations.

Admitting Human Limitation

The first limitation is the human limitation which consists of three aspects.

First, we ought not to forget the corrupting influence of the sinful nature on our minds. Sometimes, we just don't want to give others the satisfaction of informing them that they are right, and we are wrong. (I know this well from my marriage.) This is a formidable limitation that we may not always be aware of. Therefore, we must imitate the psalmist who prayed, "Search me, O God, and know my heart! Try me and know my thoughts! And see if there be any grievous way in me, and lead me in the way everlasting!" (Ps 139:23–24).

Second, we must admit that no one on account of his or her airtight, logical, and tidy theology, has a perfect knowledge of the Bible because human intellect alone cannot understand God's word. We must keep in mind that "no one comprehends the thoughts of God except the Spirit of God," and "we have received not the spirit of the world, but the Spirit who is from God, that we might understand the things freely given us by God" (1 Cor 2:11b–12). Therefore, we ought to develop a habit of studying while praying and praying while studying, constantly asking the Lord to illuminate our minds and purify the motives of our hearts as we read God's word.

Third, we should not feel too confident about human language to believe that what we know about God as contained in our language is exhaustive and beyond analogy. No, I am not one of those deconstructionists who believe that human language is so unstable that there is no "fixed center of meaning,"[24] or if there is, it is unknowable. Nevertheless, we should not think that human language can perfectly capture all that has been revealed from above. When Paul was "caught up into paradise," he was held speechless upon hearing "inexpressible things, things that man is not permitted to tell" (2 Cor 12:4 NIV). Like a caveman lacking vocabulary to describe a computer he saw in his dream, neither Paul nor his audience at that time had the adequate language to capture what was going on in the heavenlies. The same goes for us. While Scripture is more than adequate to inform us of the things of God to hold us responsible, language itself is representational, meaning our knowledge is "a copy and shadow of the heavenly things" (Heb 8:5b). Thus, "now I know in part; then I shall know fully" (1 Cor 13:12b).

24. Markos, *From Plato to Postmodernism*, 5.

These three factors should humble us concerning what we think we know. Therefore, we should feel comfortable saying, "I do not have all the answers; others may know that which I do not understand; what I know may be incorrect; others may know it correctly." This will surely create tension that reduces the comfort level we feel toward our competence, knowledge, and preferred positions, while increasing our tolerance of those who may think differently.

Recognizing the Limits God Places around Us

The second limit is the one that God has placed around us.

My colleague Keith often says that theology is like a fence to guard the mystery of God. This is essentially what God tells Moses to do before he "[came] down on Mount Sinai in the sight of all the people" (Exod 19:11b). Then the Lord declares, "And you shall set limits for the people all around, saying, 'Take care not to go up into the mountain or touch the edge of it. Whoever touches the mountain shall be put to death" (Exod 19:12). From this we gather that limits were placed to keep the Israelites from seeing God shrouded "in fire" and "smoke" (Exod 19:18). Therefore, as far as the Israelites were concerned, besides being spared from death for seeing God, the Lord ensured that he remained a mystery to them.

Fences are placed around a property to keep people out; therefore, while onlookers may know something about the property, they do not and cannot know everything, especially about things beyond their purview. In that sense, antinomic revelation (i.e., two contradicting propositions that are in themselves reasonable) serves as a fence to guard the mystery of God, or as Packer puts it, "to recognize that here is a mystery which we cannot expect to solve in this world,"[25] including our seminaries and theological tomes. It is as if God is saying: "Don't ever think that you have figured me out. Don't trespass by trying to figure out my word down to minute details by way of ignoring or distorting Scriptures that are inconvenient in justifying your preferred theology."

While no one actually says, "I have God figured out," when our teaching implies, "God does not do this or that anymore because my theology (based on selective citing of Scriptures) will not allow that," this is equivalent to saying, "I have God figured out." And that is making a mockery of what the Lord declares in Isaiah 55:8–9: "My thoughts are

25. Packer, *Evangelism and the Sovereignty of God*, 24.

not your thoughts, neither are your ways my ways, declares the Lord. For as the heavens are higher than the earth, so are my ways higher than your ways and my thoughts than your thoughts." No, this does not mean anything goes lest some continuationists justify their bizarre behaviors or interpretations; we have the Scripture to help us to discern. But the same Scripture also tells us that God may do things that will shock us at any given moment. When God told Hosea to marry "a wife of whoredom" (Hos 1:2b), it stunned the prophet; when the one hundred twenty spoke in linguistic tongues, it "amazed and astonished" the onlookers (Acts 2:7b); and when we see Samson the playboy and Rahab the harlot mentioned along with David and Samuel (Heb 11:31, 32) in the Hall of "Saving" Faith, such amazing grace of God should shock us all!

Love

While humility is needed to embrace the Radical Middle and is indispensable to spiritual growth prompted by our sense of inadequacy (John 15:5) and Christ's sufficiency (Phil 4:13, 19), the disposition necessary to increase the desire for the Radical Middle and spiritual growth is love. How so?

A Key Understanding to be Able to Love

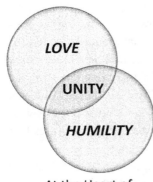

At the Heart of
the Radical Middle

As cited earlier, "knowledge puffs up but love builds up" (1 Cor. 8:1b). In the famous love chapter of 1 Corinthians 13 are found several negative characteristics that typically manifest when theological arguments become heated: impatience, unkindness, boasting, pride, rudeness, and anger. Paul's point is that love is being patient, kind, humble, not being rude and angry.

So what awareness can pacify those who are feuding and then goad them toward "the most excellent way" of love? (1 Cor 12:31 NIV). While we go to 1 Corinthians 13:12 again, the question raised here is different: How does the realization that "now we see in a mirror dimly . . . now I know in part" help us to be more patient, kind, humble, and not be rude and angry when discussing theological matters (or in dealing with any conflicts)? It is as if Paul is saying,

> Your lack of love toward those with whom you disagree, including theological disagreements—which is emblematic of spiritual immaturity (1 Cor 1:12, 3:4)—is because you are too sure of the rightness of what you believe, and the wrongness of what others believe. Unless you admit that you do not see everything clearly and correctly, you cannot help but be impatient, unkind, and rude to those who oppose your viewpoint.

In short, Paul is saying that we cannot love others apart from recognizing our own limitations. At the same time, when we disagree over theology (or, again, over anything else), we ought to make a concerted effort to find out what the opposing side truly believes, instead of demonizing them based on hearsay or a secondhand source. Ignorance breeds fear and contempt of those with whom we disagree, but an informed discussion tends to result in dialogues that can lead to, at the very least, an agreement to disagree. And carrying ourselves in this manner shows spiritual maturity.

"But Have Not Love, I Am Nothing"

For many of us who love knowledge, we need to constantly remind ourselves that ultimately, love triumphs over knowledge. Paul says in his prayer to the Ephesians, "And I pray that you, being rooted and established in love, may have power, together with all the saints, to grasp how wide and long and high and deep is the love of Christ, and to know this love that surpasses knowledge . . ." (Eph 3:17b–19a NIV). He reminds the Corinthians, "If I have the gift of prophecy and can fathom all mysteries and all knowledge . . . but do not have love, I am nothing" (1 Cor 13:2 NIV); "love never ends" (1 Cor 13:8a); and again, "knowledge puffs up, but love builds up" (1 Cor 8:1b). So whatever the conflict that drives a wedge among believers who are passionate about what they believe, particularly those who privilege word and those who favor Spirit, we say, "Brothers and sisters, 'Let us love one another, for love is from God, and whoever loves has been born of God and knows God'" (1 John 4:7). Without love there is neither the Radical Middle nor authentic spiritual growth. The fact that I am saying this is a true irony because I don't do love very well. (Thank God that I have a wife who does that well!)

WHY HUMILITY AND LOVE? IT'S FOR UNITY

Humility and love, for what? An undeniable fact is that all make mistakes in their theology. This includes pastors, whether they are American, Korean, or Mexican. While a few are renowned, like John MacArthur among cessationists and Fred Price among charismatics, most of us are ordinary. Thus, unifying the body of Christ is always hard because of differences in our beliefs and because we are people who can still act like mere men, being given to "jealousy and strife" (1 Cor 3:3a). But none of us should ever be allowed to ignore what Jesus said to the Father the night before his crucifixion: "The glory that you have given me I have given to them, that they may be one even as we are one, I in them and you in me, that they may become perfectly one, so that the world may know that you sent me and loved them even as you loved me" (John 17:22–23). Unity is essential for an authentic witness in a world full of critics, like Dawkins and Ehrman, who want nothing more than to topple our faith. As this book draws to its end, I feel it is fitting to end with two stories that show how unity is possible in Christ despite our differences. The first story is about the organization to which I belong to, and the second story concerns my time in Mexico as a missionary.

AMI in the Radical Middle

AMI is a community of churches that seeks to theologize and minister according to the Radical Middle. It stems from valuing unity that is inherent in the Triune God. So we agree on our statements of faith, purpose, and mission in order to have a common foundation and framework as we work together. We also agree to remove any obstacles that weaken our unity in Christ.

First, AMI upholds unity with respect to the essentials of the Christian faith. No time is really spent discussing the essentials because we simply accept the fundamental dogma of the church. It is a short list, but no compromise is made here. Thus, we believe it is Christ who saves us by faith alone through his substitutionary atonement. We plant new churches and send missionaries to proclaim the gospel, followed by faithfully declaring the "whole counsel of God" through proclaiming the word (Act 20:27b) and exercising all spiritual gifts by the Spirit "for the common good" (1 Cor 12:7b). Some churches are more charismatic, some pastors are more expository, some services are more hipster, but all the same, we serve under a common vision and unity in Christ.

Second, we allow liberty regarding important, but ultimately nonessential, matters, such as the ordination of women. Some of us are for it and some are not; all the same we are constantly dialoguing to explore the best way to serve together without allowing this or other important, but not-so-essential, matters to drive a wedge between us. Again, unity is valued. At the end of 2015, the annual meeting of AMI pastors was marked by a rather heated debate over the ordination of women. So afterward I spoke to all our pastors (through phone calls, emails, even a personal visit), trying to find a common ground expressed in an agreed statement and the following official statement was the fruit of this effort: "All AMI pastors acknowledge the validity of women ordained in other AMI churches; however, in light of the fact that not all agree doctrinally on this matter, it is understood that some pastors do so out of respect but without necessarily affirming it." In response, one pastor who does not support women's ordination, wrote, "I don't personally affirm or believe in women's ordination, but for the sake of fellowship and unity, I choose not to make it a primary issue . . . I can be the strongest supporter and proponent of AMI while disagreeing on this."

Third, above all, we strive to place love as the undergirding of all our theologizing and serving in the Radical Middle so that we remain in Christ who "first loved us "(1 John 4:19b). Amid all our shortcomings and deficiencies, we lean on the Lord for forgiveness, thereby being unified in his amazing grace. Against this backdrop, AMI's desire is to passionately pursue God to bring us together as it is expressed in worship, prayer, and ministry. This spirituality keeps us going in the same direction as we do ministry.

Mexican Pastors of Chihuahua in the Radical Middle

Now as I have reached the end of this book, I would like to share what the Lord led me to see and experience while serving in Chihuahua, Mexico, from 2001–11.

Contentious Pastors

The strongest denomination in Mexico is the Assemblies of God, part of the Pentecostal movement that is almost synonymous with the charismatic movement. As indicated in chapter 1, an international study discovered that more than 90 percent of Pentecostals (some in name only, since they are not open to the Spirit) around the world believe in prosperity teaching. This, along with the disorderly manner in which some gifts are practiced and overemphasized among them, bothers me as much as it bothers Pastor MacArthur. However, I am just as bothered by those who deny the spiritual gifts while justifying their stance with a rationalized theology that tends to attract people with a Western mindset. Yet what is most disturbing is the infighting among the believers over this issue of spiritual gifts, which was the case in Chihuahua, Mexico, between the Baptists and the Pentecostals.

Divorce or Reconciliation

So what shall we do in light of Christ who prayed "that they may all be one, just as you, Father, are in me, and I in you, that they also may be in us" (John 17:21a)? I opt for reconciliation. On Wednesdays, most Baptist pastors in the city came to my class, and on Thursdays, as many as thirty Assemblies of God pastors came, and this pattern went on from 2003 to 2011. One of the last courses that I produced in Mexico was "Comparative Systematic Theologies," in which several leading theologies are thoroughly compared and analyzed. As mentioned in chapter 8, this course took a year and half to go through in a weekly class lasting three to four hours. Why this course? I wanted to demonstrate in a concrete way that, first, regardless of how theologically different we may be, our agreement on the essentials of the Christian faith should unite us; second, by firmly grasping not only our preferred systematic theology but also that of others, our disagreement can be expressed in a cogent and respectable manner, instead of throwing barbs at each other.

By the time I was teaching course, I had become good friends with most of the pastors, and they knew I had their best interests at heart. Regardless, it was still hard telling the Pentecostal pastors that some of their beliefs, such as prosperity teaching and tongues as the only sign of baptism of the Holy Spirit, were not biblical. One time, after a rather brutal discussion in which several Pentecostal pastors let me have it, three of them came to me during break to offer their apology. And they all came back for the next class. It was even harder telling the Baptist pastors that all the gifts are still in operation, even though these have not always been well practiced. And to the Baptist pastor, a friend, who asked in a class whether I spoke in tongues, I said, "You have known me for all these years as your advocate; does it really matter whether I speak in tongues?" He nodded in agreement. (Later, he would serve the Lord in Egypt; now he is in Spain as a missionary.) No one walked out of the class that day; in fact, our study continued for several years more.

The Fruit of Unity

After finally finishing the course with the Baptists, I asked Pastor Javier, then the president of the Baptist Convention, to pray. Being aware of how he had felt about the Pentecostals before this course, I was both curious and nervous of how he might pray, but I was relieved when he prayed, "Dear Lord, bless the Pentecostal brothers." Later, he not only took an invitation to speak at a Pentecostal church but hosted, as mentioned before, a prayer meeting of pastors, most of whom were Pentecostals and charismatics. A year after I had left Mexico to return to the States, I received an email from Pastor Heriberto of the Assemblies of God, who, after teaching my "Comparative Systematic Theologies" course to twenty-five leaders, invited the Baptist Pastor Javier to speak at the graduation service.[26] Yes, I was very moved and gratified by Heriberto's gracious gesture toward someone on the other side of theological divide. In Spanish, we say "Se puede"— "Can be done!"

The final meeting when we all gathered as one:
the Baptists, Methodists, Pentecostals

26. I left Chihuahua in June of 2011. The email from Pastor Heriberto was sent on November 17, 2012.

FINAL WORDS

I said earlier that I would talk about the danger of my view at the end. Admittedly, I too must be on guard from converting the Radical Middle paradigm into a tidy, airtight system ("I am right and everyone is wrong") and reverting to the hermeneutics of logocentrism. A critic may argue that by advocating the Radical Middle paradigm over others, I've inherently established a similar dichotomy of right and wrong as other systematic theologies. To that end I may have done so, and my apologies for that. Not all other systems are wrong, particularly in the essentials of our faith. And the Radical Middle takes seriously the viewpoints of Reformism, Pentecostalism, Dispensationalism, and cessationism; it retains most or some of their theologies as necessary but not entirely sufficient interpretations of God's word. Here, I borrow the words of Richard Gaffin who articulated at the end of his essay, "A Cessationist View," "I am aware that I may have unintentionally misrepresented the views of others or am guilty of talking by them. Where that has happened, I apologize and look to be corrected."[27] What words of humility (because humility understands limitations), love (because love is not rude), and unity (because cessationists and continuationists are one in Christ), and I second them here. Thank you.

QUESTIONS FOR REFLECTION AND DISCUSSION

1. What has been your experience as you have studied and discussed the Bible with those who think differently on theology? Have there been some unpleasant moments?

2. What does it mean to agree to disagree? When discussing doctrinal matters, why is that disposition so important when there is an earnest disagreement among the participants?

3. What is so unsettling about finite humans trying to know everything there is to know about God? How does that look to God? What does it mean for us to enjoy the mystery of God (Isa 55:8–9; Job 42:1–3)?

4. Why is humility so important when we try to theologize?

5. Let's imagine that the person with whom you are discussing doctrinal matters doesn't know the Bible as well as you do and is using poor

27. Gaffin, "Cessationist View," 63.

arguments. How would you love that person in that moment? Why would you want to do that? Ultimately, why is love so important?

Appendix A

"The Enemy is So United, but the Church, So Divided"

ON THE SECOND FRIDAY of June 2010, before heading to my class to teach, I was about to drop off my daughter, Christy, who was teaching English in Mexico for her summer break during college, in front of a drug rehab place (one of five centers operated by *Templo Cristiano Fe y Vida* church). Just then, a man came out to inform us that the English class was canceled because of the shooting that occurred the night before. To our horror, we learned that gunmen in several suburbans came to rehab centers and proceeded to kill nineteen people. There had been other shootings in the city, but this one hit home because I was close to Pastor Rene, who ran this ministry to help more than 250 men who were trying desperately to leave the life of drugs. He also had graciously lent his church to me so that I could hold classes every Thursday with the Assemblies of God pastors at his church (which was also used as a rehab center).

The following Thursday was the final Greek class before the summer break, and I wasn't sure exactly what to do. With the other classes, I had thoroughly reviewed everything we had learned throughout the year ahead of time, using mountains of PowerPoint slides, but somehow doing that did not seem appropriate for this day. I soon had my answer as I caught sight of a workman removing the drug rehab sign from the top of the metal gate that led to the church's courtyard. He informed me that Rene decided to close down all five rehab centers because it was just too dangerous; in turf battles among the drug cartels, rehab centers were quickly becoming an easy target to get rid of their rival gangs. My heart was now really aching for my friend, who must have agonized over letting go of these men, many of whom didn't have places to go. But what choice did he have? After entering the classroom, I said to the pastors, "No Greek today, but we need to pray." And as we prayed, the grown men in the room began to sob for the people of Mexico. If there ever was a moment when I felt like I was a Mexican, it was that moment.

After praying, Rene, a burly and rough looking man, stood before us and began sharing from his heart, saying, "This is not an attack against my church or my ministry; it is an assault against all of us (the church). The enemy just recruited another 250 people to his side because these folks who left my facilities are liable to rob and kill to get drugs." At this point, Rene broke down in tears, admitting that this horrific carnage made him realize how selfish he had been as a pastor, because he prayed for God's blessing upon *his* ministry, but rarely for the other churches. "The enemy is so united," Pastor Rene quipped, "but the church, so divided, and as long there is absence of unity among us, we will remain weak."

During the following Sunday service of our Baptist church, I got a little annoyed that none of the prayers offered during the worship even hinted at what happened to this Assemblies of God church not too far from them. Being a close friend of the pastor, I got his permission to speak to the congregation for a moment. After sharing what Rene said about the absence of unity, I said, "Don't think for a moment that what happened to this Pentecostal church is just their problem, because it is our problem also. Your street and mine just got that much more dangerous because there are now more people roaming around our city, willing to do anything to get drugs." Then, I pleaded with them to pray for Rene and for the Pentecostal churches in general.

Many of us belong to good churches; I belong to Acts Ministries International and I consider it a great privilege to be part of it. However, don't forget that we are a small part of a greater movement of the kingdom of God, which is likened to a mustard seed that eventually becomes a tree under which "the birds of the air come and perch in its branches" (Matt 13:32a). Become a kingdom Christian, whose concerns extend beyond the four walls of his home or church; reach out to those who agonize, suffer, and live without hope in Christ, both here and abroad. The enemy is so united and active in their efforts to destroy people's lives, even closing down ministries that give hope, but what are we doing?

Appendix B

What a Really Good Arminian Pastor Taught Me about Unity and Humility

MANY PASTORS WHOM I had the privilege to teach in Mexico were in their forties and fifties, and some of them were in poor health. One of them was Pastor Armando, a United Methodist Church pastor and an Arminian who believes that believers can lose their salvation, which is not what I believe.

Last Friday, I received an email that Armando just passed away, and my reaction caught me by surprise: I became very emotional and began weeping profusely. This man, barely five feet tall, was the first pastor whom I had met in Juarez (a violent city bordering El Paso) while learning Spanish there in 2000. I had known about Armando's deteriorating health; he began receiving dialysis four times a day in 2010. So when I had a farewell pastoral conference before leaving Mexico in 2011, his presence was very special. Revealing how small of a person I am, I remember being peeved by a few pastors who didn't show up, especially one guy who was always asking me for favors. And this is where Armando separated himself from those who might have befriended me for what I could do for them. As I wept for him, I remembered his giving. No, not money, but many opportunities to preach at his church. A former student, who told me about his passing, said in an email (in English): "Pastor Ryun, I know how helpful Pastor Armando was to your ministry. I remember you telling us several times how he let you give the sermon in his church, even when you did not speak Spanish well in those days."

In fact, I preached seven times that year, twice in broken Spanish, because Armando wanted me to get some experience before heading to our new destination in Chihuahua (about 250 miles away).

That wasn't all. I remember being invited to his home and eating the "quietest" lunch ever: He didn't know English and my Spanish was so bad at that time that I could have been arrested for abusing it. And his counsel: I believe in eternal security (not the Free Grace type), but this Methodist pastor did not, so what was the topic of my seventh sermon? Eternal security (thinking that I was actually doing him a favor). Although I was slightly worried about his reaction, I said to myself, *Who cares, since I am about to move away?* I saw him a few days later, at which time he said earnestly, "Ryun, don't let that sermon be your first one in Chihuahua." I just knew that his concern was not theological but more pastoral; he was just looking out for me. Not long after our move, I was invited to speak at the annual Methodist men's retreat, because Armando had put in a good word for me to its organizers. Several years later, we were reunited in my city, after he was assigned to the largest Methodist church there. Soon followed dinners at each other's house (this time talking), and several more preachings and classes offered at his church. Then, he got sick and had to vacate his position.

While I hadn't thought about Armando for a while, my surprise reaction to his passing revealed how deeply I had been touched by him, because I was reminded that he was always looking out for my best interest, believing that I could be useful to God for service in his country. Despite our theological differences, he never let go of our unity in Christ; seeing me as his brother in the Lord, he did all he could to prepare me to serve in his country. So he gave me what I desperately needed: opportunities to preach even when I was brash, theologically not Methodist, and butchering Spanish. If that's not true humility, then I don't know what is.

And this got me to think about how I would like to be remembered after I am gone. It would be really heartening if someone cried because he remembered that I "look[ed] not only to [my] own interests, but also to the interests of others." Actually, Paul said that in Philippians 2:4 (NIV), adding, "Your attitude should be the same as that of Christ Jesus . . . [who] humbled himself and became obedient to death—even death on a cross" (Phil. 2:5, 8b NIV). In other words, Christ spared no expense in looking to our best interests. So thank you Jesus for sending a man into my life who embodied your heart of humility, love, and unity, to help me.

Appendix C

A Correct Understanding of Inspiration Can Resolve Many Discrepancies in the Bible

How should we deal with so-called contradictions in the Bible?

First, note that the following apparent contradiction is easy to harmonize: the differing accounts of the death of Judas Iscariot in the Gospels and Acts. Picture a situation in which the driver of a car was killed due to massive internal injuries as a result of crashing into a tree. However, during an autopsy, the coroner discovered that a heart attack would have likely killed him first before the accident. In a similar way, Judas died from having hung himself (Matt 27:5), likely on a tree at the edge of a cliff. Subsequently, once the branch was no longer able to support the weight of Judas, it broke off, causing the dead body to fall headlong in the very field he had purchased with the money he obtained from betraying Jesus. Luke, noticing that this field then became known as "Field of Blood," focused on the fall in order to connect it to Psalm 69:25: "Let his dwelling place be desolate and let no one live in it."

Of course, not every case of alleged contradiction in the Bible is easy to solve. But, plausible responses can be found as long as the inspiration of Scripture is correctly understood. While no one knows the exact nature of inspiration, it was neither mechanical (e.g., robotic) nor merely dictation. (There are exceptions such as direct quotes from God following phrases like "Thus says the Lord.") If it were so, then factors in writing that typically result in differences in style, description, and emphasis would be irrelevant to inspiration. This would imply that two authors writing about the same event must produce exactly the same account. However, the inspired writers were fully in control of their own faculties, which means that they had differences in their objectives, audience, and even cultural orientation. All these factors helped to produce distinctive writings in the Bible. These distinctions may appear as discrepancies, but nothing can be further from the truth.

For instance, take the example of the invasion of Judah by King Nebuchadnezzar of Babylon. While according to Daniel it occurred in the third year of the reign of King Jehoiakim of Judah (Dan 1:1), Jeremiah reported that it happened "in the fourth year of Jehoiakim" (Jer 25:1b). This appears contradictory since both cannot be historically true: the invasion took place either in the third or the fourth year. But when cultural factors are considered, this apparent difference is easily explained. Whereas the Babylonians counted the ascension year (when the king takes up the throne) as the year zero in their calendars, the Jews considered that as year one. Thus, the fourth year according to Jeremiah in Judah is equal to the third year according to Daniel living in Babylonia; thus, both accounts are true.

If the definition of inspiration does not allow cultural and individual idiosyncrasies, then we are forced to either question inerrancy or come up with an explanation that creates more problems. For example, as mentioned in chapter 11, a renowned theologian, noting the numeric discrepancy between Mark and Luke in their account of Peter's denial of Jesus, said that he denied him six times. While Mark reported that the rooster crowed twice upon Peter's denial of Jesus, both Matthew and Luke simply stated that "the rooster crowed" (Luke 22:60b). Instead of recognizing that no two people tell the same story exactly the same way, the mechanical view of inspiration held by this theologian caused him to react irrationally to what he deemed a contradiction. It can be argued, then, that Peter, being the main source for Mark's Gospel, vividly recalled the details of what was a personally devastating event, while Matthew and Luke simply noted the most important aspect of the event: Peter's denial of Jesus.

With respect to the discrepancy regarding who was the high priest in Nob when David went there to look for food and a sword, even though, according to Mark, it was Abiathar (Mark 2:26), it was actually Ahimelech. This certainly is a discrepancy in a factual sense, but this story should be understood from the standpoint that, again, no two people tell a story the same, and that the Holy Spirit did not interfere with this process. The fact is that Abiathar and his high priest father, Ahimelech, are at Nob when David comes there (1 Sam 21:1) to escape from Saul. Later, Abiathar does become the high priest (2 Sam 20:25). What does this mean? Jesus, while telling this story, did something we all do from time-to-time when talking about an event that happened in the past.

Let me offer this example. My wife and I were dating while we were attending seminary. Once during that time I changed the oil in her car. Now listen to how I tell this story: "Once, when my wife and I were attending Talbot, I changed the oil in my wife's car and . . ." Is there anything wrong with how I told this story? Some may say, "She was not your wife when you changed the oil for her." While that is very true in a technical sense, no one will object to that story since the owner of the car whose oil I changed indeed became my wife.

So, apparently, Jesus' statement that David entered the house of God in the days of Abiathar the high priest, was not problematic to the Jewish audience; otherwise some scribes would have redacted this story later. As to why he mentions Abiathar instead of Ahimelech, I offer three reasons. First, Abiathar was present when David ate the bread (1 Sam 22:17, 20); second, Abiathar did become the high priest later; and third, Abiathar became more renowned than his father, Ahimelech (thus, it was easier to recall his days as the high priest than those of his father). Sadly, people who grow up in churches with an inerrancy view entrenched in the Western logic of "either/or" and numeric precision that eliminates human elements involved in inspiration are susceptible to a big shock that may result in losing confidence in the Bible.

Seeing the inspiration of Scripture in this manner, it stands to reason that the Bible is a both humanly and divinely ordained book, in some ways like the humanity and divinity of Christ. Through "being carried along by the Holy Spirit" (2 Pet 1:21b), the human writers were able to pen *exactly* what the Lord wanted them to record, without compromising their individuality and cultural orientation. The word of God is inspired, as well as reliable to correctly instruct us toward "the way of the LORD" (Prov 10:29a). "It is written, 'Man shall not live by bread alone, but by every word that comes from the mouth of God'" (Matt 4:4).

Bibliography

Atkinson, Sam, et al., eds. *The Philosophy Book.* 1st Amer. ed. New York: DK, 2011.

Barclay, William. *The Gospel of John.* Vol. 1. Rev. ed. Philadelphia: Westminster, 1975.

———. *The Letters to the Corinthians.* Rev. ed. Philadelphia: Westminster, 1975.

Barker, Kenneth, ed. *The NIV Study Bible.* Grand Rapids: Zondervan, 1995.

Barro, Antonio Carlos. "Wrestling with Success." *Christianity Today* 13 (November 16, 1998) 70–71.

Bass, Clarence B. *Backgrounds to Dispensationalism: Its Historical Genesis and Ecclesiastical Implications.* Grand Rapids: Baker, 1960.

Beckwith, Francis. "Q&A: Francis Beckwith." Interview by David Neff. Christianity Today, May 9, 2007. http://www.christianitytoday.com/ct/2007/mayweb-only/119-33.0.html.

Bennett, Dennis, and Rita Bennett. *The Holy Spirit and You: A Study Guide to the Spirit-Filled Life.* Plainsfield. NJ, 1971.

Berkhof, Louis. *The History of Christian Doctrines.* Grand Rapids: Baker, 1986.

———. *Systematic Theology.* Combined ed. Grand Rapids: Eerdmans, 1996.

Bettenson, Henry, ed. *Documents of the Christian Church.* 2nd ed. London: Oxford University Press, 1967.

Blomberg, Craig. "You Asked: Are the Differing Narratives of Peter's Denials Reconcilable?" https://www.thegospelcoalition.org/article/you-asked-are-the-differing-narratives-of-peters-denials-reconcilable/.

Bloom, John A. "Theistic Evolution Isn't Fit for Survival." *Biola Magazine* (Fall 2011) 28.

Brann, Eva. *The Logos of Heraclitus.* Philadelphia: Paul Dry, 2011. Kindle.

Brown, Colin. *Philosophy & the Christian Faith.* Downers Grove, IL: InterVarsity, 1968.

Brown, Michael. Review of *Authentic Fire*, by John King. *Pneuma Review*, May 26, 2014. http://pneumareview.com/michael-browns-authentic-fire-reviewed-by-john-king/.

Burge, Gary. "The Lapsed Evangelical Critic." *Christianity Today* 6 (June 2006) 26.

Cairns, Earle E. *Christianity through the Centuries.* Grand Rapids: Zondervan, 1967.

Chang, Ryun. "Hola, the Koreans are Here! Asian Missions in Latin America Today." In *The Reshaping of Mission in Latin America*, edited by Miguel Alvarez, 178–90. Oxford, UK: Regnum, 2015.

Clark, Randy. "Strange Fire: Analysis of Introduction, Appendix, and General Method." In *Strangers to Fire: When Tradition Trumps Scripture*, edited by Robert W. Graves, 59–68. Tulsa: Empoweredlife, 2014.

Clayton, Christal. *My Faith: Series I Teacher's Book*. Covina, CA: Self-published, 1962.

Cowan, Steven B., and Terry L. Wilder, eds. *In Defense of the Bible: A Comprehensive Apologetic for the Authority of Scripture*. Nashville: Broadman and Holman, 2013.

Craig, William Lane. "Tough Questions about Science." In *Who Made God?*, edited by Ravi Zacharias and Norman Geisler, 49–72. Grand Rapids: Zondervan, 2003.

Dana, H. E., and Julius R. Mantey. *A Manual Grammar of the Greek New Testament*. New York: Macmillan, 1955.

Dawkins, Richard. *The God Delusion*. New York: Houghton Mifflin, 2008.

Deere, Jack. "Were there Only Three Periods of Miracles?" In *Strangers to Fire: When Tradition Trumps Scripture*, edited by Robert W. Graves, 209–24. Tulsa: Empoweredlife, 2014.

Dennis, Lane T., et al, eds. *ESV Study Bible*. Wheaton, IL: Crossway, 2008.

De Young, James B. "1–3 John." In *Evangelical Commentary on the Bible*, edited by Walter A. Elwell, 1177–87. Grand Rapids: Baker, 1989.

DeYoung, Kevin, and Greg Gilbert. *What is the Mission of the Church?* Wheaton, IL: Crossway, 2011.

Elbert, Paul. "Face to Face: Then or Now? An Exegesis of First Corinthians 13:8–13." In *Strange to Fire: When Tradition Trumps Scripture*, edited by Robert W. Graves, 493–520. Tulsa: Empoweredlife Academic, 2014.

Ellul, Jacque. *The Subversion of Christianity*. Translated by Geoffrey W. Bromiley. Grand Rapids: Eerdmans, 1986.

"Evangelism Antagonism." *Christianity Today* 2 (February 2003) 32–33.

Faust, Michael. "T. D. Jakes Embraces Doctrine of the Trinity, Moves Away from 'Oneness' View." http://www.christianitytoday.com/news/2012/january/td-jakes-embraces-doctrine-of-trinity-moves-away-from.html.

Frankowski, Nathan, dir. *Expelled: No Intelligence Allowed*. Dallas: Premise Media Corporation, 2008. DVD.

Fuller, Daniel Payton. "The Hermeneutics of Dispensationalism." ThD diss., Northern Baptist Theological Seminary, Chicago, 1957.

Gaffin, Richard B., Jr. "A Cessationist View." In *Are Miraculous Gifts for Today? Four Views*, edited by Wayne Grudem, 25–64. Grand Rapids: Zondervan, 1996. Kindle.

———. *Perspective on Pentecost: Studies in New Testament Teaching on the Gifts of the Holy Spirit*. Philipsburg, NJ: Presbyterian and Reformed, 1979.

González, Ondina E., and Justo L. González. *Christianity in Latin America*. Cambridge: Cambridge University Press, 2008.

Green, Michael. *I Believe in the Holy Spirit*. London: Hodder & Stoughton, 1979.

Greer, Thomas. *A Brief History of the Western World*. 4th ed. New York: Harcourt Brace Jovanovich, 1982.

Grudem, Wayne. *Systematic Theology: An Introduction to Biblical Doctrine*. Grand Rapids: Zondervan, 1994.

Hagin, Kenneth E. *Why Tongues?* Tulsa: RHEMA Bible Church, 2011. Kindle.

Hammond, T. C. *In Understanding Be Men*, 6th ed. London: IVP, 1968.

Harris, Sam. *The End of Faith*. New York: W. W. Norton, 2004.

Henry, Carl F. H. *The Uneasy Conscience of Modern Fundamentalism*. Grand Rapids: Eerdmans, 1947.

Hodges, Louis I. *Reformed Theology Today*. Columbus, GA: Brentwood Christian, 1995.

Hodges, Zane. *The Gospel Under Siege*. Dallas: Redención Viva, 1992.

Hoekema, Anthony A. "Amillennialism." In *The Meaning of the Millennium*, edited by Robert G. Clouse, 155–87. Downers Grove, IL: InterVarsity, 1977.

———. *Tongues and Spirit-Baptism: A Biblical and Theological Foundation*. Reprint. Grand Rapids: Baker, 1981.

Hollomon, H. W. "Theology II: Anthropology, Hamartiology, Christology, Soteriology." Rev. ed. ST603 Syllabus, Talbot School of Theology, 1987.

Horton, Michael, ed. *Christ the Lord: The Reformation and Lordship Salvation*. Grand Rapids: Baker, 1992

Houghton, S. M. *Sketches from Church History*. Edinburgh: The Banner of Truth Trust, 1980.

Hoyt, Herman A. "Dispensational Premillennialism." In *The Meaning of the Millennium*, edited by Robert G. Clouse, 63–92. Downers Grove, IL: InterVarsity, 1977.

———. *The End Times*. Chicago: Moody, 1969.

Ice, Thomas. "When Will the Rapture Come?" *Calvary Chapel Prophecy Conference: Israel and Final Days*. Chino Hills, CA, August 2006. CD.

Jackson, Bill. *The Quest for the Radical Middle: A History of the Vineyard*. Cape Town: Vineyard International, 1999.

Kaiser, Walter, Jr., et al. *Hard Sayings of the Bible*. Downers Grove, IL: InterVarsity, 1996.

Keener, Craig S. "Are Spiritual Gifts for Today?" In *Strangers to Fire: When Tradition Trumps Scripture*, edited by Robert W. Graves, 135–62. Tulsa: Empoweredlife, 2014.

———. "A Review of MacArthur's *Strange Fire*." In *Strangers to Fire: When Tradition Trumps Scripture*, edited by Robert W. Graves, 35–58. Tulsa: Empoweredlife, 2014.

Kendall, R. T. Review of *Holy Fire*, by Craig S. Keener. *Pneuma Review*, February 26, 2014. http://pneumareview.com/rtkendall-holy-fire-ckeener/2/.

Koukl, Greg. "Experiencing God." *Solid Ground Newsletter* (January/February 1999) 1–8.

———. "What's Wrong with 'Experiencing God?'" http://www.str.org/free/commentaries/theology/whatswro.htm (dead link).

Kroeger, Richard, and Catherine Kroeger. "Pandemonium and Silence at Corinth." https://www.bibliotecapleyades.net/sumer_anunnaki/reptiles/reptiles11.htm.

Kubo, Sakae. *A Reader's Greek-English Lexicon of the New Testament*. Berrien Springs, MI: Andrews University Press, 1971.

Ladd, George Eldon. *The Gospel of the Kingdom: Scriptural Studies in the Kingdom of God*. Grand Rapids: Eerdmans, 1959.

———. "Historic Premillennialism." In *The Meaning of the Millennium*, edited by Robert G. Clouse, 17–40. Downers Grove, IL: InterVarsity, 1977.

Lane, Tony, and Hilary Osborne, eds. *The Institutes of Christian Religion*. Grand Rapids: John Calvin, 1987.

Larson, Warren. "Unveiling the Truth about Islam." *Christianity Today* 6 (June 2006) 39–40.

Latourette, Kenneth Scott. *A History of Christianity, Volume I: Beginning to 1500*. San Francisco: Harper & Row, 1975.

Lindsey, Hal. *The Rapture*. New York: Bantam, 1985.

Lovelace, Libby. "LifeWay Releases Prayer Language Study." http://www.bpnews.net/25765/lifeway-releases-prayer-language-study.

M., Jonathan. "Is Intelligent Design 'Apologetics?'" https://evolutionnews.org/2015/10/is_intelligent_3/

MacArthur, John F., Jr. *Charismatic Chaos*. Grand Rapids: Zondervan, 1992.

———. *The Charismatics: A Doctrinal Perspective*. Grand Rapids: Academie, 1978.

———. *The MacArthur New Testament Commentary: James*. Chicago: Moody, 1998.

———. *The MacArthur Study Bible*. Nashville: Word, 1997.

———. *Strange Fire: The Danger of Offending the Holy Spirit with Counterfeit Worship*. Nashville: Nelson, 2013.

Mandryk, Jason, ed. *Operation World*. 6th ed. Colorado Springs: Biblical, 2010.

Markos, Louis. *From Plato to Postmodernism: Understanding the Essence of Literature and the Role of the Author: Glossary and Bibliography*. Chantilly, VA: The Teaching Company, 1999.

Marshall, Alfred. *The R. S. V. Interlinear Greek-English New Testament*. Grand Rapids: Zondervan, 1970.

Martin, Walter, and Norman Klann. *Jehovah of the Watchtower*. Minneapolis: Bethany House, 1981.

McCraken, Brett. "The Rise of Reformed Charismatics." http://www.christianitytoday.com/ct/2018/january-february/rise-of-reformed-charismatics.html.

McGrath, Alister. *The Journey: A Pilgrim in the Lands of the Spirit*. New York: Doubleday, 2000.

Metzger, Bruce M. *Lexical Aids for Students of New Testament Greek*. Princeton: Self-published, 1983.

Moreland, J. P. *Love Your God with All Your Mind*. Colorado Springs: Navpress, 1977.

Myers, Allen C., ed. *The Eerdmans Bible Dictionary*. Grand Rapids: Eerdmans, 1987.

Neill, Stephen. *A History of Christian Missions*. Rev. ed. Reprint. London: Penguin, 1987.

Olsen, Ted. "What Really Unites Pentecostals?" *Christianity Today* 12 (December 2006) 18–19.

Packer, J. I. *Evangelism and the Sovereignty of God*. Downers Grove, IL: InterVarsity, 1961.

Park, Keith. "Introduction to AMI: Philosophy & Structure." Lecture presented at the AMI Institute, Los Angeles, CA, May 27, 2013.

Pausch, Randy. *The Last Lecture*. New York: Hyperion, 2008.

Pierson, Paul. "Historical Development of the Christian Movement." MH 520 Syllabus, Fuller Theological Seminary, 2000.

Pivec, Holly. "The 'D' Word: Has Doctrines Become the New Dirty Word?" *Biola Connection* (Summer 2006) 13–17.

Postman, Neil. *Amusing Ourselves to Death: Public Discourse in the Age of Show Business*. New York: Penguin, 1986.

Price, Frederick K. C. *Is Healing for All?* Los Angeles: Faith One, 2015. Nook.

Prince, Joseph. *Destined to Reign*. Tulsa: Harrison House, 2007.

Provine, W. B. "Darwinism: Science or Naturalistic Philosophy?" http://www.arn.org/docs/orpages/or161/161main.htm.

Rambo, Shelly. *Spirit and Trauma: A Theology of Remaining*. Louisville: Westminster John Knox, 2010.

Ramm, Bernard. *Protestant Biblical Interpretation*. 2nd ed. Grand Rapids: Baker, 1970.

Reynolds, Gregory Edward. "Old, Content, Reformed: The Resurgence of Calvinism?" *Ordained Servant* 8 (2006) 31–35.

Ryrie, Charles C. *Dispensationalism Today*. Chicago: The Moody Bible Institute, 1965.

Sainsbury, Howard. "Jonathan Edwards." In *Eerdmans' Handbook of the History of Christianity*, 1st Amer. ed., edited by Tim Dowley et al., 438. Grand Rapids: Eerdmans, 1977.

Saucy, Robert L. *The Church in God's Program*. Chicago: Moody, 1972.

———. "An Open but Cautious View." In *Are Miraculous Gifts for Today? Four Views*, edited by Wayne Grudem, 96–148. Grand Rapids: Zondervan, 1996. Kindle.

Saucy, Robert L., and Alan Gomez. "Justification and the New Perspective." *Sundoulos* (Spring 2011) 12–21.

Schaeffer, Francis. *The God Who is There*. Downers Grove, IL: InterVarsity, 1968.

Shepherd, Ken. "For the 'Poor, Uneducated and Easy to Command' File." https://www.newsbusters.org/blogs/nb/ken-shepherd/2007/04/09/poor-uneducated-and-easy-command-file.

Sherrill, John L. *They Speak with Other Tongues*. Old Tappan, NJ: Fleming H. Revell, 1964.

Smietna, Bob. "International Mission Board Drops Ban on Speaking in Tongues." http://www.christianitytoday.com/ct/2015/may-web-only/imb-ban-speaking-in-tongues-baptism-baptist-missionary.html?start=2

Spring, Beth. "Carl F. H. Henry Dies at 90." *Christianity Today* 2 (February 2004) 20.

Sproul, R. C. "Israel's Temporary Hardening." https://www.ligonier.org/learn/devotionals/israels-temporary-hardening/

———. *What is Reformed Theology?: Understanding the Basics*. Grand Rapids: Baker, 1997.

Steele, David N., and Curtin C. Thomas. *Romans: An Interpretive Outline*. Reprint. Philipsburg, NJ: Presbyterian and Reformed, 1967.

Stott, John R. *Baptism & Fullness: The Work of the Holy Spirit Today*. Downers Grove, IL: InterVarsity, 1975.

Strong, James. "Greek Dictionary of the New Testament." In *Strong's Greek Exhaustive Concordance of the Bible*, 7–79. Nashville: Crusade Bible, 1980.

Summers, Ray. *Essentials of New Testament Greek*. Nashville: Broadman, 1950.

Synan, Vinson. *The Spirit Said "Grow."* Monrovia, CA: MARC, 1992.

Tasker, R. V. G. *The Gospel According to St. John*. Grand Rapids: Eerdmans, 1960.

Taylor, LaTonya. "Heresy Charge Torpedoes Pastor's Political Debut." *Christianity Today* 7 (June 2002) 19.

Vine, W. E., et al. *An Expository Dictionary of Biblical Words*. Nashville: Thomas Nelson, 1985.

Vos, J. G. *Biblical Theology: Old and New Testaments*. Grand Rapids: Eerdmans, 1948.

Wagner, C. Peter. *Your Spirit Gifts Can Help Your Church Grow*. Ventura, CA: Regal, 1979.

Walker, Williston. *A History of the Christian Church*. New York: Charles Scribner's Sons, 1970.

Wallace, Daniel B. *Greek Grammar: Beyond the Basics*. Grand Rapids: Zondervan, 1996.

Wesley, John. "The Use of Money." http://wesley.nnu.edu/john-wesley/the-sermons-of-john-wesley-1872-edition/sermon-50-the-use-of-money/

Wilkin, Robert N. *Confident in Christ: Living by Faith Really Works*. Irving, TX: Grace Evangelical Society, 1999.

Witherington, Ben. "What Calvin Gets Right." *Christianity Today* 9 (September 2009) 33–34.

Wright, Christopher J. H. *The Mission of God's People: A Biblical Theology of the Church's Mission*. Grand Rapids: Zondervan, 2010.

Wright, David F. "What the First Christians Believed." In *Eerdman's Handbook to the History of Christianity*, 1st Amer. ed., edited by Tim Dowley et al., 96–121. Grand Rapids: Eerdmans, 1977.

Wright, N. T. *Justification: God's Plan and Paul's Vision*. London: Society for Promoting Christian Knowledge, 2009.

Wycliffe, "Why Bible Translation?" https://www.wycliffe.org/about/why.

Yoder, John H., and Alan Kreider. "The Anabaptists." In *Eerdman's Handbook to the History of Christianity*, 1st Amer. ed., edited by Tim Dowley et al., 399–403. Grand Rapids: Eerdmans, 1977.

Zodhiates, Spiros, ed. *The Complete Word Study: New Testament*. Chattanooga, TN: AMG International, 1992.

Scripture Index

OLD TESTAMENT

NEW TESTAMENT

Matthew

Romans

EARLY CHRISTIAN WRITINGS

QUORAN

Subject Index

salvation and baptism, occurring
simultaneously in the Spirit, 164
Samaritan(s)
described, 197
imparting the Holy Spirit to, 163n4
receiving the Holy Spirit later, 163
showing Jimenez the way in India, 196
Samson, 256
Samuel, 256
sanctification, 243, 244
Sarah, 126n14
Satan. *See also* devil
angel of sent to harass and bug Paul,
228
under God's sovereign control, 122
inciting David to take a census, 30–31,
119–22
sickness from, 223, 231
Saucy, Mark, xviiin5
Saucy, Robert L.
on behavior within the corporate
church, 169
on the gift of tongues, 140
on the ministry of the prophets,
190–91, 205
not including prophets like Judas and
Silas, 206
on Paul's prayer for "Israel," 78
on personal edification coming
through speaking in tongues,
152–53
presenting opposing views in a fair
manner, xviii
on the proper ministry of any gift,
174–75
on prophecies never included in the
canonical Scriptures, 182n11
on prophecy less than fully inspired
and authoritative, 207
on the prophetic ministry of Judas and
Silas, 185
on secondary prophets, 186, 189–90,
206
on spiritual gifts, 41
on two categories of apostles, 210, 213
King Saul, 183
Schaeffer, Francis, 89
Scripture(s)

applying antithesis and antinomy to, 26
applying in every circumstance, 192
calling Barnabas and others as
"apostles," 214
characteristics of, 248
considering to study sign gifts, 252
different approaches to interpreting, 4
entire context of, 108
framed antithetically and antinomically, xx
full of antithetic and antinomic revelations, 54
full of antithetic/antinomic propositions, 49
as full of factual errors, 240
ignoring or distorting inconvenient,
249
interpreting Scripture, 24, 24n6, 187
justifying both sides of word versus
Spirit, 36–37
not allowing to speak for itself, xvii, 52
pairs of in binary opposition, 107
pairs of opposite contradicting each
other, 27
pitting word and Spirit against each
another, 36–38
presenting a category of noncanonical
prophecy, 182
presenting two types of tongues, 140
primary intent of, 248–49
privileging God's sovereignty and human responsibility, 61
privileging those supporting one's preferred systematic theology, 55
Radical Middle paradigm of both/and
in, 58–63
recognizing the antithetic and antinomic nature of, xxi
recognizing the validity of inconvenient, 55–56
seeming to present conflicting truths,
22–23
seen through a Western mindset,
240–41
selective reading by Pentecostals and
charismatics in the book of Acts,
166
spiritual benefits of studying, 103

CPSIA information can be obtained
at www.ICGtesting.com
Printed in the USA
FSHW02n0755061018
52689FS